Distributing Condoms and Hope

Distributing Condoms and Hope

THE RACIALIZED POLITICS OF YOUTH SEXUAL HEALTH

Chris A. Barcelos

UNIVERSITY OF CALIFORNIA PRESS

University of California Press
Oakland, California

© 2020 by Chris A. Barcelos

Library of Congress Cataloging-in-Publication Data

Names: Barcelos, Chris A., author.
Title: Distributing condoms and hope : the racialized politics of youth
    sexual health / Chris A. Barcelos.
Other titles: Reproductive justice ; 3.
Description: Oakland, California : University of California Press, [2020] |
    Series: Reproductive justice : a new vision for the twenty-first
    century ; 3 | Includes bibliographical references and index.
Identifiers: LCCN 2020022312 (print) | LCCN 2020022313 (ebook) |
    ISBN 9780520306707 (hardback) | ISBN 9780520306714
    (paperback) | ISBN 9780520973732 (ebook)
Subjects: LCSH: Teenage pregnancy—United States—Prevention—Case
    studies. Teenagers—Sexual behavior. | Teenage pregnancy—
    Prevention—Government policy—United States.
Classification: LCC HQ759.4 .B366 2020 (print) | LCC HQ759.4
    (ebook) | DDC 306.874/3—dc23
LC record available at https://lccn.loc.gov/2020022312
LC ebook record available at https://lccn.loc.gov/2020022313

Manufactured in the United States of America

27 26 25 24 23 22 21 20
10 9 8 7 6 5 4 3 2 1

For my father, Celso Anthony Barcelos,
and my son, Clay Anthony Barcelos,
without whom none of this would have been possible

Contents

Illustrations

Acknowledgments

Over the years I've heard numerous analogies comparing the process of writing a book to that of giving birth or raising a child. Such a comparison seems particularly apt for a book about the politics of reproduction, but I'll simply say that this book was raised up by a number of mentors, colleagues, family members, comrades, organizations, and a couple of fluffy cats.

First and foremost, the utmost respect, acknowledgement, and gratitude go to the people who participated in the research for this book. A sincere thanks to the professional stakeholders interviewed for this book, who face abundant constraints in their work to improve the lives of marginalized young people. I realize that not all stakeholders will agree with everything in this book, and I invite us all to use it as a provocation to continue to advocate and agitate on behalf of young people. Thanks especially to "Lourdes Navarro" for your fierce determination and tenacious support of Towne House students. Thank you as well to the executive director of the Towne House, for your persistence in keeping the doors open as well as for supporting the various research projects that have taken place there over the years.

Thanks to the students at the Towne House—and teen mamas everywhere—for being smart and fabulous in the face of so much shame and stigma; I would not have written this book were it not for the opportunity to amplify your voices and tell a different kind of story about teen pregnancy and parenting. A special shout-out goes as well to all the teen moms, young moms, slutmoms, queer families, welfare queens, and everyone else out there who dares to live fabulously and authentically in a world where our existence is abject. You all keep doing you. I've been inspired by many kick-ass teen or young parents over the years, and in particular I send a big thank-you to Lindsey Campbell, Allison Crews, Ariel Gore, China Martens, and Alicia Randolph.

The support of my colleagues at a variety of institutions of higher education made possible the researching, writing, and revising of this book. At the University of Massachusetts Amherst, Aline Gubrium provided invaluable training in visual and sensory methodologies and recognized the importance of teen moms in sexual and reproductive justice scholarship. Robert Zussman encouraged me to see this project as a book from the very beginning, no doubt saving me countless hours in the revision stages. David Buchanan greatly shaped my thinking on how to envision an emancipatory health promotion practice. A very special thanks to Laura Briggs for encouraging me to think about race, reproduction, and science in the context of empire; for supporting my career throughout multiple stages; for connecting me to the Reproductive Justice series; and for showing up in queer family solidarity in ways that totally surpassed the typical academic mentor-mentee relationship. I cannot express how influential your mentorship has been as I have cultivated relationships with my own graduate students. Many thanks to Svati P. Shah for providing invaluable insights about the politics of intervening in topics that are overdetermined in research and policy. Dan Gerber has served as a teaching mentor, cheerleader, and advocate since the very beginning of my doctoral work. Alice Fiddian-Green started out as one of my students and went on to become a valued friend and fellow PhD student. Josefa Scherer taught me about doing radical public health work while navigating the same structures of oppression that we are trying to work against; you are awesome and I love you to pieces.

While I was a visiting assistant professor at Oberlin College, my work benefited from the intellectual community of many fierce and brilliant scholars. Thank you to Jacinthe Assad, Cal Biruk, Meiver de la Cruz, Irene

Garza, Vange Heiliger, Greggor Mattson, and Kathryn Miller for providing intellectual community, Bee's Knees at the hotel, and beers at the Feve. My gratitude to Cal Biruk for providing much-needed feedback and perspective on the original book proposal. Greggor Mattson read and commented on several chapters, even long after I'd left Oberlin, and has supported me in countless other ways from providing ongoing career advice to cocreating excellent memes about sociological hanky codes.

Many thanks to all of my colleagues at the University of Wisconsin Madison who helped move this book through its adolescence. Annie Menzel provided much-appreciated feedback at the proposal stage. I am delighted and honored that my book sits alongside Annie's in the Reproductive Justice series. Thanks to Claire Wendland for providing important feedback on chapter 4. An enormous thank-you to Finn Enke for serving as my mentor and for his commitment to trans and racial justice in our department and in the world as a whole.

Thank you as well to my colleagues in Women's, Gender, and Sexuality Studies at the University of Massachusetts Boston, who welcomed me into the department as this book was finally making its way out into the world.

I wrote a large part of this book (OK, probably most of it) at coffee shops, and I want to acknowledge the underpaid and precarious labor of the workers who served me coffee all these years. A big thanks to every staff person at the Lady Killigrew Cafe (Montague, Massachusetts), Rao's (Amherst), Slow Train Cafe (Oberlin, Ohio), and Barriques (Madison, Wisconsin).

I am very fortunate to have found a home for this book at the University of California Press. I am extremely grateful for the constructive and kind feedback provided by two anonymous reviewers. As I tell my students, the anxiety over having other people critique your work never really goes away, and I am blessed to have had reviewers who saw the strengths and weaknesses in my manuscript and helped me improve it with clear and thoughtful feedback. Thank you to the editors of the Reproductive Justice series, Khiara M. Bridges, Zakiya Luna, Rickie Solinger, and Ruby Tapia, for your work in bringing this series to fruition and for the honor of having my work included. Thank you to Naomi Schneider for your work in bringing this and so many other important books to life. Thank you as well to editorial assistants Benjy Malings and Summer Farah for your crucial labor in this process.

This book also benefited from the feedback of audiences at several academic conferences, including the annual meetings of the National Women's Studies Association, the American Sociological Association, the Eastern Sociological Association, and the American Public Health Association. An earlier version of chapter 3 was published in *Gender & Society* as "Culture, Contraception, and Colorblindness: Youth Sexual Health Promotion as a Gendered Racial Project" (vol. 32, no. 2 [2018]). The research for this book was supported through a research assistantship funded by the Ford Foundation Sexuality Research Initiative and a University of Massachusetts Amherst Graduate School Dissertation Grant, both of which provided necessary financial support in bringing this project to completion. Faculty start-up funds from the University of Wisconsin Madison enabled me to push the book past the finish line.

It is my time in the classroom that feeds my soul in order to continue my research and writing. My students at the University of Massachusetts Amherst, Greenfield Community College, Oberlin College, and the University of Wisconsin Madison deserve my deepest gratitude for their willingness to be students and teachers alongside me. Thank you to the graduate students I've had the pleasure of working closely with at UW Madison—including Devon Betts, Frankie Frank, Malú Machuca Rose, and Diana Madrigal—for being valued interlocutors as I launched myself into being a full-time professor.

I often call myself an "accidental academic," and I am immensely grateful for the folks I've met along the way who maintain a critique of the work we do and the institutions we do it under. Thank you to Stephanie Budge, Cáel Keegan, Ghassan Moussawi, Z Nicolazzo, and many others whose names I'm forgetting, for your solidarity and support. Thanks to Jessica Fields for providing generative feedback on chapter 2 and for her significant contributions to the critical literature on sexuality education, contributions that made mine possible. Thank you as well to Clare Forstie for providing last-minute comments on my methods appendix.

Stevie, Wondernicks, and Patti Smith provided company, head butts, and moral support during the writing of this book. I would thank them for keeping my lap warm while I sat and wrote, but actually what they did was sit on the keyboard and knock stuff off the desk. I love you more than I love most humans.

My partner, Davey Shlasko, is not only a professional editor who has already read this book about a hundred times, but is also the kindest, most loving person to ever come into my life. Words in a book acknowledgment are not sufficient to express how thankful I am to have you as a lover, friend, partner, comrade, and editor.

My father, Celso Barcelos, passed away during the first year of my doctoral program. When I was a pregnant teenager, he was the first, and for a long time only, person who believed in me. Without his support, I would not be here today, and it makes my heart heavy that he cannot be here to witness this publication.

Finally, my son, Clay Barcelos, was along for the ride through college, graduate school (twice), and numerous moves across the country. This book has been gestating since he was seven years old, and it seems fitting that it was finished just in time for his eighteenth birthday. Clay, thank you so very much for "ruining" my life, because otherwise I would never have gone from a high school dropout to a university professor, much less have written a book. This is for you.

Introduction

THIS IS WHAT HAPPENS WHEN YOU
GET PREGNANT AS A TEENAGER

On a gray day in early winter, I parked my car outside the unassuming brick building that housed the Millerston Youth Center.[1] The bleak December sky mirrored the drab landscape of abandoned mills and boarded-up row housing. The youth center stood at the edge of Millerston's downtown, where health and human service organizations occupied many of the buildings, along with a scattering of storefront churches, bodegas, and discount stores. Across the canal from the youth center was the "Canals" neighborhood, crowded with the now-empty or repurposed factories that had made Millerston a vibrant city at the height of the manufacturing economy. Nowadays, the median income in the neighborhood was the lowest in the city, at only $13,000.[2] Like most deindustrialized cities in the United States, Millerston's neighborhoods are racially and economically segregated; approximately 90% of the Canal's residents are Puerto Rican. The neighborhood has the highest teen birthrate in the city, at 154 births per 1,000 women ages fifteen to nineteen each year. In contrast, less than three miles away in the "Heights" neighborhood, the population is 89% white non-Hispanic, the median annual income is $65,000, and the teen birthrate is 34 births per 1,000 young women ages fifteen to nineteen annually.

I was at the youth center to attend a meeting of the Millerston Adolescent Sexual Health Promotion Committee (MASHPC), a group composed of representatives from city government, health clinics, and social service organizations. MASHPC's mission was to develop multifaceted community-based approaches to decrease teen pregnancy and sexually transmitted infections (STIs) in Millerston. Millerston was well known in the region for its high teen pregnancy rate among Latinas, and I was interested in telling a different sort of story about teen pregnancy prevention and the lives of teen mothers. As I got out of my car, I greeted Hannah McNeil, a white former nurse in her sixties who served as commissioner of the Millerston Board of Health and the chair of MASHPC. Offering to help her unload meeting supplies from her luxury sports car, I found myself carrying cookies and fruit piled into a tote bag from an upscale athletic wear company whose $100 yoga pants would represent 12.5 hours of labor for a worker making $8 an hour, then the state minimum wage. We made small talk as we carried the items inside the building and found our way to the meeting room. Throughout my fieldwork, I spent many hours sitting in on meetings such as this one, where groups of mostly white, economically privileged, middle-age professional women lamented the "problem" of teen pregnancy in the city. They saw themselves engaged in a valiant battle against this problem.

Often in these meetings I felt as if I was in the Bill Murray movie *Groundhog Day*, where a time warp forces the main character to relive the same day over and over again. In MASHPC meetings, and in other coalitions and committees I observed during my research for this book, participants discussed the same issues, made identical critiques, and proposed similar strategies. Later, when my archival research turned up meeting minutes from earlier incarnations of the group, I learned that the focus of these efforts had changed little since the beginnings of Millerston's teen pregnancy prevention work in the 1990s. At this particular MASHPC meeting, members were celebrating the just-released data showing that the teen birthrate in the city had declined. They viewed the committee's work as having directly caused this declining rate, and discussed their next steps to ensure the rate would continue to go down. Hannah shared that this work had always been a "passion" of hers that she held "close to the heart." I scribbled in my notebook, "I don't even know what to say about that." As a white, economically privileged older woman who viewed the prevention of pregnancy among economically marginalized young women of color "close to her heart," Hannah invoked a deep legacy of professional white women's benevolence in managing racialized and economically marginalized women's fertility and childrearing practices.[3] She went on to tell the group that the city had "had a chance in the [19]90s" to get a handle on the teen birthrate. "We didn't get it done then," she lamented, "but we're doing it now." Moving to the next item on the meeting's agenda, Hannah informed the group that the district superintendent had given them permission to hold a "National Day to Prevent Teen Pregnancy" rally at the Millerston high schools. Hannah hoped that the group could also organize a parade for teen pregnancy prevention in the city's downtown. Beth Emmerson, a white nurse and researcher in her fifties, chimed in to share her thoughts on additional tactics the group could employ, such as hosting an event in which community members help clean up a city park to "promote change from within." Along with other committee members, the majority of whom were white women in their forties and fifties, Beth lauded the importance of engaging Latinx parents as a strategy to prevent teen pregnancy.[4] She argued, "We need community members to say to their kids, 'You're not going to have sex; you're going to school!'"

Earlier that fall, I had joined students and staff for lunch in a small break room at the Towne House, a community-based school for pregnant and parenting young women in Millerston. We were participating in a multiday workshop in which students used storytelling to push back against the stigmatization of young mothers. A buffet of rice, beans, pork, yucca, and tostones from a local restaurant lined the middle of the table. As we ate, Tabitha, a Black 19-year-old mother to a 1-year-old who lived in a shelter for homeless teen mothers and their children, gazed out the windows at the large, weathered but elaborate Victorian homes lining the street. "If I stayed living in Millerston," she remarked, "I'd want to live in one of those." Emma, a 21-year-old Latina mother to a baby, disagreed with Tabitha's remark, proclaiming that she wanted to move away from Millerston because "everywhere you look there's girls with babies." In response, Cristina, a 21-year old Latina mother of a toddler, mentioned that she had heard that the teen pregnancy rate in Millerston was going down. Cristina thought that prenatal care providers in the city were unhappy about this change because, she argued, "they are trying to make money off us." Lourdes Colón Cruz, the Towne House's education director, immediately jumped into the conversation. Lourdes was a Latina in her early fifties and had had her children in her late teens. "I'm just gonna say something," she said, "I think a teen mom is like, 14, 15, 16 years old, not 18 or 19. When I was young, you got married right out of high school, you had a June wedding and a baby 9 months later. And nobody had any problem with that. It was normal." The young mothers around the lunch table, most of them 18 to 22 years old, nodded in consensus. Before the group turned their conversation to the various side effects and downsides of contraception, Lourdes imparted a final bit of wisdom about inequality in Millerston. "Let me tell you something," she said; "there are people in the world—there are rich people and there are poor people, and the rich people need the poor people to stay poor."

The conversations at these two events demonstrate the divide in how privileged service providers and marginalized young people make sense of sexuality, reproduction, and power. Although the service providers, most of them privileged along the intersections of race and social class, were oblivious to the workings of disciplinary social power and their complicity in reproducing it, the young mothers at the Towne House had no choice but to negotiate their positions in a system of domination. The conversations at the MASHPC meeting relied on common tropes of young women of color as hyper-reproductive and of poor people as lazy; the conversations at the Towne House illustrated how multiply marginalized people make sense of the discourses that produce them.

In placing these vignettes side by side, I do not mean to imply that *Distributing Condoms and Hope* is a story about "good" professionals trying to do right by young people versus "bad" professionals intent on regulating young people's sexuality and reproduction. The story of youth sexuality and reproduction in Millerston is much more complicated than such an easy dichotomy suggests. Instead, these vignettes provide a backdrop for understanding the politics of youth sexuality and reproduction in Millerston and frame the ways of thinking about and doing public health that I analyze in this book. *Distributing Condoms and Hope* demonstrates how discourses of race, reproduction, and science play out in the youth sexual health promotion efforts of this racially and economically stratified small city in the northeastern United States. Health care providers and educators in Millerston acknowledge the social determinants of health, but privatize responsibility for race, class, and gender inequalities by advocating for individual-level solutions, such as distributing condoms and promoting "hope." Since the early 2000s, teen pregnancy prevention campaigns based in shame and stigma have ignited conversations among scholars, service providers, and the public surrounding the politics of youth sexual health. Meanwhile, reproductive justice activists have worked to amplify the voices of pregnant and parenting youth.[5] *Distributing Condoms and Hope* brings together the perspectives of these disparate groups. By making space for the stories of young mothers alongside an analysis of youth sexual health promotion, I aim to create a platform for affecting policy and practice. Moreover, I want us to imagine and theorize different kinds of futures, ones that neither use young mothers' lives as the basis for disciplinary public policies nor romanticize their struggles.

This book makes visible the operation of power in youth sexual and reproductive health and reimagines what health promotion would look like through the lens of reproductive justice. Women of color feminist activists developed the concept of reproductive justice (RJ) in the mid-1990s as a framework, vision, and social movement. Reproductive justice refocuses individual-level debates about reproductive "rights" and "choice" so as to emphasize a broader analysis of racial, economic, and structural constraints on power.[6] The approach expands a singular focus on white, economically privileged women's access to contraception and abortion to include the right to have children and to parent them with dignity and support. In the RJ vision, reproductive freedom involves the ability to prevent or terminate a pregnancy alongside access to affordable child care and the ability to raise children without the threat of state violence.[7] In Millerston, most professionals focused narrowly on promoting contraception and did not view expanding abortion access as part of their work. Rather than supporting teen mothers' right to parent with dignity and resources, professional stakeholders considered their lives only in regard to their potential to serve as a "warning" about the dangers of teen pregnancy. Although they used "youth sexual health promotion" as an umbrella term to refer to their work, their efforts emphasized preventing pregnancy much more than promoting a holistic understanding of "sexual health."[8]

Although I critique the absence of a reproductive justice framework in Millerston's youth sexual health promotion efforts, I have no doubt that the professionals in the city were sincere in their beliefs and conducted their work without explicit maliciousness. This sincerity, however, does not erase or diminish their complicity in structures of racial domination and the very real implications it has for racially and economically marginalized young people. Likewise, although I critique how the efforts pathologized teen pregnancy and parenting, I have no doubt that the teen parents I worked with experienced both joy and hardship. I call attention to how health promotion mobilizes discourses of race, reproduction, and science to justify intervention in the sexual and reproductive lives of marginalized young people. I also analyze how young parents negotiate the politics of teen pregnancy and make sense of the dominant understandings of their lives. By focusing on discourse, I am interested in how people in Millerston—public health professionals and young mothers alike—organize and create knowledge. I understand discourse in the Foucauldian sense, as composed of circulating forms of knowledge-power that produce and regulate language, bodies, populations, and so on. What makes power so useful, according to Foucault, is that it is not merely repressive but also "traverses and produces things, it induces pleasure, forms knowledge, [and] produces discourse."[9] Discourses of youth sexual health promotion produce particular ideas about race, class, gender, and sexuality—for example, that there is something about Latinx culture that leads to high rates of teen pregnancy in Millerston. Critiquing these discourses is more than a strategy by which to understand or eliminate health inequalities. It is a way to envision new ways of thinking about and doing public health, ways that center the people most impacted by interlocking systems of oppression.

"HOW DO YOU SUPPOSE YOU'RE GOING TO DO THAT?"

It is often difficult to locate the precise bounds of an ethnographic research project, or even identify when it began. To trace this project to its origins, I would have to return to my own unintended pregnancy at age 19. Shortly after I gave birth, a visiting nurse came to my father's house, where I lived at the time, on a routine postpartum follow-up visit. Looking back, I don't know if she read me as just another Latina teen mom or a white girl who had made an unfortunate mistake. I do vividly recall the all too noticeable derision in her words when she asked what I planned to do now that I had a baby. I replied that I wanted to go to college. "Well," she snorted, "how do you suppose you're going to do that?" I can't recall what I said. Whatever it was, it was a lie, because I really had no idea. Now, looking back, it's almost as if I flouted her assumptions by going to college and never really leaving. I was a postsecondary student from the time my son was a toddler through the beginning of his teenage years; now I am a university professor. Like many of the young mothers in Millerston, and contrary to the dominant narrative, my "teen pregnancy" was not what ruined my life. It was what saved it. Yet I would be remiss if I let this anecdote pass without naming the considerable privilege and cultural capital that enabled me to become an academic who studies sexuality and reproduction, rather than a marginalized parent whom academics target to participate in their research projects. The path to academia is not equally open to all young people experiencing pregnancy while young, single, and poor, and it's not the result of a meritocratic system that allowed me to follow this path. In large part, it is my access to white-passing privilege that facilitated this path.

For now, it is sufficient to say that I got pregnant as a teenager and made a career out of it in the form of researching, writing, and teaching about the politics of sexuality and reproduction. I'm hardly the first scholar whose research topic chose them, and my professional connections to Millerston's public health circles made it a logical choice. Over the years I have frequently joked that I got knocked up as a teenager and now I'm stuck talking about teen pregnancy for the rest of my life. I have come to appreciate that, although the politics of teen pregnancy is not new to me, the social and political context of youth sexuality and reproduction is fertile ground for a feminist social scientist. Although teen pregnancy, and the moral panic surrounding it, is not a recent development, it remains a timely and deeply contested issue for communities, politicians, feminists, health and human service professionals, and cultural observers. Ultimately, however, *Distributing Condoms and Hope* is more an analysis of the politics of race, class, gender, and sexuality than a study of teen pregnancy and parenting per se.

PRODUCING YOUTH SEXUALITY AND REPRODUCTION
IN RESEARCH AND POLICY

A November 2014 *New York Times* op-ed by Nicholas Kristof exemplifies the dominant way of understanding teen sexuality and reproduction in the United States.[10] In this editorial, Kristof invokes responsibility and greatly oversimplifies the social and political context of youth sexual health. To his credit, Kristof attempts to redirect the burden of responsibility toward the state and away from young people themselves. However, his argument elides the racial politics of sexuality, contraception, and family formation:

> Here's a story of utter irresponsibility: About one-third of American girls become pregnant as teenagers.[11] But it's not just a story of heedless girls and boys who don't take precautions. This is also a tale of national irresponsibility and political irresponsibility—of us as a country failing our kids by refusing to invest in comprehensive sex education and birth control because we, too, don't plan ahead. I kind of understand how a teenage couple stuffed with hormones and enveloped in each other's arms could get carried away. But I'm just bewildered that American politicians, stuffed with sanctimony and enveloped in self-righteousness, don't adequately invest at home or abroad in birth-control programs that would save the government money, chip away at poverty, reduce abortions and empower young people.[12]

This brief piece touches on nearly all of the taken-for-granted "truths" that constitute commonsense understandings about teen sexuality and reproduction. By invoking "responsibility," Kristof mobilizes a keyword that signals deeply held American cultural values of individualism, self-sufficiency, and personal responsibility.[13] Whether intentional or not, invoking responsibility also reifies a well-worn trope in American politics: the irresponsible, nonwhite, promiscuous woman who keeps having babies in order to increase the value of her welfare check.

I encountered these assumptions over and over again both in my field research and in my analysis of policy documents, committee reports, and health promotion campaigns—as well as in my own life as a young parent. These "truths" include the assumptions that teen pregnancy is inherently problematic; that having children within a two-parent heterosexual middle-class marriage is the only legitimate family formation; that teens are ignorant about their bodies and unable to make healthy decisions; that abortion is undesirable; that contraception is apolitical and uncomplicated; and that teen pregnancy causes poverty, rather than the other way around. Kristof also deploys another common strategy I encountered in my research, one that academics, activists, and professionals also use. He attempts to reframe teen pregnancy from an individual-level issue (blaming teens for being sexually irresponsible) to a structural-level issue (casting misguided public policies regarding sex education and contraception as irresponsible). Like many people involved in this work, however, Kristof is unsuccessful. Because he fails to acknowledge the influence of racial and sexual politics, he does little to address the structural inequalities that might promote sexual and reproductive justice and increase the well-being of vulnerable families.

Kristof is correct that young people in the United States are disproportionately likely to become pregnant as teenagers, at least in relation to our peer countries. The United States has one of the highest adolescent birthrates in the Global North, at approximately 22.3 births per 1,000 women ages 15–19 each year.[14] In comparison, Western European countries such as France and the Netherlands have dramatically lower rates, at 6 and 5 births per 1,000 women under the age of 20, respectively.[15] The rate of sexually transmitted infections among young people in the United States is also dramatically higher than in European countries. For example, the rate of syphilis among US teens is twice that of teens in the Netherlands, the rate of gonorrhea is 33 times higher, and the rate of chlamydia is 19 times higher.[16] Both scientific and popular literature have tried to make sense of this discrepancy, mostly by placing the blame on poverty, lack of comprehensive sex education, and lack of access to contraceptive services.[17]

Teen pregnancy, abortion, and birthrates in the United States have been on the decline for several decades. This decline has occurred in most US states and among all racial and ethnic groups. The 2015 teen birthrate (22.3 births per 1,000 women ages 15–19) represents a 64% decline from its peak in 1991 (61.8 births per 1,000 ages women 15–19). In 2010, the US teen pregnancy rate reached its lowest point in over 30 years (57.4 per 1,000),[18] a 51% decline from its apex in 1990 (116.9 per 1,000).[19] The pregnancy rates for Hispanic/Latina and Black/African American teens remain about twice as high as their white, non-Hispanic counterparts, though they have fallen 51% and 56%, respectively, since their peaks in the early 1990s.[20] The 2010 teen abortion rate was 14.7 abortions per 1,000 women ages 15–19, the lowest rate since *Roe v. Wade* legalized first-trimester abortion in 1973.[21]

The preoccupation with teen pregnancy as a social, economic, and public health issue is not on the decline, despite the fact that the teen birthrate continues to drop.[22] Federal, state, and local governments, nongovernmental organizations, scholars, and the general public remain focused on determining the causes of teen pregnancy and what to do to prevent it. The 1981 Adolescent Family Life (AFL) program (Title XX of the Public Health Service Act) first brought preventing adolescent pregnancy under the purview of the federal government. This law authorized grants for programming that included prevention (in the form of promoting sexual health education and contraception) and supports for pregnant and parenting teens. However, with passage of the Personal Responsibility and Work Opportunity Reconciliation Act (commonly referred to as "welfare reform") in 1996, the promotion of sexual abstinence became the primary strategy of most federal teen pregnancy prevention efforts. In 2010 the Obama administration shifted away from the focus on abstinence with the establishment of two programs that provided federal funding for "evidence-based" teen pregnancy prevention initiatives: Teen Pregnancy Prevention (TPP) and the Personal Responsibility Education Program (PREP). The TPP, funded in its first year at $110 million, was a discretionary project that provided competitive grants to both public and private entities to fund "medically accurate and age appropriate" programs to reduce teen pregnancy. PREP, established through the Patient Protection and Affordable Care Act (ACA; also known as "Obamacare"), created a new state grant initiative that appropriated $375 million over 5 years for broad-approach programs to educate young people on both abstinence and contraception.[23] President Obama's fiscal year 2017 federal budget was the first since 1996 to eliminate all funding for abstinence-focused programs. Other federal programs related to teen pregnancy include the Title X family planning program, which provides preventive care and family planning services to low-income and uninsured individuals ($286 million in fiscal year 2017)[24] and various public and private funding streams to support teen pregnancy prevention research. Teen pregnancy prevention therefore occurs throughout multiple sites and levels, including clinics, schools, academic and private research institutions, and community-based organizations, and in state and federal funding mechanisms.

The academic and policy literature is replete with reports, data, interpretation, and polemics that detail the scope of adolescent childbearing from perspectives that assume teen pregnancy and parenting are dire social, economic, health, and educational problems (and, more recently, health disparity problems).[25] For example, the National Campaign to Prevent Teen and Unplanned Pregnancy's "Counting It Up" project reports that preventing adolescent childbearing could save American taxpayers $9.4 billion dollars per year in public assistance expenditures.[26] Their "Why It Matters" series states that the sons of teenage mothers are more than twice as likely to be incarcerated as the sons of older mothers, that teenage mothers are significantly more likely than mothers over the age of 20 to be reported for child abuse or neglect, and that children born to teen parents score significantly lower on measures of reading and math ability. They also emphasize that teen pregnancy is linked to other "risky behaviors," such as substance abuse, and that teen parents are disproportionately likely to not finish high school and to experience poverty. Language from their website echoes a common cultural sentiment on teen pregnancy: "By preventing teen and unplanned pregnancy, we can significantly improve other serious social problems including poverty (especially child poverty), child abuse and neglect, father-absence, low birth weight, school failure, and poor preparation for the workforce."[27]

Amid such grim predictions on social, economic, and health outcomes for young mothers and their children, researchers have called attention to epistemological and methodological issues in constructing the teen pregnancy "problem."[28] First, as Arline Geronimus points out, "teen pregnancy" is less a valid construct than it is a political tool that signifies "an absorptive shorthand that strikes exposed dominant cultural nerves about race, responsibility, and sexuality."[29] She argues that the sustained social problem construction of early childbearing among economically marginalized women of color serves to reinforce elite cultural interests and allows for the reproduction of privilege in advantaged social groups.[30] These epistemological issues produce and constrain research and policy making on teen childbearing, an issue that is at the heart of *Distributing Condoms and Hope*. Second, empirical findings on outcomes related to teen pregnancy are equivocal, and some research finds that early childbearing can even have *positive* effects. Scholars have criticized research that finds considerable negative outcomes of adolescent childbearing for methodological problems such as confounding factors,[31] selection bias,[32] and inappropriate comparison groups.[33] To take one example, researchers find that many of these negative outcomes are minimal or disappear altogether when studies use an appropriate comparison group to assess the consequences of teen childbearing.[34] Much research has tended to overstate the deleterious social, health, educational, and economic outcomes for teen mothers and their families.[35] In reality, these negative effects are minimal and often short-lived, rather than sustained throughout the life course of the mother and her children.[36] What is more, research increasingly suggests that poor educational and economic outcomes among young mothers are the result of preexisting poverty, not of early motherhood itself.[37] As a result, policy strategies over the past several decades that sought to reduce poverty by reducing the teen birthrate were not only misguided but also ineffective.[38]

The scholarly research on youth sexuality and reproduction falls into three broad approaches. These strategies are not mutually exclusive or homogenous, but are instead rubrics for thinking about how research makes sense of teen sexual and reproductive behavior and what to do about it. The *pathology* approach frames teen sexuality and reproduction as inherent problems. Research grounded in this approach constructs adolescent childbearing as a disastrous social, health, and economic problem and focuses on preventing teen pregnancy to alleviate the supposed costs and consequences to society.[39] The *reform* approach frames teen pregnancy and sexually transmitted infections as the symptoms or outcomes of a problem. This body of research attributes the potential negative outcomes of adolescent sexuality to the underlying socioeconomic inequality that results in negative social, economic, and health outcomes.[40] Finally, the *critical* approach frames teen pregnancy as a discursively constructed problem. This approach centers an analysis of power that challenges easy assumptions about the causes and consequences of teen pregnancy or adverse sexual health outcomes rather than focusing on what causes these outcomes and how to prevent them.[41]

Distributing Condoms and Hope employs the critical approach to analyze youth sexuality and reproduction from within the field of community-based public health.[42] Critical public health critiques the dominant (bio-medical and positivist) paradigms in health promotion and emphasizes their epistemological, ontological, and methodological failures to account for power.[43] For instance, although the field of health promotion empha-sizes the explanatory power of social determinants of health, it continues to rely on individual-level behavior change strategies.[44] Groups with social, economic, and political power tend to impose these strategies on marginalized populations.[45] It is important to interrogate why public health scholars and practitioners focus on manipulating individual behav-iors when we know that population-level changes in health status are best achieved by policy changes and large-scale social emancipation.[46] Critical public health scholars call attention to the contradiction of this reliance on positivist biomedical and behavioral science to solve health problems that are political in nature.[47] This critique argues that there is no "value-free" state of health. Indeed, the discipline of public health and the social production of knowledge around health are replete with value making. Public health's unquestioning assumption that teen pregnancy is a signifi-cant public health problem limits what is and can be known about youth sexuality and reproduction. Inquiry based on that assumption rarely devi-ates from attempts to understand *why* young people become pregnant and how to prevent them from doing so. An analysis of the power relations inherent in the regulation of youth sexuality and reproduction is absent from taken-for-granted understandings and inquiries, in particular how youth sexual health promotion indexes racial logics. As a result, we come to see the social and health problem construction as neutral and value-free. Viewing teen childbearing through the lenses of critical public health and reproductive justice enables us to take seriously the political nature of teen sexuality and reproduction.

RESEARCHING YOUTH SEXUAL HEALTH PROMOTION
Millerston

Millerston is a deindustrialized northeastern city that sustains a long-held reputation as a place with high levels of poverty, high school dropout, unemployment, substance abuse, and violence. Like many other former mill towns, the city is among many in the United States that suffered considerable economic depression following the decline of manufacturing. Millerston experienced several waves of immigration and migration throughout the nineteenth and twentieth centuries, and today nearly half of the population in the city is Puerto Rican. Millerston consistently ranks poorly in terms of socioeconomic and educational indicators. The median annual household income in Millerston is approximately $35,500, compared to $67,800 for the state overall. The US Census Bureau estimates that 27% of all families in Millerston live below the federal poverty level, compared to 8% statewide. Forty-two percent of families with children under 18 years of age in the city live below the federal poverty level, compared to 12% statewide. Fourteen percent of residents over the age of 25 have not completed high school or an equivalency, compared to 6% in the state as a whole. Whereas 40% of people in the state hold a bachelor's degree or higher, in Millerston that figure is only 23%.

Millerston also fares poorly across numerous health status indicators. The city's rates of overall age-adjusted mortality, cancer mortality, and cardiovascular-related mortality are all higher than those for the state as a whole. In terms of sexual health indicators, the HIV/AIDS prevalence rate in the city is nearly three times higher than in the state (705.8 cases per 100,000 versus 261 per 100,000). The rate of gonorrhea infection among persons 15–19 years of age is 2.5 times higher than the state rate (193.4 per 100,000 versus 76.6 per 100,000), and the rate of chlamydia infection in that age group is 3.5 times higher (4,771 per 100,000 versus 1,310 per 100,000).[48]

Professionals, the media, academics, and community members throughout the region recognize Millerston as the city with the highest teen birthrate in the state, a position it has held since 2002.[49] When I began fieldwork in Millerston in 2012, the teen birthrate for the most recent year available (2009) was 96.8 births per 1,000 women ages 15–19, compared to 19.5 per 1,000 for the state as a whole. As in the United States overall, the teen birthrate is on the decline in both the state and in Millerston. The state has one of the lowest teen birthrates in the nation, one 50% lower than the US rate.[50] Racial differences in teen birthrates in Millerston and the state mirror those nationally. In 2010, the state birthrate among Hispanic women ages 15–19 was five times higher

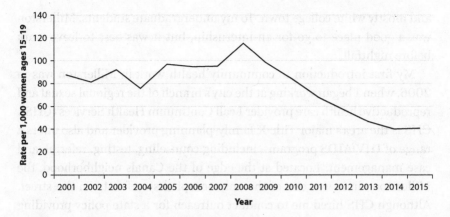

Figure 1. Teen birthrate in Millerston, 2001–2014.

than the rate for whites (49.3 per 1,000 versus 10.4 per 1,000).[51] In Millerston, the rate among Hispanic teens was three times higher than whites (99.3 per 1,000 versus 36 per 1,000).

During the years I was an employee and researcher in Millerston, I frequently heard professionals and community members express the sentiment that there was just "something about Millerston" that resulted in this disproportionately high teen birthrate. Amanda Rodríquez, a Latina in her late twenties who worked as the director of Millerston's transitional living program for homeless teen mothers, called attention to outsiders' perception of Millerston as a "dirty" place. "I think there is this stigma in the city," she explained to me: "You live in Millerston, you're a parent, you're just 'fast' and you have kids." When I asked Ana Reyes Rivera, a Latina in her early twenties who grew up in Millerston and conducted teen pregnancy prevention programs in youth residential homes, about the first thing that came to her mind about Millerston, she replied without hesitation, "A lot of babies." I often heard community outsiders talk about Millerston as if there was something in the water or the air that made young people pregnant or families poor. If you lived in the towns surrounding Millerston, it was not unusual to hear people refer to the city as a "joke." To many outsiders, Millerston is a place where you go to work in a nonprofit organization, buy drugs, or rent a cheap apartment because you got priced out of the rental market in Hatherleigh, a nearby affluent and mostly white college town. To my undergraduate students, Millerston was a good place to go for an internship, but it was best to leave work before nightfall.

My first introduction to community health work in Millerston was in 2006, when I began working at the city's branch of the regional sexual and reproductive health care provider I call Continuum Health Services (CHS). CHS is the area's major Title X family-planning provider and also offers a range of HIV/AIDS programs, including counseling, testing, referral, and case management. Located at the edge of the Canals neighborhood, the Millerston clinic was one of the only occupied storefronts on the street. Although CHS hired me to conduct outreach for a state policy providing pharmacy access to emergency contraception,[52] I mostly languished in the clinic, occasionally clearing expired condoms out of the storeroom closet or fielding phone calls from people with anxious questions. CHS employed many staff from the community, including Latina family-planning counselors at their Millerston site, though the senior and middle management at the regional office in Hatherleigh was almost entirely white. I later worked at the Millerston Community Health Center (MCHC), the city's federally qualified community health center. Located on a busy downtown intersection, MCHC is one of the main clinical providers in the area, offering Millerston residents primary care, urgent care, dental care, behavioral health counseling, a pharmacy, and a variety of community health education programs, including youth sexual health promotion. I wore a variety of hats at MCHC, including writing grants to fund health education programming, coordinating campus-community partnerships, and conducting research related to issues ranging from pediatric dental care access to food and fitness policy. As a result, I became well acquainted with the politics of health in Millerston and the various community players.

Working at the Millerston Community Health Center provided a significant part of the impetus to shift my career from nonprofit management to academic research. I recall sitting at my cubicle one day thinking, *If I have to write one more grant describing how "Latino cultural food practices" contribute to the obesity rate in this city, I might just explode.* MCHC staff and their organizational practices mostly failed to examine how power relations and racial politics operated in their work. For example, although we always included a statement in our grant proposals that over half our staff were "bilingual and bicultural members of the community," these people held mostly low-level and low-wage positions such as medical assistants and administrative assistants. During the time I worked there, approximately 10% of the medical providers (MDs and nurse practitioners) and 12% of senior management staff were Latinx. Although in principle MCHC was committed to alleviating racial inequalities, in practice it failed to put that goal into action within the organization.

Although *Distributing Condoms and Hope* is grounded in a specific city and time period, the politics I describe in this book are certainly germane to locations beyond Millerston. Growing wealth inequality has troubled deeply held beliefs in the American dream, particularly after the 2008 financial collapse. Racial justice movements have gained increasing visibility in the mainstream culture, specifically around mass incarceration, police brutality, and health inequalities. Meanwhile, the results of the 2016 presidential election have exacerbated attacks on contraception and abortion access, welfare assistance, the Affordable Care Act, and school-based sex education. The politics of youth sexual health promotion in Millerston are undoubtedly transferrable to other settings in which sexual and reproductive health issues play out in complex power dynamics. There are many Millerstons.

Methodologies and Methods

Distributing Condoms and Hope uses ethnographic and discursive research in Millerston, situated in a critical feminist methodology, to understand how the politics of knowledge influence community-based public health. As Wanda Pillow and Cris Mayo suggest, a key aspect of a feminist ethnographic approach is looking at what is missing, what is passed over, and what is avoided in the situation of inquiry.[53] What is often missing, passed over, or avoided in accounts of youth sexuality and reproduction is how power plays out in health promotion efforts. Pillow and Mayo also argue that feminist ethnography begins from a different place than traditional ethnographic approaches, "a place that questions the power, authority, and subjectivity of the researcher as it questions the purposes of the research." Rather than attempting to tell the objective, neutral "truth" of youth sexual health promotion in Millerston, this book interrogates the production of knowledge itself. I understand the research "problem" in this inquiry not as youth sexuality or reproduction itself, but rather as the discursive contexts that limit critical ways of knowing, constructing policies, and providing programs and services. Moreover, I consider how my social positionalities and political commitments function in the politics of knowledge production.

Prior to beginning an official research project, I had been an informal participant observer in Millerston for several years as an employee in various community-based health organizations. From 2012 to 2015, I conducted formal observation by participating in a wide variety of community groups and organizations related to youth sexuality and reproduction in Millerston. These included the quarterly meetings of the Millerston Adolescent Sexual Health Promotion Committee (MASHPC), Millerston's annual events for the National Day to Prevent Teen Pregnancy, and events organized through the Promoting Adolescent Sexual Health (PASH) network and its multipartner *Teens Count* initiative. I participated in events such as community conferences, provider trainings, and "collective impact" meetings (see chapter 1 for further description of these groups). I also conducted participant observation at the Towne House, where I cofacilitated a youth engagement group, MAMA (Mothers Are Majorly Awesome), which used digital storytelling to push back against stigmatizing images of young mothers (see chapter 2). Finally, I participated in policy meetings, the Teen Parent Statewide Lobby day, and provider trainings with the Statewide Organization on Adolescent Pregnancy (SOAP), a policy advocacy and provider training organization (see appendix A for a description of organizations and projects in Millerston).

In addition to participant observation, I conducted in-depth, semi-structured interviews with professional stakeholders working in clinical, educational, administrative, and policy domains. Interviews focused on stakeholders' perceptions of teen pregnancy in Millerston and their beliefs about how to best develop health promotion programs and policies. I also conducted interviews with pregnant and parenting young women at the Towne House. These interviews centered on their experiences as young parents and their thoughts concerning the social context of youth sexuality and reproduction more generally. In addition to these semistructured interviews, I engaged in countless informal conversations over the years with professional stakeholders and young parents in the city.

I collected a wide range of documents that provided context for my interview and participant observation data. According to Adele Clarke, using existing visual and textual materials is one strategy for moving beyond the "knowing subject" of the qualitative interview and "be fully on the situation of inquiry broadly conceived, including the turn to discourse."[54] I located and analyzed all of the sexual health curricula in use in the Millerston public schools and community-based organizations at the time of my research (see chapter 4 for analysis of two of these curricula, "Making Proud Choices" and "*¡Cuídate!*"). I also collected print, web, and audiovisual sexual health education materials in use in Millerston, as well as documents such as grant progress reports, data briefs, policy papers, and meeting minutes.

Finally, I conducted archival research to contextualize and add history to the present-day health promotion efforts in the city. First, I searched the database of a local newspaper for the years 1950–2015 using keyword searches to locate articles from three time periods: the mid-twentieth-century influx of Puerto Ricans to Millerston, the beginning of organized efforts toward teen pregnancy prevention in the early 1990s, and prevention efforts at the time of my fieldwork in the 2010s. Second, I used two collections at a local archive that included industry, government, civic, and personal materials. I analyzed archival materials concerning Puerto Rican migration to Millerston, which consisted mainly of newspaper clippings, census reports, and maps. Although there are several published manuscripts related to European immigration to Millerston, the history of Puerto Ricans' migration is less well documented. Therefore, this collection was integral to teasing out the history of racial politics in the city that I trace in chapter 1. I also analyzed archival materials donated by the estate of a longtime civic leader in the city that included administrative files, electoral and legal documents, scholarly works, memorabilia, and news clippings related to Latinxs in the city. The minutes, budgets, memoranda, and reports related to a variety of community health task forces and projects in Millerston were particularly valuable. The most important of these were materials related to the Millerston Infant Mortality Task Force, which later morphed into the first organized teen pregnancy prevention efforts in the city (see chapter 1).

Uncomfortable Reflexivities

In the tradition of feminist research, the ethical concerns in this project extend beyond traditional social science and biomedical issues regarding a favorable risk-benefit ratio and informed consent as understood though institutional review boards. Rather, for this project I understand research ethics as situated in a field of power relations.[55] These relations structure the selection of research topics and participants, the research encounters, and the practices of writing, representation, and dissemination. As a mixed Latinx and white former teen parent with a background in nonprofit work and a university affiliation, I shared positions in a matrix of domination with *both* the professionals and the young people in this study. In chapter 2, I discuss in more detail how I navigated my "insider-outsider" status as alongside my (sometimes disclosed) status a former pregnant teen, as well as the racial-ethnic ambiguity that allowed professional stakeholders and teen parents alike to unevenly understand me as "one of them." My positioning as an "insider-outsider" makes issues of power and representation in this research even more complex.[56] However, as Nancy Naples reminds us, "insider- and outsiderness are not fixed or static positions; rather, they are ever-shifting and permeable social locations that are differently experienced and expressed by community members."[57] Conducting research that assumes an "insider" perspective masks intersecting relations of power. Because in most cases researchers maintain control over the interpretation of results and responsibility for the task of representation, power is always present.[58] This power is not a responsibility I take lightly. Similarly, in this project I do not attempt to "give voice" to marginalized young people or to expose any particular "truth" about their lives. I wish to complicate the notion that researchers can "give" voice to research participants. As Joey Sprague notes, such a position problematically assumes that researchers have power, that research participants do not, and that voice is something that researchers can give downward in relations of power.[59]

Throughout the process of conceptualizing, researching, and writing this book, I have aimed for what Wanda Pillow calls "uncomfortable reflexivity," that is, a "reflexivity that seeks to know while at the same time situates this knowing as tenuous."[60] My strategy for practicing an uncomfortable reflexivity has been to engage with the "messiness" of knowledge production in ethnographic inquiry.[61] In particular, I have wrestled with the messiness of my status as person who was not part of the Millerston community, held tremendous cultural capital as a university researcher, and yet had been subjected to stigmatizing and hegemonic teen pregnancy discourses. This messiness means that I cannot claim stable truths about professional stakeholders, young mothers, or myself. Like all knowledges, my analysis in this book is partial, incomplete, and slippery. I view this mess as productive for our understanding of the workings of power.

Despite the issues of representation and potential exploitation that ethnographic work with marginalized young people might entail, this project facilitates a space where the embodied knowledges of young mothers can emerge.[62] The stories of young people, however, are not the main focus of *Distributing Condoms and Hope*. I have chosen to focus primarily on how professional stakeholders take up and transform youth sexual health promotion discourses related to race, sex, and science for two main reasons. First, I have sought to create a space for young people's voices while simultaneously deemphasizing them in an attempt to avoid so-called "poverty porn" and the duty of marginalized subjects to constantly "confess." There is an emancipatory potential in *not* always being the focus of research and policy interventions and a privilege in *not* having to constantly tell your story.[63] Second, and relatedly, the decision to emphasize professionals' discursive constructions is part of a strategy of "studying up."[64] Focusing on those in power, rather than the default social science approach of studying oppressed and marginalized groups, is one strategy by which to "shift the way we see who is 'the problem' from those who are the victims of power to those who wield it disproportionately."[65] Studying up is a method of working toward redressing power imbalances by researching those who have the power to affect the lives of disadvantaged people. However, like "insider" or "outsider" research positions, studying "up" versus "down" is a false dichotomy. *Distributing Condoms and Hope* is an attempt to study up, down, sideways, and all around.

A NOTE ON LANGUAGE AND TERMINOLOGY

Language is always political and fraught with meaning. Throughout *Distributing Condoms and Hope*, I discuss how the deployment of language serves various discursive projects. I want to make clear to the reader some important choices about my use of language and terminology. First, I believe that gender-inclusive language is an important political practice. In addition to working against sexism in everyday conversation, such language also avoids making assumptions about a person's gender identity or expression. In this book, however, I use gendered terminology (in particular "mothers") intentionally. Academics and professionals increasingly replace *teen mothers* with *expectant and parenting teens* in an attempt to call attention to the role of young men in pregnancy prevention. Sometimes they use this language as a conscious attempt to avoid the stigmatized term *teen mother*. I mainly use the term *mothers* to highlight the political stakes of this issue. Generally, when we are referring to teen *parents,* we are really talking about teen *mothers* (and often teen mothers of color). Using a gender-neutral term can elide the racially coded and gendered meanings associated with young people who become parents. In addition, although reproductive justice movements have made important strides toward being more inclusive of trans and gender-non-conforming individuals, to the best of my knowledge the participants in this project were most comfortable with the terms *mothers* and *women*. My writing reflects the language they used to describe themselves.

A related language issue concerns how we refer to the age of reproductive subjects using terms such as *teen* or *young mom*. I refer to the youth participants in this study as both "young" and "teen" moms because these were the terms they most often used to describe themselves. Some strongly identified with *teen mom,* while others distanced themselves from it due to its negative connotations. I use *teen pregnancy* or *adolescent pregnancy* to connote the discursive context of childbearing outside culturally sanctioned norms, rather than the chronological age of the parent. The scholarly literature generally uses *teen* and *adolescent pregnancy* interchangeably. Public health research usually does not acknowledge that *adolescence* is a relatively recent social construct thought to reflect a particular and unique developmental period of the life course. On the contrary, public health literature typically uses *teen* or *adolescence* to refer to anyone under the age of 21.[66] This is not a neutral choice given that the majority of "teen" births in the United States occur to women who are 18 or 19 years of age and are thus legal adults. For example, some of the young mothers in *Distributing Condoms and Hope* were 22 years old but self-identified as "teen" or "young" moms, either because they became pregnant as a teenager or because they identified with the construct of teen parent. I also distinguish between "youth" and "professional" participants, even though some "youth" were over the age of majority and some professionals were not much older than them. This distinction reflects the ways that health promotion discourses position young people, rather than revealing anything absolute about either group of participants.

Finally, unlike most of the researchers who have worked in Millerston over the years, I have chosen to use a pseudonym for the city itself, as well as for participants, places, and organizations. This is a complicated choice, as making a place-based social inquiry anonymous is quite difficult. More than once I have presented my research at academic conferences nowhere near Millerston only to have an audience member raise their hand and say, "Oh, you mean [name of the city]?" Despite the difficulties, I have attempted to protect the privacy of my participants and those associated with the city in general. This decision is related both to confidentiality and to the politics of knowledge production. I chose my nonrandom sample of key informant interviews because they were primary stakeholders in Millerston's public health work. These participants include the heads of public committees, well-known educators and health care providers, and the mayor and the superintendent of schools. Because I was interested in teasing out how these actors understand the social and political context of the work they do, providing even the smallest degree of confidentiality was important in order for them to be able to speak freely. In this way, such confidentiality helped to promote the quality of my data. With all public figures, I offered to refer to them in the text as an "elected city official," rather than by their actual title, but all consented to my using their specific position. Most offered to use their real name in the text, but I have chosen to use pseudonyms in an effort to protect the identity of many others who requested confidentiality.[67]

The decision to use pseudonyms is also political, as are many other ethical choices in social research. Intervening in an issue that is already overdetermined and overrepresented, like teen pregnancy, entails a complicated negotiation. Taking steps to protect the confidentiality of participants, those directly involved in the research and those simply implicated in it, is a strategy by which to avoid reifying Millerston as "the" place with the teen pregnancy problem. The story of teen pregnancy in Millerston is not a new story, nor is it a story that "ends." It is not even really my story to tell, but I have chosen to tell it and want to do so in a way that is mindful of a wide range of interlocutor needs and desires. I believe that it is an important story to tell, especially in a critical way, despite these complexities and constraints. I recognize the intricacies of these choices, and I know that "Millerston" will be immediately recognizable to many readers. If you are one of those readers, I encourage you to see Millerston with a beginner's mind, to set aside what you already know to be true about its teen pregnancy "problem," and to view the city, its people, and its problems in a new way.

A Compulsory Caveat

Invariably, when I discuss this project at conferences or in casual conversations, other scholars call on me to clarify whether or not I am "promoting" teen pregnancy or to adjudicate its status as a "problem." The consistency with which colleagues and acquaintances ask these questions speaks to how strongly discourses surrounding adolescent childbearing constrain what is and can be known about young people's sexuality and reproduction. Nonetheless, it is worth stating explicitly: I do not think teen pregnancy is a problem, not least of all because I refuse to engage in the redemptive narrative that requires me to frame my own teen pregnancy as a mistake that I should have prevented. I do not care how many infants are born to mothers under 20 years of age, but I am quite interested in why public health is so obsessed with teen pregnancy and what that tells us about race, science, and sex. I do think that cultural framings of the sexuality and reproduction of economically marginalized women and women of color are a problem, as I believe that racism, economic inequality, heterosexism, transphobia, and so on are problems. What I want to "promote" is nothing less than a critical public health theory and practice that reenvisions sexual health promotion in terms of social and political transformation.

ORGANIZATION OF CHAPTERS

Chapter 1, "Race, Pregnancy, and Power in Millerston," locates my place-based inquiry in both historical and contemporary context through an analysis of the politics of race and reproduction. I illustrate how the present-day youth sexual health promotion work in Millerston grew out of infant mortality prevention efforts that began in the 1980s. The chapter also introduces the teen pregnancy prevention industrial complex (TPPIC), details the term's advantages and disadvantages, and makes a case for its political utility. I build on critiques of the "nonprofit industrial complex" offered by scholars such as Ruth Wilson Gilmore, Dylan Rodríguez, and Dean Spade. The TPPIC is composed of the webs and relationships of service providers, organizations, coalitions, programs, and funding at work in Millerston and elsewhere. It functions as a neoliberal regime that promotes individual behavior change (e.g., use of long-acting reversible contraceptives, or LARCs) for remedying structural inequality (e.g., racial health disparities). I argue that it is not the economic impact of the "industry" nor the size of the "complex" per se that is most relevant, but rather its discursive effects. These effects are significant, though not totalizing or immune to resistance.

In chapter 2, "The Messy Narratives of Disidentifying with Teen Motherhood," I engage the tradition of queer of color critique as an analytic lens through which to make sense of young mothers' lives and imagine new political futures. Using the concepts of disidentification, temporality, and mess, I illustrate how teen childbearing works to queer—or "mess up"—normative sexuality and reproduction. Pregnant and parenting young women's strategic narratives both reproduce and reinterpret dominant narratives about teen childbearing. They reproduce common stories of teen pregnancy as a social pathology, while disidentifying with these narratives in an attempt to assuage stigma. For example, young mothers tell stories of redemption through hard work and self-sacrifice while simultaneously critiquing their location within a hierarchy of stratified reproduction. The chapter concludes by stressing the importance and limitations of young mothers' personal narratives within a reproductive justice vision. In particular, their stories can function as a strategy for critiquing and reforming prescriptive public policies (e.g., increased access to contraceptives or comprehensive sex education) that do not meet their actual needs (for, e.g., increased access to child care and safe, affordable housing). I highlight the political possibilities of acknowledging the queer mess of their lives in a way that resists pathologizing or romanticizing their quotidian struggles.

Chapter 3, "'It's Their Culture': Youth Sexual Health Promotion as a Gendered Racial Project," introduces the notion of a gendered racial project, meaning the processes by which race and gender interact to structure social meanings, experiences, and inequalities. The concept names and interrogates how the lived experiences of race and gender are bound up in social significations of race and gender. Gendered racial projects in Millerston conflate the socially constructed, political concept of race with a deterministic conception of Latino culture that dictates gender, sexuality, and health. Simultaneously, an ideology of colorblindness anchored in the idea of a "postracial" society permits the uncritical promotion of long-acting reversible contraception. The strategy of promoting LARC as a magic bullet to lower teen pregnancy rates restricts user agency by minimizing the interpersonal complexities of contraceptive use and eclipses the history of LARC in reproductive coercion. The chapter concludes with a discussion of the seeds of resistance to racial and reproductive regulation among professional stakeholders in the city.

Building on chapter 3's analysis of how race organizes youth sexual health promotion, chapter 4, "Sex, Science, and What Teens Do When It's Dark Outside," uses the framework of feminist science studies to explore how discourses of sex and science produce what can be known about youth sexuality. First, particular and authoritative forms of knowledge at work in Millerston emphasize responsibility, values, and choice while obscuring silences about pleasure, abortion, and LGBTQ youth. Second, professional stakeholders utilize what I term *causal fantasies* about the causes and consequences of teen pregnancy. Causal fantasies attribute declining teen birthrates directly to stakeholders' work and disregard evidence of the equivocal outcomes of teen childbearing while promoting evidence-based sexual health education. I detail how causal fantasies enable community health strategies based on magical thinking, including the notion that a lack of daylight produces an increased risk of unprotected sex because teens have nothing else to do when the sun sets earlier. Taken together, these discourses construct a social world of youth sexual health promotion that centers sexual and scientific "progress" while maintaining sexual and reproductive hierarchies. Scientific discourses in the city reflect stakeholders' belief that their work enables young people to progress to a middle-class, heteronormative life course.

Distributing Condoms and Hope concludes by reframing hope as a mode of critique that imagines how to integrate a reproductive justice framework into youth sexual health promotion work in Millerston and elsewhere. A reproductive justice framework helps us to envision how we might open up the overlapping forms of power operating in Millerston to make more space for a critical practice of youth sexual health promotion. This practice centers on the needs that young people identify for themselves, prioritizes youth leadership, and includes the sexual and reproductive health needs of LGBTQ youth. It accounts for pleasure and desire while valuing a full range of sexual and reproductive choices, including abortion and young parenting. I consider how utilizing a reproductive justice framework, vision, and movement in Millerston would enable new ways of knowing and doing that account for multiple and intersecting systems of oppression and envision new forms of agency for marginalized young people. Finally, the text describes specific strategies that youth sexual health promotion efforts in Millerston and elsewhere can employ in order to move toward this vision, including training, collaboration, and coalition work with racial justice groups and reproductive justice umbrella organizations.

1 Race, Pregnancy, and Power in Millerston

During my research for this book, the disparate collection of youth sexual health promotion activities in Millerston coalesced into a grant-funded coalition called the Teens Count initiative. As a strategy to streamline their work, the initiative began to host "collective impact" meetings to bring together the numerous professional stakeholders in the city.[1] The email invitation to the first of these meetings addressed the invitee as a "community champion in adolescent sexual health" and asked them to participate in a high-impact collaboration to improve the sexual health of youth. It noted that community partners were already taking "bold steps to begin to develop a high impact sustainability plan to fundamentally change how our communities address the high rates of teen births and sexually transmitted infections among youth." The invitation went on to state that this new collaboration would foster relationships among diverse sectors, including community-based organizations, human-service providers, medical clinics, youth leaders, and federal and state teen pregnancy prevention initiatives to "merge their collective strength into one highly disciplined, coordinated, collaborative group," and concluded by proclaiming that "by addressing teen pregnancy and other adverse sexual health outcomes, we will help eliminate barriers so that youth can reach their full potential."

As I entered the meeting space to attend the first collective impact session, a cheery staff person from the PASH Network, the host organization, greeted me and handed me a name tag that read "sexual health superhero" under my name. A major player in the area's youth sexual health promotion work, the PASH Network (Promoting Adolescent Sexual Health), served as a visible organizing presence in the area with the goal of using "research, advocacy, and community education and collaboration to influence policy and practice in adolescent sexual health." Jenny Díaz, a Latina obstetrician-gynecologist in her forties with a background in public health, was the founder and executive director of PASH and had sent out the meeting invitation to a large number of professional stakeholders in the area. The meeting room was set up with chairs arranged in an oval shape and side tables bearing refreshments, including cheese, crackers, fruit, coffee, and water bottles. Under each seat was a goody bag containing noisemakers, candies, and a mug with the PASH Network logo on it. The walls were covered in posters from various PASH Network events, as well as foam-core standouts presenting data on teen pregnancy and STIs in the greater Millerston area. As participants milled about, some in scrubs, some in jeans, others in suits, I could hear smooth blues music coming from the overhead speakers. I could not discern the objective of this elaborate setup. Was it an attempt to make yet another meeting at the end of a long workday more pleasant for the participants? Was it part of the cheerleading strategy Jenny often employed, a sort of reward for all the sexual health superheroes who were engaged in valiant battles against teen pregnancies and sexually transmitted infections?

As I took my seat and idly played with the items in my goody bag, I noted who was and was not in attendance. The "usual suspects" were accounted for: members of MASHPC (Millerston Adolescent Sexual Health Promotion Committee), staff from the family planning clinic Continuum Health Services, staff from the Millerston Community Health Center, and a variety of city health officials. Lourdes Colón Cruz, the educational director at the Towne House, was there, but she was one of the few service providers who worked for an organization that supported pregnant and parenting teens (as distinguished from those that focused on preventing teen pregnancy). A group of young people were in attendance, but it was not clear what their role would be. To the best of my knowledge, there were no current pregnant or parenting teens at the meeting. The Center for Reproductive Justice, a local organization that works nationally to advance the movement for reproductive freedom, did not have a presence at the meeting, even though their work certainly fell under the rubric of "sexual health superheroes."

Jenny Díaz cofacilitated the meeting with Gerald, a staff member from a capacity-building consulting firm that was advising the Teens Count initiative. The two began with a speech reviewing the recent history of teen pregnancy prevention work in Millerston that used a progress narrative to bring us to the current moment, when the hard work was beginning to pay off and we would engage in the collective impact process to protect our investment. Every time someone mentioned declining rates of teen pregnancy in the community, the facilitators encouraged us to cheer and wave the noisemakers from our goody bags. The facilitators then invited preselected members of the audience to stand and share their history of involvement with youth sexual health promotion in the area. These speakers emphasized the important win of implementing comprehensive sex education in the public schools, the promotion of long-acting reversible contraception use among adolescents, and the relationship between high teen pregnancy rates and high school dropout.[2] These stakeholders lauded the importance of recognizing the structural factors—poverty in particular—that contributed to problems in the community, but discussed only individual-level solutions, such as sex education and contraceptive promotion. They shared numerous data points without context or elaboration of their significance, statistical or otherwise. The youth did not speak until the end of the meeting, when one of them thanked the adults for inviting them. To wrap up the meeting, Gerald asked the audience to stand and dance to the Teddy Pendergrass song "Wake Up Everybody" while he shouted, "Say hello to the new collective impact team!"

How did we get here? How did it come to pass that health professionals viewed preventing teen pregnancy through a large and complex set of relationships between national, state, and local players—in a community with a rapidly declining teen pregnancy rate—as the solution to an urgent social problem? What factors contributed to the practices and technologies they employed to reduce this rate? Data and evidence figured heavily in the meeting, as did talk of the structural factors that contributed to high teen birthrates, yet the proposed solutions were all individual-level modifications of young, racially and economically marginalized people's sexual and reproductive behavior. Youth were invited into the room, but did not speak until spoken to. A local reproductive justice organization was not present.

This meeting helps to illustrate the *teen pregnancy prevention industrial complex* (TPPIC) in Millerston, the term I introduce in this chapter to describe the set of relationships, practices, and technologies that constrain the liberatory potential of youth sexual health promotion and serve the interests of those in power. This chapter interrogates the relationship between race, pregnancy, and power in Millerston in order to frame the chapters that follow. First, I provide a historical sketch that traces mid-twentieth-century discourses of reproduction in Puerto Rico to present-day understandings of teen pregnancy in Millerston. Next, I describe how infant mortality prevention work in Millerston in the 1980s transitioned into a focus on preventing teen pregnancy. Lastly, I introduce the teen pregnancy prevention industrial complex in Millerston and detail its relations and effects in connection with other forms of the nonprofit industrial complex.

HISTORICAL CONTEXTS OF RACE, PREGNANCY, AND POWER IN MILLERSTON

Millerston has long been a city of migrants and immigrants.[3] In the eighteenth century, a group of venture capitalists selected the city for a planned industrial community because Millerston's geography was ideal for building a canal system and harnessing the power of the Algonquin River.[4] The first workers hired to dig the canal system arrived from Ireland seeking relief from the religious oppression and economic exploitation of British rule and its resulting potato famine. Later, French Canadians and Europeans seeking factory work found their way to Millerston. Soon thereafter, the canals begot multiple cotton mills, a machine shop, and several textile and paper factories. The factories, and by extension the city's residential patterns, were ethnically segregated, with textile mill workers largely French Canadian and paper mill workers Irish. Millerston's most recent wave of newcomers began arriving in the late 1950s when Puerto Ricans began to constitute an increasing percentage of Millerston's population. By 1980, 13% of the city's population was born in Puerto Rico. By 1990, that figure had risen to 31%, and by 2000 it had climbed to 41%. Today about half the city claims Puerto Rican descent. Like their predecessors, Puerto Ricans initially came to Millerston seeking employment and housing. What sets Puerto Ricans apart from other racially or ethnically marked groups in Millerston's history, however, relates to a complex web of US imperialism, racialization, economic exploitation, geographical displacement, and gendered ideologies. Teasing out these complexities allows us to more clearly understand how sexuality and reproduction, and in particular teen pregnancy, become emblematic of this racialized, deindustrialized city.

A series of legislative maneuvers in the late nineteenth and early twentieth centuries, notably the Chinese Exclusion Act of 1882 and the Quota Act of 1921, slowed immigrant flows to the United States. Both acts were based on a xenophobic reaction to the perceived threat posed by outsiders, a reaction that continues to structure immigration responses today. These restrictions decreased the availability of immigrant labor, creating a demand that Puerto Rican migrants eventually filled. A convergence of economic and political factors (described in depth below) prompted several waves of Puerto Rican migration from the island to New York and other parts of the Northeast. Puerto Rican migrants to Millerston arrived, and continue to arrive, directly from the island but also by way of New York City and other major US cities in the Northeast.[5] Migration to the Algonquin River Valley area also intensified between 1948 and 1982 as increasing numbers of farmworkers sought work in the tobacco fields. During this time the Puerto Rican Department of Labor and Human Resources helped arrange contracts for more than 400,000 seasonal workers in the region. Simultaneously, in the late 1950s, demolition of housing in the nearby city of Carlsborough, part of urban renewal programs promoted by the Lyndon Johnson administration, prompted massive relocation to Millerston. These displaced residents settled into the former tenement row houses built at the height of Millerston's industrial economy.

The particular historical moment when Puerto Ricans arrived in Millerston helped shape a trajectory of racialization that informs the discursive context of youth sexuality and reproduction today. Although the Irish were once a racialized ethnic other, they arrived at a time of economic growth and prosperity. In particular, as fair-skinned, Anglophone Europeans, the Irish were able to access whiteness in ways that Puerto Ricans, as Spanish-speaking, diasporic Caribbeans, did not.[6] Moreover, although the Irish came to Millerston as a racialized class of workers, factory owners valued their labor for the construction of the canal system. In contrast, despite the pull of seasonal migrant farmworker jobs in the region, Puerto Ricans arrived at a time when the city's overall economy was declining. Unlike earlier groups, Puerto Ricans came to Millerston at a time of significantly changed economic structures and declining population in the city. Millerston's paper and textile industries had decayed throughout the twentieth century as technological advancements introduced new techniques for producing paper and fabric and companies began outsourcing labor overseas. Millerston didn't need Puerto Rican workers in the way they had needed the Irish, but other places needed to "get rid of" Puerto Ricans.

Reproduction and Modernity Converge in Millerston

The convergence of US colonialist development policy and eugenic ideology helped push migration from the island to the mainland, and lack of economic opportunities and affordable housing eventually brought Puerto Ricans to Millerston. The persistent colonial status of Puerto Rico has structured the economic and political events that prompted mass migration to the mainland.[7] Sexuality and reproduction are key to understanding these processes.[8] Indeed, Puerto Rico has long served as a literal and metaphorical "test tube" for the United States in producing knowledge about women's lives and bodies.[9] Examining these histories enables us to more fully understand how youth sexual health promotion constructs teen pregnancy in Millerston specifically as a *Puerto Rican* problem. It also makes visible how that construction elides histories of racism, economic exploitation, and the production of Latina sexual deviance. This history provides an important backdrop for the emergence of the teen pregnancy prevention industrial complex.[10]

Beginning with the 1898 occupation of the island, mainland US interests prompted the implementation of sweeping economic policy changes.[11]

At that time, the island's agricultural economy was balanced among coffee, tobacco, and sugar production, but by the 1930s sugar production grew by more than 250%, and mainland corporations controlled two-thirds of the sugar industry. Becoming a monocrop economy had significant effects on unemployment and poverty in Puerto Rico, which transmogrified into concerns about "overpopulation" on the island. Initially this concern referred to the idea that the working class was reproducing "too much," and later became a way for mainland health officials to describe the condition of Puerto Rico as a whole.[12] In their view, excessive sexuality and fertility were to blame for poverty on the island, which almost perfectly parallels understandings of teen pregnancy in Millerston today. Then as now, hyperbolic panic about excess brown and Black babies were discursive productions rather than statistical facts. As historian Laura Briggs points out, although population increased on the island during the 1940s and '50s, so did per capita income. Population growth was not a sufficient explanation for island poverty, yet the "argument that uncontrolled Puerto Rican sexuality and reproduction were dangerous had sufficient force that it persisted even in the face of evidence that flatly contradicted it."[13] Similarly, in Millerston in the 1990s, 2000s, and 2010s, the teen birthrate rapidly declined in a state with one of the nation's lowest rates, yet policy makers, health care providers, and the media considered it a significant social, health, and economic issue with grave consequences for the city's well-being.

By the mid-twentieth century, mainland government officials viewed migration and contraception as solutions for island poverty and overpopulation. Addressing the perceived problems of overpopulation on the island through reforming Puerto Rican sexualities and families was key to becoming a "modern" nation. First, in 1947 the US government set into motion "Operation Bootstrap," a series of policies and programs aimed at transforming Puerto Rico's economy by attracting foreign investment and promoting export-oriented industrialization. Although ostensibly neutral with regard to migration, the Bureau of Employment and Migration opened its first mainland office in New York City in 1948 and "actively encouraged migration to the mainland by facilitating settlement and employment, thus laying the groundwork for subsequent chain migration."[14] Second, as Iris López notes, "the application of neo-Malthusian and eugenic approaches to population and development within the colonial relationship between Puerto Rico and the U.S. played a critical role in the development of the island's birth control movement."[15] Puerto Rico served as a site for early clinical trials of hormonal contraceptives—in what we now know were deleteriously high doses of estrogen and progesterone—in part because public health officials believed the dangers of overpopulation outweighed the potential risks the medications posed. Puerto Rico also became entangled in the politics of population control through the ubiquity of surgical sterilization. Although there is evidence against widespread forced sterilization campaigns,[16] researchers have found midcentury rates of sterilization as high as 35%.[17] Indeed, sterilization was so common among Puerto Rican women both on the island and the mainland that it was, and still is, referred to as *la operación*, needing no distinction from other kinds of operations.[18]

Puerto Ricans in Millerston

When Puerto Ricans displaced from urban renewal projects in Carlsborough relocated to Millerston, the local press expressed hope that these "problem families" wouldn't "pull down neighborhood standards" in their new home. A 1959 article in the *Algonquin Valley News* describes a police officer who took it upon himself to befriend the Puerto Ricans and "point out to them the necessity of education and the adjustments they must make if they were to continue to live in the United States." In 1962, the newspaper referred to the city's new arrivals as "immigrants" who were "lured" to Millerston by cheaper rents and the lesser degree of residential segregation than Carlsborough residents experienced. The article positioned Puerto Rican migrants to Millerston in familiar terms. Using the word *invasion,* the author noted that the population was increasing by three Puerto Rican families per week. Whereas these newcomers had been "very hard at work all week" in Carlsborough, the author states, upon arrival in Millerston they were putting in a lazy "2 to 3-day work week."

By the late 1960s, Puerto Ricans in Millerston became implicated in a discourse about public assistance–hungry overreproducers. In the fall of 1969 the state dispatched its "special assistant for Spanish affairs" to the city to "investigate the reported mass recruitment of Puerto Ricans to fly to [Millerston] and collect state welfare benefits." According to one *Algonquin Valley News* report, government officials were concerned about welfare coyotes who were offering charter trips from Puerto Rico to New York and then bus rides to Millerston to collect on the "nation's most liberal welfare benefits." An official quoted in the article emphasized that families with twelve children were making a dubious $750 per month (the equivalent of $5,065 in 2017 dollars) in welfare benefits without working. Journalists wrote articles with headlines such as "Out-of-State Arrivals Jam Welfare Office" whose content mirrors those written about teen pregnancy today. In these pieces, the women are always pregnant, living with their deadbeat boyfriends, and mired in intergenerational poverty exacerbated by overgenerous welfare benefits.

Millerston's complicated relationship to and thinly veiled racism toward its Puerto Rican residents continued through the 1970s and '80s. In the early 1970s, what the newspaper called "civil unrest" in the city's Canal neighborhood prompted mass arrests and a citywide curfew. Subsequent police brutality directed at Puerto Ricans in the community prompted further organizing and public protest. In 1981 the city implemented a busing program in order to desegregate the public school system. By the mid-1980s, Millerston had garnered a national reputation for its growing arson problem. Although city government blamed the Puerto Rican community for every spate of fires, many residents thought that absentee landlords trying to cash in on insurance money were responsible. Around this time, a white op-ed writer in the *Algonquin Valley News* called attention to the sentiment among some whites in the city that Millerston's problems wouldn't exist without its Puerto Rican population. He observed that white residents believed that these problems would disappear if Puerto Ricans conducted themselves the way other migrant groups did when they first arrived in the city. Although the author made the unusual move of explicitly naming racism as a problem in Millerston, he let whiteness remain invisible and partially blamed city tensions on a lack of Puerto Rican leadership. He admonished "the Puerto Rican community" to develop "an understanding . . . of the feelings of some of Millerston's non–Puerto Ricans about the habits of some members of the Puerto Rican community in such matters as litter in the streets, idleness, and noise." The article represents an apparently widely held view held by white people in Millerston that Puerto Ricans were dirty, lazy, and loud, rather than understanding tensions in the city as caused by racism, economic exploitation of migrants, and inequitable distribution of resources.

Today it is not uncommon to hear similar statements expressed by white residents of the city and the greater region. Most people will talk around the notion that Puerto Ricans are responsible for the city's problems using racially coded language, such as "inner-city poverty" or "Spanish speakers." Hannah McNeil, however, was uncharacteristically explicit. Although I saw Hannah frequently in public settings in her role as chair of MASHPC, she was particularly frank one morning prior to committee meeting when we met for an in-depth interview. "See," she told me, "I grew up here, so it's—I *know* what the city once was. And I know how the city can function, and it is going to have a different face, because it has a different population. But I would love to see the present face become the *past* face, the way it was when I grew up." When I pressed her to explain what she meant by the "face when she was growing up," she replied that it was a time when there was a high percentage of Irish Catholics in the city, something that was unifying (though ostensibly not exclusionary toward other ethnic or religious groups). Hannah continued:

> Well, it was a—it was a safe city, where you could be outside and go down-town and walk anywhere. Your schools were ranked as one of the top in the state. Education was superb. People didn't need to go to private schools. They were in the public school system. Teachers were state of the art, literally. When people came out of the schools, they went on to further themselves. Not only with education, but with job opportunities. We had a lot of unity in the city.

Hannah explained that although the city's annual St. Patrick's Day parade was a point of pride for the city that brought people together, "divisions" in the community meant that the same was not true for the annual Puerto Rican pride parade. When I asked her why she thought this division existed, Hannah framed it this way:

> Well, I think it's because the city—I think the city deteriorated too quickly. There were no controls in the housing. So there was so much inexpensive housing that it drew in, um, people that were, you know, dependent on, um, on welfare, is what it was back then. So, when you have people that aren't

working and aren't contributing to the city—as it was, everyone contributed—
there were divisions in the city. You know, you had the Heights and the Canals
neighborhoods. But all those people still worked together within their own
section of the city. And then there was, you know, integration, which then hit
the schools. Whereas now there's just too much division.

Despite her racialized understanding of Millerston's divisions, Hannah
was quick to tell me that she had an "open mind" and welcomed the
changes in her city. "But there are of course," she said, "those who aren't as
positive about, you know, the changes in the . . . in the culture. So I find
that unfortunate." When pressed, she identified these "changes" as the
presence of more Latinos in the city.

"The Two Millerstons"

In 2006, shortly after I began working at Millerston's branch of Continuum
Health Services, an article in a statewide magazine that covered politics
and civic life posed the question "Can Millerston seize the prosperity of its
college town neighbors?" Comparing the small mountain range that separates Millerston from the rest of the Algonquin River Valley to the Berlin
Wall, the article reified long-held tropes about the city as "dangerous" or
"dirty," a place where the health and human service workers who commute
from the wealthy, white college towns were afraid to remain after dark.
The article detailed the city's attempts at "revitalization" in language that
can easily be read as "gentrification" to make Millerston more like the
neighboring college towns; in other words, more white. The article pos-
ited that Millerston could be revitalized by inviting artists (who, according
to the article, are "used to cities" and aren't "afraid of Millerston") to set up
studios in the city's abandoned factories, attract tech industries to the city,
and promote commerce by opening more music venues and coffee shops.
The author also quoted a white resident who owned successful businesses
in one of the nearby college towns: "Millerston is in the business of being
poor." This sentiment captured the prevailing local understanding of
Millerston's economic condition.

This comparison of Millerston to the rest of the region mirrors understandings of the "two Millerstons." In both comparisons, one place is white,
educated, and middle-class with low teen birthrates, and the other is

Figure 2. Homes in Millerston's Heights neighborhood.
Photograph by Jena Duncan.

nonwhite, uneducated, poor, and hyperfertile. In the most basic sense, the difference between the two Millerstons is a difference in the race and social class composition of various neighborhoods. This simplification, however, obscures the fact that what divides the city into two Millerstons is not merely "difference" but rather marked and sustained power asymmetries. Ana Reyes Rivera had an unusually trenchant perspective on this asymmetry. Ana grew up in Millerston, attended a nearby liberal arts college, and returned to the city after graduating. Sitting on a bed in a spare room of her grandmother's home, we discussed the notion of the two Millerstons. "I don't know if you've seen this yet," Ana offered, "but there's two Millerstons." "Sure," I replied. "Yes. Everyone talks about the two Millerstons." Ana continued: "So, the people that are making decisions about Millerston, and the people that are in power, are not the ones that are getting pregnant. . . . They're trying to fix these problems, or have these ideas, but [the ideas] are not realistic, and they're not really fitting into the lives of the people that are affected." In our conversation, Ana articulated the politics of representation and leadership that plagued the city. She noted the phenomenon of community outsiders moving to and purchasing property in the predominately white, middle-class Heights neighborhood of the city, who then took it upon themselves to serve as representatives of Millerston. She illustrated this phenomenon by describing how one of her

Figure 3. A boarded-up building in Millerston's Canals neighborhood. Photograph by Jena Duncan.

college professors bought a house in the Heights and subsequently became the person whom newspaper reporters quoted whenever they wrote a story about Millerston's problems. Similarly, Ana recalled the election campaign of the city's mayor at the time, Ryan Brown. The campaign drew on his insider status as a person who grew up in the city in an attempt to bridge the gap between the two Millerstons. "I remember," Ana said, "it was sort of like, 'I'm from Millerston, I'm white but I speak Spanish and I went to the Millerston public [school] system like you and I was successful.' And it's like, you are a white man! The system is made for you to succeed!"

In addition to calling out the limitations of a bootstraps mentality that disregards intersecting systems of oppression, Ana clarified how one Millerston has decision-making power, the ability to escape stigma, and the privilege of being ignored in discussions about youth sexual health "problems." The other Millerston holds far less political power and is saturated with stigma and assumptions connected to race, class, sexuality, and reproduction. Those in power, including many community health workers and city policy makers, tended to see the distinction between the two Millerstons as inhering in the "choices you make," as a speaker at the high school's National Day to Prevent Teen Pregnancy rally (described in chapter 4) put it. In this view, the difference between the two Millerstons is unrelated to socioeconomic and racial inequalities. These discursive constructions of the two Millerstons, along with the colonial dimensions of Puerto Rican migration to the US Northeast and the practice of blaming economic problems on poor women's childbearing, set the stage for the emergence of the teen pregnancy prevention industrial complex.

THE TEEN PREGNANCY PREVENTION INDUSTRIAL COMPLEX

When I asked professional stakeholders about the first thing that comes to mind when they think of teen pregnancy in Millerston, most offered responses such as "There's a lot of it" or "We are number one in the state." On a visit to Millerston High School, I posed this question to Farrah Silecio, a white nurse practitioner in her fifties who worked at the school's teen health clinic. Perched on a stool in her tiny exam room, surrounded by posters inspiring young people to avoid STIs and go to college, she answered the question simply with a long sigh. Farrah's sigh reflected the ineffable taken-for-grantedness that teen pregnancy represented for many professional stakeholders in the city. The fact that Millerston was widely known for its tenure as the city with the state's highest teen birthrate escaped almost no one. As Greta McNally, a white woman in her fifties who coordinated the Millerston public schools' science and health curricula, once exclaimed at a MASHPC meeting, "We're number one for something *really bad!*" One year, during a National Day to Prevent Teen Pregnancy rally at the high school (described in chapter 4), the invited inspirational speaker asked the crowd of students, "Let's turn Millerston around. That number one spot? We don't want that. We're gonna turn that around. Are you guys with me?" The crowd cheered (the only acceptable response) and the speaker continued, "Millerston doesn't want to be number one for teen pregnancy. We don't want that. We're gonna try to get to the bottom of that list." Notwithstanding the fact that "getting to the bottom of the list" may not be possible or even desirable, the speaker's comments indicated how Millerston was synonymous with being "number one" for teen pregnancy.

From Preventing Infant Mortality to Preventing Teen Pregnancy

The historical processes described earlier in this chapter detail the marginalization of Puerto Ricans in Millerston and the pathologization of Puerto Rican women's reproduction more generally, but they do not completely explain how preventing teen pregnancy became a key feature of Millerston's public health landscape. To fully trace the emergence of the teen pregnancy prevention industrial complex in the city, we must also look to its origins in the city's infant mortality prevention efforts of the 1980s and '90s. As Annie Menzel and other scholars have shown, infant mortality has long been a racialized political problem.[19] Infant welfare advocates in the early twentieth century initially viewed high rates of Black infant mortality as the result of inheritable "race traits" that made these infants biologically susceptible to early death. In the era of the Sheppard-Towner Act, passed by Congress in 1921 to provide federal funding for maternal-child health promotion, cultural explanations for infant mortality replaced biological ones: it was the parenting practices of Black and immigrant women that was the problem.[20] Similarly, Natalia Molina shows that infant mortality prevention efforts in Los Angeles County during the 1920s allowed public health officials to deflect attention from limited resources and an underdeveloped health care infrastructure toward blaming Mexican women's parenting habits instead. Focusing on minoritized women's parenting behaviors enabled educational campaigns, rather than structural changes in housing or working conditions, to be the primary public health strategy for reducing infant death. The use of infant mortality rates as a strategy for portraying Mexican women as bad mothers had another effect: it reinforced the idea that low infant mortality rates among white women were a consequence of their good mothering habits, rather than their racial privilege and access to resources.[21] As I show in chapters 3 and 4, this tactic continues in health promotion work today. By pathologizing the sexuality and reproduction of multiply marginalized women, economically privileged white women reinforce their own sexuality and reproduction as normal and healthy.

To this day, women of color have higher rates of inadequate prenatal care, preterm birth, low birth weight, and infant mortality than white women.[22] Without a doubt, these are undesirable (and preventable) outcomes, but we ought not to let them obscure implications of the discursive work that establishes a causal link between teen pregnancy and infant mortality. Adverse perinatal outcomes across all racial groups have declined consistently since the 1960s, and the infant mortality rate for teenage mothers declined 34% between 1986 and 2006.[23] In the 1980s, fueled by growing acceptance of teenage pregnancy and parenting as significant social, economic, and health problems, public health workers, across the nation and in Millerston, conflated lowering teen pregnancy rates and preventing infant deaths. This recommendation existed despite a lack of causal evidence suggesting that changes in the teen pregnancy rate would have measurable effects on the infant mortality rate. As with infant mortality, the focus on preventing teenage pregnancy became a raced and gendered strategy to blame individuals for structural-level problems. As epidemiologist Arline Geronimus presciently noted in 1987: "If environmentally induced risk factors are the primary explanation of the association between early fertility and excess infant mortality, then policy initiatives focusing directly on altering the childbearing behavior of teenagers will not reduce infant mortality."[24]

Newspaper accounts, health reports, and task force meeting minutes from the 1980s and '90s provide clues to how infant mortality prevention work in Millerston transformed into the teen pregnancy prevention work that continues today.[25] These documents illustrate how public health workers were able to construct the prevention of teen pregnancies as key to preventing infant death: through positing Latina teen pregnancy as causally related to high infant mortality rates. However, the archival evidence demonstrates how this claim drew more on racialized understandings of economically marginalized women's reproduction than on conclusive data. For instance, a 1985 a report titled "Health Issues and Concerns of Hispanics" argued that the relationship between teenage pregnancy and infant mortality was being ignored and that "physical and mental health problems, e.g. substance abuse, teen pregnancy, and infant mortality occur at alarming levels among Hispanics." A 1983 "Community Study Project" focusing on health issues in the city stated that the "poorer areas are taken over by the Hispanic population," which was generally "young and unemployed." Noting a $1,200 program of sex education in schools, the report concluded, "Therefore it is inferred that teenage pregnancy may be a problem," though the precise correlation is unclear. In January 1989, the *Algonquin Valley News* reported on the reconvening of the Statewide Task Force on the Prevention of Low Birth Weight and Infant Mortality but chose the headline, "Millerston Has Highest Rate of Teen Pregnancy in the State." All of these documents present infant mortality among Latinas as self-evidently connected to teen pregnancy, even as they note the lack of adequate prenatal care services in the area and fail to provide evidence illustrating that high teen birthrates were causally linked to high infant mortality rates.

In December 1995, when the state released its annual vital statistics report, the data revealed that Millerston had the second highest infant mortality rate in the state, in addition to the highest teen birthrate. This report prompted the convening of the Millerston Infant Mortality and Teen Pregnancy Prevention Task Force, which formally merged earlier efforts to prevent infant mortality with new efforts to prevent teen pregnancy.[26] After about a decade of lapsed funding had stalled this combined infant mortality–teen pregnancy prevention initiative, in 2007 the Millerston City Council Redevelopment Committee took up the issues of teen pregnancy, but not infant mortality, and high rates of STIs in the city. In 2009 it called on the city to "become unified in proclaiming that education on reproductive health and sexuality is vital to the prevention of high rates of teen pregnancy and sexually transmitted diseases."

Today the association with infant mortality has faded from teen pregnancy prevention work in the city, even though Millerston Latinas of all ages continue to have lower rates of adequate prenatal care and higher rates of preterm birth than white women. The work continues under the rubric of "youth sexual health promotion," but preventing teen pregnancies is the primary focus. As I discuss earlier in this chapter, Millerston ranks much higher than the state in STI infections and HIV/AIDS. Project and organization mission statements reflect these disparities, but youth sexual health promotion activities focus almost exclusively on teen pregnancy prevention, with other sexual and reproductive health indicators (such prevention of STIs, HIV testing and treatment, and access to prenatal care) taking a backseat or barely mentioned. Latinx teens are at the center of these efforts, sometimes implicitly, sometimes explicitly, despite the fact that the rate of teen birth among white, non-Latinx youth in Millerston is three times the rate for the state overall. In addition, in terms of perinatal health indicators, white teen mothers in Millerston are worse off than their Latina peers: white teen mothers in Millerston are *less* likely than Latinas to receive adequate levels of prenatal care and *more* likely to give birth to a low–birth weight or premature baby. Despite these facts, white teen moms are barely visible in the practical or discursive work of youth sexual health promotion in Millerston. After analyzing how this work forms the "teen pregnancy prevention industrial complex," I describe the contours and webs of current youth sexual health promotion work in Millerston.

The Political Utility of "Industrial Complex"

In conceptualizing teen pregnancy prevention as an industrial complex, I draw on traditions that utilize the concept *industrial complex* to name how social institutions and processes consolidate power. Queer, of color, and disabled scholars and activists have all deployed the term *industrial complex* as an effective rhetorical strategy for critiquing the prison industrial complex, the white savior industrial complex, and the medical industrial complex, among others.[27] Legal scholar Dean Spade suggests that when "intellectuals use various terms that end in 'industrial complex,' [they] are pointing to a multivector analysis of law, power, knowledge, and norms."[28] Similarly, poet and activist Eli Clare describes industrial complexes as "intricate jumbles" in which economic interests crisscross with scientific frameworks, public and private institutions interlock, and governmental regulations sit next to cultural understandings.[29]

I understand the teen pregnancy prevention industrial complex (TPPIC) as the webs and relationships of service providers, organizations, coalitions, programs, and funding at work in Millerston and elsewhere through which groups with social, racial, and economic privilege produce and regulate reproduction among economically marginalized, racialized young people (see figure 2). The TPPIC serves as a neoliberal regime that promotes individual behavior change (e.g., using long-acting, provider-controlled contraception) for remedying structural inequality (e.g., poverty and racial health disparities). Following Spade and Clare, I argue that the TPPIC may involve and be located in many people, places, and discourses: individual policy makers, sex educators, clinicians, and program administrators; federal, state, and local funding streams; NGOs such as the National Campaign to Prevent Teen and Unplanned Pregnancy; medical clinics, high schools, and social service organizations; sexual health curricula and contraceptive technologies; and social norms surrounding race, gender, and sexuality.

Deploying *industrial complex* to describe teen pregnancy prevention efforts is neither a neutral term nor a constitutive descriptor. Rather, it is an intentional political strategy to name and push back against power. Although the concept of industrial complex has proliferated to the point of overuse and may lack conceptual clarity,[30] it is nonetheless a useful way of framing the discursive and practical effects of youth sexual health promotion in Millerston. I use the term to highlight the possibilities for social transformation that are foreclosed by depoliticizing sexuality and reproduction and focusing narrowly on preventing teen pregnancies at the expense of other sexual and reproductive health indicators. It's not the economic impact of the "industry" or the size of the "complex" that's most relevant, but rather its discursive effects. These effects are significant, though not monolithic or immune to resistance. The concept of the TPPIC illustrates the discourses and effects that cohere in and through youth sexual promotion discourse and practice, rather than through specific stakeholders.

There are sites of resistance to the TPPIC, both on the part of individual stakeholders in Millerston and through organizations working at the nexus of social justice and community health.[31] Likewise, not all individual actors in the TPPIC are white: just as nonprofit organizations run by people of color may become wrapped up in the nonprofit industrial complex, Latinas in Millerston sometimes participate in the TPPIC. Like other forms of power, industrial complexes operate by internalizing disciplinary power within us. Nonetheless, to build on Gayatri Spivak's notion of "white men saving brown women from brown men," in Millerston today white women saving brown girls from themselves are an integral part of the teen pregnancy prevention industrial complex.[32] The work of the TPPIC benefits those in power more than it does those marginalized by interlocking systems of oppression such as racism, sexism, and classism. Although representatives of the TPPIC invite young people into the work, for the most part it is only to serve as token success stories or provide a redemption narrative or warning (see chapter 2).

In theorizing the TPPIC, I draw specifically on scholarship that interrogates the "nonprofit industrial complex," the term activist-scholars use to name the professionalization of social movements in ways that dampen political dissent while serving the interests of government and private industry.[33] The notion of a nonprofit industrial complex draws on that of the "prison industrial complex," or a way of understanding mass incarceration not only in terms of material prisons, jails, and detention centers but also as a "set of relations [that] makes visible the connections among capitalism, globalization, and corporations" and "the practices of surveillance, policing, screening, profiling, and other technologies to partition people and produce 'populations.'"[34] Dylan Rodríquez defines the nonprofit industrial complex as "a set of symbiotic relationships that link political and financial technologies of state and owning class control with surveillance over public political ideology, including and especially emer-

gent progressive and leftist social movements." Rodríquez suggests that
the nonprofit industrial complex espouses a particular epistemology, a
"way of knowing social change and resistance praxis that is difficult to
escape or rupture."[35] In Millerston, the set of relations that compose the
TPPIC, described in detail below, is key to understanding the epistemology of the TPPIC. In particular, analyzing these relationships helps us to
understand how they deploy hegemonic understandings of youth sexuality and reproduction in ways that shape policy and practice. The particular epistemology of the TPPIC in Millerston leaves little room for a sexual
health promotion practice grounded in a reproductive justice framework,
vision, and social movement. Like the nonprofit industrial complex and
the prison industrial complex, the teen pregnancy prevention industrial
complex delimits what can be known about its object, that is, youth sexuality and reproduction in Millerston.

Rickie Mananzala and Dean Spade highlight key problems with the
nonprofit industrial complex (NPIC) that are especially relevant to
TPPIC.[36] First, the NPIC separates service delivery from political organizing through reliance on disparate funding streams. In the TPPIC, this
separation makes highly political services like sex education or contraception appear apolitical and disconnected from larger struggles for sexual
and reproductive autonomy. It also helps explain why the Center for
Reproductive Justice was not involved with youth sexual health promotion work in Millerston. Second, federal, state, and local funding of community-based nonprofits take the focus and direction of nonprofit work
out of the hands of the people most affected and concentrate them on the
priorities of funding agencies and service professionals. In Millerston, this
process has the effect of foregrounding teen pregnancy prevention as a key
public health objective in the city at the expense of the health issues identified by community members themselves. Because there is money in teen
pregnancy prevention, youth sexual health promotion in Millerston (and
elsewhere) must focus on preventing teen pregnancies (and not, for example, on promoting enthusiastic consent and healthy relationships). Third,
and relatedly, the NPIC reproduces racism, classism, and colonialism
within nonprofit organizations because elites, rather than people directly
affected by the issues at hand, determine the direction of the work and
make decisions about its implementation. The professional structure of

the TPPIC, and public health more generally, means that people with educational, economic, and racial capital are in charge of determining the priorities and practice of health promotion aimed at marginalized groups. Fourth, the nonprofit structure undermines and constrains the radical potential of social justice work. This process fosters individual service provision as the focus of health promotion, rather than coalitional political struggle. In the TPPIC, this process manifests as a constrained vision of "health" as fewer pregnancies, and thus forecloses the possibility of a reproductive justice vision in which young people have the ability to choose whether or not to parent and to do so with dignity and support.

It is also worth noting that academia is very much implicated in the teen pregnancy prevention industrial complex, as it is in the policing of Black and brown bodies more generally.[37] Academic knowledge production has been critical to establishing the TPPIC nationally, and to some extent locally in Millerston.[38] Teen pregnancy itself first emerged as a health concern and policy target in the United States during the late 1970s with the Guttmacher Institute's report *11 Million Teenagers: What Can Be Done about the Epidemic of Adolescent Pregnancies in the United States.*"[39] This report was instrumental in producing teen childbearing as an object of scientific inquiry and policy concern, even though, as it notes, teen fertility had declined since the 1960s. *11 Million Teenagers* achieved a major discursive move by conflating sex and pregnancy (11 million teenagers were reportedly having sex, not necessarily getting pregnant or having babies) and by identifying teen pregnancy as a problem because it was affecting *white* teenagers. The Guttmacher report instigated the first wave of quantitative social research on the distribution, determinants, and outcomes of adolescent childbearing. With tight links between scholars, research institutes, and policy makers, this research was—and continues to be—integral to establishing and maintaining the social problem construction of teen pregnancy, without which the TPPIC could not exist.[40] As I discuss in the book's introduction, there is much to critique about this body of research, both methodologically and politically. In addition, a fair number of careers have been made on trying to figure out why young women become pregnant and have babies—and how to stop them from doing so. These scholars, who are often men and almost always white, have characterized their career trajectories in teen pregnancy research as a "love affair" or "something that just happened."[41] These characterizations reflect their degree of complicity in the TPPIC, in which regulating the reproductive lives of economically marginalized women of color is reduced to a career move.

Understanding youth sexual health promotion in Millerston as a set of relationships, practices, and technologies that constrain liberatory possibilities allows us to see how health promotion can reify inequalities and serve the interests of those in power, rather than those targeted by its apparatus. The TPPIC eclipses other concerns in the city, including the needs that young people define for themselves. Perhaps most important, it forestalls the possibility that youth sexual health promotion could integrate racial and reproductive justice visions, frameworks, or movements. In the following sections, I first describe the set of relations that compose the TPPIC in Millerston and then consider their discursive and practical effects.

The Contours and Webs of the TPPIC in Millerston

Just like prisons, individual nonprofit organizations are linked to local, national, and international complexes of public-private partnerships, funding streams, special projects, research institutes, and so on. In the same way, broader teen pregnancy prevention efforts in the United States are linked to the local manifestation of the teen pregnancy prevention industrial complex in Millerston. As I explain in the introduction, despite declining rates of teen pregnancy, and the fact that researchers greatly overstate the negative effects of teen childbearing, teen pregnancy remains a major object of social, political, economic, and public health concern. As one indication, during the three years I engaged in fieldwork in Millerston, the US government spent over $700 million on teen pregnancy prevention efforts.[42] The reach of the National Campaign to Prevent Teen and Unplanned Pregnancy, a federally and privately funded nongovernmental organization concerned with preventing pregnancy among teens and young adults up to age 29, offers a useful example of the broader TPPIC in the United States. By connecting national and community-based prevention efforts, the National Campaign both produces and regulates individual teen sexual subjects and expands prevention discourses throughout the population.[43] In addition to coordinating the National Day to Prevent

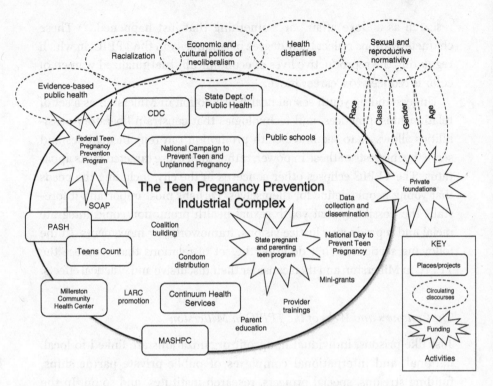

Figure 4. The teen pregnancy prevention industrial complex in Millerston.

Teen Pregnancy, which involves state and local programming (see chapter 4 for a discussion of this programming in Millerston), the National Campaign is responsible for some of the most widely cited statistics on the harm of teen pregnancy, funding the creation of the MTV reality TV series *16 and Pregnant* and *Teen Mom,* and distributing some of the most stigmatizing teen pregnancy prevention ads of the past several decades.[44] The discursive and practical work of these webs and relationships of federal, state, and local teen pregnancy prevention efforts work in tandem with those in Millerston and elsewhere.

Although the size of the "industry" isn't the most salient part of the TPPIC in Millerston, preventing teen pregnancy is a major industry in this former manufacturing city. Although numerous initiatives over the past several years have sought to attract tech industries to Millerston, the city's major employers continue to be retail and health and human services. Human service work—much of it related in some way to sexuality, reproduction, or families—is a major enterprise in deindustrialized Millerston. Indeed, the $1.1 million federal grant that funded much of the teen pregnancy work in Millerston during the years of my fieldwork represented a major infusion of cash into the region. In line with the critiques from Gilmore, Rodríquez, and Spade described above, here I sketch out the set of projects and relationships that form the teen pregnancy prevention industrial complex in Millerston.

Youth sexual health promotion in Millerston takes place through the relationships of a large variety of organizations, people, and places. As noted, in 2010 the Millerston school committee voted in favor of implementing a "comprehensive, scientifically based" sexual health curriculum in the city's public schools. Additional sexual health programming occurred at clinics, including the Millerston Community Health Center, and through community-based organizations such as Girls Inc. As described at the beginning of this chapter, the PASH Network was a major player in the area's youth sexual health promotion work during the time of my fieldwork. Jenny Díaz formed the PASH Network in 2006 and served as its executive director until 2015. PASH is not a service-providing agency, but instead consists of "diverse community stakeholders who work together to create a proactive, comprehensive response to adverse adolescent sexual health and adolescent sexuality." In addition to serving as a stakeholder umbrella, PASH provides technical assistance and holds an annual community-based conference on youth sexual health.

In partnership with the capacity-building Statewide Organization on Adolescent Pregnancy (SOAP), the CDC awarded the PASH Network a $1.1 million grant in 2010 for the Teens Count initiative, a "multi-component, community-wide" effort to reduce teen pregnancy and STIs in Millerston and the neighboring city of Carlsborough (a larger, more racially mixed community that ranked fourth in the state for teen births). The goal of Teens Count was to reduce teen birthrates in these cities by 10% in five years through community mobilization, clinical coordination, evidence-based programming, and stakeholder education. Teens Count project activities that took place during my fieldwork included the formation of the "Clinic Collaborative," which enabled medical providers to share information and resources about best practices, including the promotion of long-acting reversible contraceptives (LARCs; see chapter 3); promotion of evidence-based comprehensive sexual health curricula in area schools and community organizations; creation of a youth leadership team;[45] and establishment of the "collective impact" process to bolster the work in Millerston and Carlsborough (see also chapter 4). During the time of my fieldwork, Continuum Health Services and Millerston Community Health Center were part of the PASH Network and the Teens Count project's clinic collaboration.

SOAP works on issues related to both teen pregnancy prevention and support services for pregnant and parenting teens by administering grants, providing technical assistance and provider training, advocating for youth-friendly state policies, and organizing young parents to reframe the stigma around teen childbearing. The organization is one of a few that simultaneously engage in dissimilar activities such as training providers to implement teen pregnancy prevention curricula and organizing the annual Teen Parent Statewide Lobby Day, when providers and teen parents from across the state converge on the statehouse to advocate for policies that meet their needs. SOAP also organizes an annual conference, though unlike the PASH conference, SOAP's draws service providers from across the state who work in both teen pregnancy prevention and support for teen parents.

The Millerston Adolescent Sexual Health Promotion Committee (MASHPC) was formed in 2010 in response to a request by the mayor to formalize collaborative teen pregnancy prevention efforts between the city health department, the public school system, and the high school teen clinics. The group, officially a committee of the Millerston Board of Health, meets approximately quarterly. A rotating group of staff from area health and human service organizations, clinics, schools, and city government, and occasionally a few academics, attend MASPHC meetings. There are no official criteria for membership, and the committee has a high rate of turnover and a small core group of regular attendees. There is considerable overlap among those who are involved with the PASH Network, the Teens Count initiative, and MASHPC, making it often difficult to tease out the precise role of each. MASHPC runs three subcommittees focused on community engagement, education, and access to health services. In addition to providing recommendations and reports to the mayor, MASHPC is responsible for organizing the annual National Day to Prevent Teen Pregnancy events in Millerston. Elizabeth Randolph, the manager of Continuum Health Service's Millerston clinic, regularly participated in MASHPC meetings, as did Millerston Community Health Center's youth health coordinator, Clarisa Ortiz. One longtime, active regular member, Beth Emmerson, a white former nurse in her sixties, was not affiliated with an organization in Millerston but had conducted research in the city. Throughout the two years that I observed the MASHPC meetings, about one-quarter to one-third of the attendees on any given day were women of color.

In addition to the Towne House, a community-based educational program for pregnant and parenting young women (described in chapter 2), numerous programs provide services to pregnant and parenting young people in Millerston (most geared specifically toward teen mothers). A variety of community-based organizations (including the Towne House) implement the Young Parents GED Program, which is funded through the state Office of Welfare Assistance. In addition to GED preparation and testing, this program provides job skills training, job placement assistance, parenting classes, and case management; it also fulfills the education requirement for receiving benefits under the rules of the federal TANF (Temporary Assistance to Needy Families) program, the current form of "welfare." Young mothers eligible for welfare benefits who are homeless are also eligible for the teen parent shelter system. In Millerston, Amanda Rodríquez managed this program. Other state-funded programs provide child care assistance, case management, and parenting classes to young parents to help them "meet their responsibilities as parents, students and employees." Finally, under a federal grant from the Department of Health and Human Services Office of Adolescent Health, community-based organizations in Millerston and Carlsborough administered the State Pregnant and Parenting Teen Program. The goals of this program are to "provide pregnant and parenting teens with wrap-around services to promote graduation from high school or GED attainment, delay second pregnancy, and ensure teen parents' children are on track for healthy development." Through her work at a large, multisite health and human services provider organization, Emily Lambert, a white social worker in her forties, managed both this program and the aforementioned case management and parenting class program. Services for pregnant and parenting youth in Millerston are gender-neutral in their names, but most are available only to teen mothers. There is a fair amount of overlap and redundancy among programs. With the exception of the Towne House, most programs emphasize preparing young parents for the low-wage labor market, preventing second teen pregnancies, and begin from an assumption that young people need to be taught to be "good" parents.

THE DISCURSIVE AND PRACTICAL EFFECTS OF THE TPPIC IN MILLERSTON

When I interviewed Mayor Brown in his stately, wood-paneled City Hall office, he asked if part of my research was to quantify attitudes surrounding teen pregnancy in Millerston; for example, whether religious beliefs influenced the likelihood of young women in the city to have an abortion. I explained that my work was interpretive and that I was interested in how people made sense of teen pregnancy in the city, and particularly how it related to race, class, and gender. As a way of illustrating that my research was qualitative, not based on frequencies or distributions, I joked that I wasn't looking to quantify how many people in the city think there's something in the water making all the teens get pregnant. The joke seemed to be lost on the mayor, who told me with a corrective urgency, "Yeah, there's nothing in the water, obviously." Nevertheless, while there may not be anything in the canal water, raced and classed understandings of sexuality and reproduction no doubt saturated Millerston. Mayor Brown had illustrated these understandings during a speech at a prior year's rally for the National Day to Prevent Teen Pregnancy, held at City Hall. "As all of you know," he said to a crowded corridor filled with health and human services providers, a fair number of local media outlets, and a handful of youth, "teen pregnancy does have an economic and social impact on our community." He stated that he wanted a "healthy future" for Millerston, and that the city's future depended on resolving the issue of teen pregnancy. In the same way that mainland officials in the mid-twentieth century understood the economic and political health of Puerto Rico as dependent on curbing "overpopulation," the TPPIC in Millerston today understands the economic and political health of Millerston as dependent on reducing teen births (implied but not explicitly stated to be among the city's young Latinas). As a major industry in a deindustrialized, economically depressed city, teen pregnancy prevention becomes the key to revitalizing the city through changing "what it is about Millerston."

Understanding teen pregnancy prevention work in Millerston as an industrial complex enables a critique that mirrors those made by scholar-activists working on issues related to the prison industrial complex and the nonprofit industrial complex: the TPPIC consolidates power to define the city's problems (and solutions) and place them in the hands of those with social, economic, racial, and political power; indexes power, knowledges, and norms that pathologize sexuality and reproduction; constrains the objectives of health promotion work; and limits the possibility that youth sexual health promotion work could be integrated into a framework, vision, and movement for racial and reproductive justice. Just as individuals who work for nonprofits do not necessarily subscribe to the top-down power structures of their organizations, individual health educators and policy makers in the TPPIC do not always subscribe to views of teen pregnancy as an inherent problem plaguing the city. Yet the webs and relationships of individual and collective actors in the TPPIC together constrain a liberatory vision of sexual and reproductive health. This vision eclipses the history of regulating Puerto Rican women's reproduction throughout the twentieth century, and obscures the fact that teen pregnancies were already on a steep decline when Millerston's health and human service industry received significant federal dollars to address the "problem." These webs and relationships also redirect attention away from structural racial and economic inequalities in the city toward individual young people's sexual and reproductive behaviors.

Discursively and practically, the TPPIC reproduces a depoliticized notion of sexuality and reproduction and a narrow view of "sexual health" as simply fewer teen pregnancies. In producing racialized teen bodies and populations as always already pathological, professionals with economic, racial, and social power justify the regulation of sexuality and reproduction. Just as the prison industrial complex (PIC) disproportionately incarcerates Black and brown bodies, the TPPIC also has material consequences. Although they are more diffuse and harder to quantify than the effects of the PIC, the TPPIC in the United States has resulted in decades of research, policy making, and health promotion aimed at regulating the sexual and reproductive behavior of economically marginalized young women of color. Understanding youth sexual health promotion in Millerston as a set of relationships, practices, and technologies that constrain liberatory possibilities allows us to see how health promotion can reify inequalities and serve the interests of those in power, rather than those targeted by its apparatus. In other words, theorizing the TPPIC helps to make sense of the phenomenon of white women saving brown girls from themselves, in Millerston as elsewhere. In the following chapter, I bring in the voices of pregnant and parenting young women in Millerston to further complicate easy understandings of teen pregnancy in the city and imagine a different set of political futures.

2 The Messy Narratives of Disidentifying with Teen Motherhood

On a gray afternoon the day before Thanksgiving, I sat at my desk transcribing an interview I had conducted with a young mother, Tabitha, 19, whom I had met through the Towne House. She always seemed to feel a bit out of place, especially at the Towne House, where she was the only Black student and one of few who had not grown up in or near Millerston. Tabitha was experiencing a lot of changes in her life: struggling to complete her GED, moving around the state to take up residence in various teen parent shelter programs, negotiating tensions with family members, and questioning her sexual identity. Although many of the young women at the Towne House knew that I had had a child when I was about the same age,[1] not all of them connected with me as strongly as Tabitha. Before she met me, Tabitha had never met a teen parent who was queer. The emergence of Tabitha's queer sexuality was, as for most people, a messy process. This process unfolded over the year or so I worked with Towne House students in an elective course we titled "MAMA" (Mothers Are Majorly Awesome), which focused on mobilizing teen parent narratives for social change. Like most of the young mothers I knew in Millerston, Tabitha narrated her experiences in ways that both identified and *dis*identified with dominant cultural representations of teen motherhood. Likewise, as with all Towne House students, Tabitha was already "queer," not necessarily in the sense of her sexual desires or behaviors, but as someone whose reproductive temporality messed up normative social expectations.[2]

Earlier in November, I had accompanied Tabitha and other members of the MAMA group to the annual SOAP (Statewide Organization on Adolescent Pregnancy) conference, where we presented personal narratives from our storytelling workshops. The conference theme that year focused on dismantling taken-for-granted truths about pregnant and parenting teens in order to push back against shame and stigma. Attendees included stakeholders working in teen pregnancy prevention and service providers who worked with pregnant and parenting youth. Tabitha had been incredibly nervous during our session, despite encouragement from young mothers who had presented at another community-based conference, which it was "not so scary." Speaking to a roomful of health and human service providers, most of them white, many of them about 20 years older than she was, Tabitha emphasized that teen mothers' personal narratives illustrate that they can be good moms. "I'm almost done my GED," she insisted; "I'm getting off welfare." This positioning was both similar to and divergent from the message we would hear from a panel of young moms who presented at the large plenary luncheon later that day. Those young mothers played more directly into respectability politics, emphasizing that they were married to the fathers of their children, identified as Christian, or had graduated from college. After the plenary, they distributed notecards with quotations intended to inspire empathy in service providers who worked with young parents. One quotation particularly resonated with me as I rushed back across the state to make sure I could pick up my own child from his after-school program: "Recognize that most of us are *exhausted* and just trying to survive our complicated lives." I was tired from a long day and still had a "second shift" of single parenting to do before typing up my field notes.

During the conference, I remarked to Tabitha that I often drove to this part of the state to visit friends. She seemed surprised to hear this, just as she had been surprised that I drove a truck, had been to the Millerston welfare office as a client (rather than as an employee), and that I was queer. On the day before Thanksgiving, after I was finished transcribing my interview with Tabitha, I planned to drive back to that part of the state to meet up with an old friend. It occurred to me that Tabitha was likely taking a bus there to visit her family. When I texted her to ask if she would like to ride with me, she responded immediately, "Yes, please!" When my son got home from school, we rushed into the car and drove to Millerston to pick up Tabitha and her child at the annual Towne House Thanksgiving meal. We then promptly got stuck in terrible holiday traffic. As our children whined and complained about the traffic in their various toddler and preteen ways, Tabitha repeatedly asked me whether the friend I was meeting was my girlfriend (she wasn't) and whether I was afraid to drive her to "the ghetto." I responded by sharing stories about when I was in college and lived in a public housing project that was, remarkably, occupied by several queer single moms.

A month later, in mid-December, with one day's notice, Tabitha learned that she was once again being transferred to a teen parent shelter in another part of the state. On the last day of the MAMA group, I gave her a ride back to her current shelter so that she would not have to walk with the stack of moving boxes one of her teachers had given her. Tabitha had been hinting to several Towne House staff members that she really wanted a particular red-framed mirror she had seen at the discount store down the street. We stopped there on the way back to the shelter, and I bought one for each of us. The mirrors were flimsy and plastic. Buying her the mirror felt like the least I could do to make her sudden upheaval slightly less awful. I had recently experienced one of many stints of housing insta-bility, and the cheap consumer good felt grounding to bring back to my new bedroom. When I dropped Tabitha off at the shelter, she seemed unu-sually down. I encouraged her to stay in touch and to let me know if she changed her phone number. I empathized with the familiar apprehension of not knowing where you would be living, not knowing how you would continue going to school, and the general instability of life when you are reliant on an oppressive system for your basic survival. In a short time, you're shipped back across the state with a cheap plastic mirror, all of your things in just two boxes, and your first queer friend driving away. Messy, indeed.

I saw Tabitha several months later at the statehouse during Teen Parent Statewide Lobby Day, when pregnant and parenting youth visited with elected officials to lobby for policies that support their lives. Tabitha was there with the new teen parent program she'd enrolled in once she moved to the new shelter. She told me she was doing well and making progress on her GED but didn't like her roommate. She asked if the colleague I'd brought with me was my girlfriend (she wasn't), and I told her again to stay in touch if she wanted to. We lost touch shortly after that.

Making space for the stories of young mothers like Tabitha alongside an analysis of the teen pregnancy prevention industrial complex is a strategy for imagining and theorizing a different sort of politics around teen childbearing. These politics neither romanticize teen parents' struggles nor use their lives to implement punitive public policies. As I explain in the introduction, *Distributing Condoms and Hope* purposely shifts the analytic gaze away from the lives of pregnant and parenting teens and toward the teen pregnancy prevention industrial complex. Pregnant and parenting teens are an absent presence in the TPPIC, what feminist science studies scholars call implicated or silent actors.[3] Therefore, the stories in this chapter are a sort of interlude that responds to Sara McClelland and Michelle Fine's call for feminist researchers to "trouble the consensus that can be heard between dominant discourses and those who speak about them."[4]

In this chapter, I use concepts from queer theory and queer of color critique, including *disidentification, temporality,* and *mess,* to understand Towne House students' narratives as sites for the articulation of coalitional politics. Their narratives illustrate how teen childbearing works to queer—or "mess up"—normative notions of reproductive futurity. In their failure to adhere to normative sexual and reproductive trajectories, as well as patterns of worker productivity and capital accumulation, racialized young mothers "mess up" sexual normativity. I begin by describing how professional stakeholders in Millerston make sense of the teen pregnancy problem in order to ground young mothers' narratives in the local social construction of teen pregnancy as a problem. Next, I introduce the Towne House and use students' narratives to demonstrate how the "messiness" of their lives highlights possibilities for coalitional politics between racialized and nonnormative sexual subjects.[5] The chapter concludes with a consideration of how to incorporate young mothers' messy narratives in developing policies and practices that better meet their needs.

TEEN PARENTS AND THE TEEN PREGNANCY PROBLEM

The circulating knowledges that seek to make sense of the teen pregnancy "problem" in Millerston are integral to sustaining the teen pregnancy prevention industrial complex. These knowledges also form the particular context in which young mothers like Tabitha must negotiate their lives. Before considering the messy narratives of pregnant and parenting young women in Millerston, it is necessary to contextualize how professional stakeholders understood the problem of teen pregnancy in Millerston. Whereas some easily reproduced well-worn narratives of teen pregnancy as a threat to the very social fabric of the community, others worked to tease out the complexities of the issues at hand. Like teen parents themselves, professionals charged with promoting youth sexual health cannot completely step outside the discourses that produce meanings, practices, and identities related to their work. Rather, they must negotiate and work within them.

Professional stakeholders struggled to make sense of multiple circulating discourses about teen pregnancy as a problem; they both reproduced and reshaped common discourses, often contradicting themselves. The major contradiction involved a disconnect between arguing for a structural understanding of the causes and consequences of teen pregnancy while proposing and utilizing individual-level strategies for preventing it, such as sex education and contraceptive use. These strategies cannot possibly address the structural issues endemic to Millerston and many communities across the United States: lack of employment opportunities, inadequate public schools, racism in health care, and so on. While professional stakeholders were aware of and drew on the framework of "social determinants of health," most did not name racism or the distribution of wealth and power in society as key to addressing the issues they encountered in their professional work. Stakeholders quixotically spoke of needing to foster "hope" and "opportunity" in young people so as to prevent unintended pregnancy, but failed to connect the absence of hope and opportunity to a lack of social, economic, and political power among marginalized peoples.[6]

Many professional stakeholders positioned teen pregnancy in Millerston in much the way Mayor Brown described it to me: "It's a very complicated topic [with] so many different variables." Such stakeholders found it difficult to tease out whether teen pregnancy was a health problem, a social problem, an economic problem, a political problem, or an educational problem—often they thought it was all of the above. Farrah Silecio told me, "It's all of them. It's a no brainer—I think teen pregnancy in Millerston is a very complex problem. That's why you can't solve it all. If you get enough approaches, sooner or later you'll, you know, you'll [reach] more and more people, but it is a poverty problem." Farrah went on to say that teen pregnancy was also a "school problem," a "family problem," and a problem that Millerston had long ignored. Emily Lambert, who coordinated primary and secondary teen pregnancy prevention programs through a health and human services organization, also saw teen pregnancy in Millerston as a multifaceted issue. "I wouldn't say it's the largest problem in Millerston," she said; "I think it's the largest *result* of problems in Millerston. . . . You know, there's a drug issue, there's a violence issue, there's a lack of supervision issue, a boredom issue, and there's a lot of adolescents in this town, so if you put all of those together, somebody's gonna get pregnant." She laughed, "Right?"

In contrast to the ways these stakeholders framed teen pregnancy as a complicated, multifaceted problem, Jenny Díaz surprised me by referring to teen pregnancy as a "quote-unquote problem." Jenny was the founder of the Promoting Sexual Health (PASH) Network and a widely recognized leader in the area's community public health circles; much of her career had focused on reducing the teen birthrates in Millerston and Carlsborough. Yet during our interview Jenny questioned whether teen pregnancy was a problem at all. We sat at a conference table at the PASH office, located in a renovated former mill building on the canal, while her assistant answered a constantly ringing telephone. Jenny told me that *problem* was not a word she liked to use about teen pregnancy, but often defaulted to it in her work and public presentations. "You know," she said, "I even kick myself when the word *problem* comes out of my mouth because I'm like, that's not really what I want to say." Jenny went on to take an ostensibly neutral position on teen pregnancy and parenting—a position quite divergent from the rhetoric she used in committee and coalition settings. Was she adjusting her rhetoric because of the highly educated teen parent sitting in front of her? Was she struggling to articulate how her personal beliefs conflicted with her professional work? Jenny explained:

The reason I struggle and you hear me hesitate is because on one end, and I still haven't figured this part out, we need to be able to help those that are most impacted by the situation [of teen pregnancy] just to give them resources. . . . I'm not passing judgment but, hey, if you want to be a teen parent, let me give you everything you might need to succeed because I want you to. Or, if you're not a teen parent but hope to [be a parent later in life], let me help you be the best youth you can so that you develop the skills to be the best parent you want to become.

Using the word *situation* to stand in for *problem,* overall Jenny framed the issue in terms of the racial and socioeconomic disparities in the antecedents and outcomes of teen pregnancy and parenting. Yet she stopped short of naming racial or economic justice as solutions. Similar tensions were also evident in her position as an insider-outsider to the issues and the community: although she was quick to note that she is Latina, I never heard her acknowledge her class privilege as a physician who lived in a wealthy white suburb of Carlsborough. Jenny's framing of the problem of teen pregnancy in terms of disparities was common among professional stakeholders in Millerston. Even those who clearly articulated teen pregnancy as a problem tended to invoke something else as the "real problem." In Jenny's case, the real problem was racial and socioeconomic disparities in teen birthrates. As I discuss in chapter 3, this invoking of racial disparities was a common way for Millerston professionals to talk about race without ever specifically naming *racism.*

Finally, in a slightly different, and important, frame on the teen pregnancy problem in Millerston, Ana Reyes Rivera called attention to the limitations of a binary construction of teen pregnancy as either wholly problematic or wholly empowering. Ana was referencing a trend in academic and activist framings of teen pregnancy that attempt to mitigate stigma by pointing to the empowering aspects of the experience, such as a renewed motivation to finish school, start a career, or leave an abusive relationship.[7] Drawing on her academic and professional work, Ana understood this shift away from stigma toward empowerment as a form of romanticization. "I don't think [teen pregnancy] is a problem," she explained, "but I also don't think the flip side to it is too accurate either. . . . I think in Millerston we're still looking at it as a problem. And we haven't shifted to romanticizing it yet. But I'm afraid that that's going to be the shift." Among teen mothers in

Millerston, however, these binaries of pathologization and romanticization did not account for the messy realities of their lives—realities that were simultaneously oppressive and liberating—just as professional stakeholders' understandings of the teen pregnancy problem failed to capture the ways young mothers must strategically negotiate it.

Although Ana had a keen sense of shifting ideas about teen parents in Millerston, for the most part teen parents were an absent presence in the teen pregnancy prevention industrial complex. They were the invisible manifestations of the teen pregnancy problem. Occasionally an organization or committee would invite a teen parent to a teen pregnancy prevention event, such as the National Day to Prevent Teen Pregnancy, to tell a story of how difficult their life was and how they had redeemed themselves through hard work and self-sacrifice. Although professional stakeholders, the media, and community members almost obsessively talked about pregnant and parenting teens in Millerston, they did so only in terms of the problem of the city's high teen birthrate. It was rare to see young mothers and their families represented in any form except to serve as a warning sign or to tell a story of redemption. As I show in the previous chapter, there were a great number of health, human service, and education programs for young mothers in Millerston, most of which focused on preparing teens for the low-wage labor market, preventing additional teen pregnancies, and imparting parenting skills.[8] Such programs reflected the general approach to educational and health services for teen parents in the United States and reveal the ideological underpinnings whereby providing services is an ostensible means to the end of benefiting the children of teen parents, reducing taxpayer burden, and promoting adherence to normative fertility patterns. Paying attention to teen mothers' narratives, and understanding them outside the pathology-romanticization binary, is a strategy for beginning to build policies and programs that better meet their needs.

The Towne House

The Towne House is a useful site for exploring the tensions between the social construction of teen pregnancy as a problem and the strategies that pregnant and parenting teens mobilize to narrate their lives. Although it is part of the nonprofit industrial complex, the Towne House gestures toward an emancipatory vision of serving pregnant and parenting youth. Nestled in a residential neighborhood midway between the Heights and Canals neighborhoods, the Towne House sits among several old, dilapidated Victorian buildings that were homes for wealthy factory owners back in the days when Millerston was a thriving industrial city. It houses several programs for young mothers and their children but is primarily an alternative education high school equivalency (GED) program. The program is a notable outlier in the landscape of services for teen mothers, both in Millerston and across the nation. Its program is unique in that it enables students to complete their GED within a college-preparatory curriculum that emphasizes the arts, humanities, and athletics, subjects usually deemed unnecessary for preparing teen mothers for low-wage, service-sector employment. In fact, the school has received national recognition for its excellence in the arts and humanities. The program also provides wraparound services, including transportation, free on-site child care, lunch, basic medical services, and college and career counseling. It serves primarily young Latinas from the greater Millerston area. According to the Towne House, approximately 70% to 85% of graduates go on to college—a figure higher than that for the city's public school system. The program serves about one hundred young women each year. Most of these students are "pushouts" (rather than "dropouts"): before becoming pregnant, they were pushed out of public school by policies and procedures that failed to meet their needs.[9] Nearly all came to the Towne House as the result of the welfare assistance school attendance requirement.[10]

In the spirit of this chapter's focus on theorizing messiness, I caution against an uncomplicated view of the Towne House. Like all nonprofit organizations caught up in the webs of the nonprofit industrial complex, the Towne House is beholden to the directives and priorities of a variety of funders, including public and private sources. Its programming focuses on increasing educational access framed in terms of individual achievement and self-sufficiency. Although along the way many students receive a political education—recall Lourdes's words of wisdom about inequality that I quote in the introduction—the primary objective of the Towne House is not consciousness raising. Similarly, although its curriculum and pedagogy made the organization a far outlier in the world of education for pregnant and parenting teens, they nonetheless articulated a respectability politics in which education was a tool for productive citizenship. As I explain later in this chapter, sometimes this linear narrative of pregnancy-education-redemption bumped up against the messy realities of marginalized teen mothers' lives.

I first learned of the Towne House when I was in college and a friend sent me a news article about the school's success in serving teen mothers. Several years later, when I visited for the first time, walking through the narrow corridors accompanied by the executive director, I hesitantly decided to share my own identity and experiences as a teen parent. I got precisely the response I feared: I became an example of what the students can accomplish if they worked hard enough. By the time we reached the front stoop of the building, the director had remarked that my presence as a "success story" would help show the students "what they might be able to achieve." Over the next few years, while working in various capacities with students and staff, I tried my best to resist being held up as an exemplar of a "good" teen parent. I simultaneously had to negotiate my status as an outsider to the community, my association with a university, sometimes being read as Latinx but usually not Puerto Rican, my queer gender presentation, and my status as a former pregnant teenager. Sometimes this status allowed students to connect more closely with me, and other times it simply confused them. Sometimes they teased me for looking so young and having a child so old: they were shocked to learn I was in my early thirties and thought that I must have had my son when was I was 14 or 15. Nevertheless, each time I climbed the steep concrete stairs, walked past the parking lot of strollers, and wandered through halls cluttered with student art, poetry, and award certificates, I confronted the peculiar privilege of being an "outsider" and not a student at the Towne House.[11]

QUEERING THE RACIALIZED TEEN MOM

Ana Reyes Rivera pointed out that health promotion professionals tended to view teen childbearing as binary: they either pathologized it or romanticized it. Scholarly research and media representations often present teen mothers' stories in a similar binary, according to which, teen moms have either "ruined" their lives by having a child (thereby limiting their educational, economic, and social potential) or have "saved" their lives through resilience and redemption.[12] To work against these binaries, I consider how the "messiness" of their lives highlights possibilities for coalitional politics between racial and sexual others. This reframing requires theoretical tools that allow for a robust analysis of teen mother's lives and stories in relation to the discourses circulating in the teen pregnancy prevention industrial complex. Amid understandings of teen pregnancy as a pathology, the landscape of punitive social policies, and the binaries of prevention-redemption and pathologization-romanticization, how can we avoid analyses that oversimplify the complex politics and experiences of teen pregnancy and parenting?

In the following sections, I engage concepts from queer theory, and in particular the tradition of queer of color critique, as analytic lenses through which to make sense of young mothers' lives and imagine new political futures. Queer of color critique is a mode of analysis with roots in women of color feminisms that is grounded in the struggles and world-making of LGBTQ people of color.[13] Activists, artists, and theorists have mobilized queer of color critique to interrogate the intersections of race, gender, sexuality, class, nation, and diaspora as a response to the inherent whiteness of mainstream queer theory and the persistent heterosexism in ethnic studies.[14] The lens provides a set of theoretical tools with which to consider how racialization is central to the regulation of nonheteronormative sexuality and reproduction. Viewed through queer of color critique, attempts to naturalize categories of gender, sexuality, or reproduction by promoting specific family formations or health behaviors are strategies to maintain normative sexual, racial, and reproductive hierarchies. As Martin Manalansan puts it, queer of color critique provides a "view from below" whose mission is to "understand the traffic and travel of sexual matters, how certain bodies matter and certain bodies are located on the wayside."[15]

Queer of color critique helps us to think capaciously about "universalizing tendencies" that imagine lesbian, gay, bisexual, queer, transgender, and others as specific historical and cultural categories with linked behaviors, identities, or bodies.[16] Likewise, it is a productive framework for disrupting the analytic binaries surrounding teen pregnancy and parenting, such as "good" versus "bad," "queer" versus "not queer," and even "teen" versus "not teen" moms. In addition to providing strategies for linking processes of racialization with nonnormative sexualities and reproductive practices, it pushes back against dominant narratives around sexuality and race—an analytic project at the heart of *Distributing Condoms and Hope*. Disrupting binaries and pushing back against dominant narratives are not sufficient to dismantle the TPPIC, but it is a step on the path to an emancipatory vision of youth sexual health promotion.

Although I open this chapter with the example of a young mother negotiating her queerness, the sexual identities of teen moms are not the subject of my analysis in this chapter. Instead, I mobilize queer of color critique to analyze how nonnormative sexualities and reproduction are always already racialized.[17] Like Cathy Cohen, I use *queer* as a provocation to "imagine how we might organize across varied communities defined as 'other' by the state and/or racial capitalism."[18] Roderick Ferguson uses the figure of the Black drag queen prostitute to illustrate this point. According to Ferguson, this figure is "reviled by leftist-radicals, conservatives, heterosexuals, and mainstream queers alike, erased by those who wish to present or make African American culture the embodiment of all that she is not—respectability, domesticity, heterosexuality, normativity, nationality, universality, and progress."[19] Queer of color critique likewise allows us to consider how the figure of the racialized teen mother, lacking in respectability, normative heterosexuality, and socioeconomic progress, becomes the embodiment of a public health problem in which there is little room to understand teen motherhood outside a binary of pathology or romanticization. In the analysis that follows, I ask: What does queer of color critique teach us about the lives of racialized teen moms? I interpret teen mothers' narratives through the concepts of disidentification, temporality, and mess as strategies to think more complexly about the workings of power in teen mothers' lives.

Disidentification

At the same time that professional stakeholders work to sort out whether teen pregnancy is a problem—and if so, what kind of problem it is—teen parents must navigate dominant representations and constructions of teen childbearing. Through strategic, often messy narratives, teen mothers at the Towne House disidentified with "teen motherhood" as a tactic in navigating hegemonic discourses of race, sexuality, and reproduction. Disidentification is a strategic survival strategy for, of, and by minoritarian subjects, or those with multiple intersecting marginalized identities.[20] Jose Esteban Muñoz argues that disidentification is an alternative political resistance strategy that works both with and against dominant norms or modes of representation. Disidentification is neither an assimilation to dominant norms nor an anti-assimilationist position, but instead is a "third way" of responding to power.[21] Young parents at the Towne House disidentified with circulating discourses such as teen pregnancy as pathology, teen pregnancy as motivation, or even *teen pregnancy* as a discursive category itself. Although they rejected representations of teen mothers as bad parents or "children having children," they strongly identified with young motherhood as a motivating and redemptive force in their lives. Thus, their disidentificatory stance both reproduced *and* resisted dominant narratives on teen childbearing.

A MAMA session where we critiqued a teen pregnancy prevention video produced by Millerston High School illustrates how Towne House students disidentified with dominant discourses of teen pregnancy as pathology. The MAMA group had formed out of a larger project that used digital storytelling to push back against shameful and stigmatizing discourses of teen parenthood.[22] Our goals were to map out how to use students' narratives as a community education tool in the Millerston area and in youth sexual health promotion more generally. We also aimed to serve as a consciousness-raising space for young mothers on issues related to young parenting and reproductive justice.[23] In contrast, the purpose of the 30-minute Millerston High pregnancy prevention film is to "shine a light on the issue of teen pregnancy." It does so by combining interviews with professional stakeholders from MASHPC, PASH, and Millerston High and interviews with Millerston High students who were not pregnant or parenting. The majority of the adults in the film are white, and almost all of the youth are Latinx or Black. The adults cite statistics about teen birth in Millerston, describe how reducing the rate is key to a healthy city, and laud the importance of various youth sexual health promotion initiatives they have worked on. The second half of the film features interviews with three sets of young parents (one couple and two single mothers) about the struggles they experienced as a result of having their children, such as difficulty finishing school, making ends meet, and maintaining friendships. The production is melodramatic, with violin music playing in the background and soft-focus fades from one frame to the next.

I structured the screening and discussion of the film by asking the students—using the format of a Freirean culture circle—what they saw going on in the film, how it related (or not) to their own experiences, and what they would like to say to the people in the film or its creators.[24] Although I suspected that the students would have a lot to say about the film, I did not anticipate their visceral reactions. I assumed the video was just another example of a stigmatizing representation of young parenthood that they were well inured to. In fact, this representation hit close to home, and the students swiftly condemned the video for its over-the-top, inaccurate, and stigmatizing portrayal of teen childbearing. When the teen parents in the film referred to their children as "mistakes," Towne House students yelled at the screen, exclaiming things like, "My son was *not* a mistake!" Others yelled, "Shut up!" and "I want to punch them!" In particular, students bristled at the notion that teen pregnancy and parenting were unequivocally negative, that teens are inherently bad parents, and that school-based sex education was a magic bullet for prevention. They critiqued the blaming of high school dropout on teen pregnancy, rather than on "pushout" environments, the hypocrisy of white, middle-class adults telling them what to do, and the absence of any discussion about the positive aspects of teen motherhood. When asked what they might say to the producers of the film, one student exclaimed, "Get your facts straight! I bet a lot of those people who made the film are teen parents too!"

In addition to rejecting negative portrayals of teen parents, students at the Towne House also worked to disidentify with "bad" teen moms—those who were complacent in relying on public assistance or putting their needs ahead of their children's. By constructing other teen moms as "bad," students at the Towne House reinforced their status as "good" teen moms, evoking what Ranita Ray calls "identities of distance."[25] When Tabitha insisted at the SOAP conference, "I'm almost done my GED; I'm getting off welfare," she strategically positioned herself as distinct from the bad teen moms, those who were content to receive welfare benefits in lieu of working at a paid job outside the home. Similarly, Valeria, a 21-year-old Latina mother to a newborn and a toddler, told me, "I obviously want to finish school, go to college, have a wonderful career that's gonna support me and my kids, have a beautiful house one day and have nice cars, and . . . not have to worry about, I guess, like living off the government and—or, if I am living off the government, not being on it so long that—I just want better for me and my kids." Emma, a 21-year-old Latina mother of a baby who also had custody of her 15-year-old sister, emphasized how she prioritized the needs of her daughter over her own. "Everybody tells me that I'm a good mom," she explained, "so, everything—all the money I get—goes to my daughter. I've been slacking and my eyebrows look horrible, I usually don't look like this [sloppy]. I mean, ever since I gave birth I've been slacking on the way that I look. Also, I pretty much spend every dime that I get on her." For these young women, disidentifying with teen motherhood meant working to distance themselves from pathology by emphasizing their hard work, career aspirations, and selfless mothering practices.

Although they rejected the normative discourses of teen pregnancy depicted in the Millerston High video and worked to distance themselves from the identity of a "bad" teen mom, Towne House students also reproduced elements of dominant teen pregnancy discourses when narrating aspects of their own lives. Nearly all of them named early childbearing as the factor that *saved*, rather than "ended," their lives. They identified with the experience of teen mothering as a motivating factor that helped them to leave abusive relationships, go back to school, and so on.[26] As Ferguson puts it, to "disidentify" means to take up with revisions, and Towne House students strategically took up and revised the narrative of teen parent redemption.[27]

Isabel, a 19-year-old Black and Latina mother to a toddler, told me that she thought teen pregnancy was a problem but that "it's kind of hypocritical to come out of my mouth because, I mean, I have a baby." She also positioned her son as her motivation: "My son is two years-old and he is everything that I need him to be. And I know for a fact that I did that by myself, against the odds. He pushes me to wanna do something better." Similarly, Andrea, an 18-year-old Latina mother to a 1-year-old, reproduced dominant stories about teen pregnancy and parenting as social pathologies, but later disidentified with them. She explained, "I don't think being a teen mom is a problem but it's hard. Like, it's not easy. So I don't know, for me, I think it's not a problem because I'm a mother myself but if I would've had the time to go back and think about stuff right, I wouldn't get pregnant." Like Isabel, Karelma, also a Black and Latina 19-year-old mother to a 1-year-old, identified with this narrative of motivation and redemption. When I spoke to her one day at the Towne House she told me:

> I came [to the school] three months after I had my son. So I've been here ever since, and at first I was kind of messing up in the beginning. I wasn't coming a lot but then I started to realize like, hold on, I have to get it together. I have to do something because I have a baby now and want to be able to give my son whatever he wants and in order to do that, I have to have a good paying job and in order to do that I have to have some type of education. So that's when I just started getting like on, I have to do this, I have to do that, and this is all going to be for my son. So that's why I do it.

Yara, an 18-year-old Latina mother to a toddler, also identified with teen parenting as a motivational force that inspired resilience. She explained, "I got kicked out [of my house], and then when I found out I was pregnant it was different, because you want a future for you and your kid. You want to change. You're not going to be as ignorant, because that's ignorant, you know? You're going to be more mature and do what you got to do for you and for your kid, [and do] the best for your kid."[28]

As these narratives demonstrate, teen mothers at the Town House worked to strategically negotiate circulating discourses about pathology, redemption, and resilience. In taking up these discourses with revisions, their narratives often contradict themselves.[29] Like Isabel, many students I spoke to characterized teen pregnancy as a problem, but quickly elaborated that statement to exclude themselves from it, or to clarify the parameters of who teen pregnancy was or was not a problem for. Disidentifying with teen pregnancy as pathology meant separating their own reproductive decisions from those of other young women who were younger than them, were unmotivated to finish school, or were complacent in staying on welfare. In this sense, the young mothers' strategies actually helped to reproduce pathological constructions and representations of teen childbearing. I have to imagine that they likely even disidentified with *me* and my presence in their lives. Although they knew I was also a young mom, because many of them thought I had my son at a much younger age than they did, students often believed I fell into the category of the "bad" teen mom. They may have identified with my progress narrative of proving myself through higher education, but didn't understand what "graduate" school was. Although they identified with me as a single parent—and the stigma, hardship, and joy that may come with it—many of them disidentified with my queerness, even if they didn't articulate that stance.

Temporality

During another MAMA session, I led a brainstorm on how film, television, and news media portray teen mothers. The young women participating that day discussed how reality TV shows such as MTV's *Teen Mom* and *16 & Pregnant* presented a wholly *un*realistic portrayal of life as a young parent; in general, participants observed that the media represent pregnant and parenting young women as promiscuous welfare frauds. As part of this conversation, the students pointed out that whereas nowadays the media—and society in general—consider teen childbearing to be a "big deal," this was not the case a generation ago. Noting that older women in their families had had children in their teens but weren't excoriated as "teen moms," the participants drew attention to the fairly recent temporal construction of "teen" motherhood.[30] Recall that Towne House educational director Lourdes Colón Cruz pointed out to students that, in her view, "teen" mothers are young women who are 14- or 15-years-old, not 18- to 20-years-old, like most of the Towne House students (described in the introduction). Lourdes also explained to me that she did not learn that she was a "teen" mother herself until she began working in Millerston as an adult and was exposed to discursive constructions of normative childbearing time. "I realized that I had been a teen mom all my life! I never knew! Because I think the age range is like sixteen to nineteen?" she said.[31] "In public health research a teen parent is usually anyone under 20 years old," I explained. Lourdes continued, "And so a lot of the teen mothers that we have here [at the Towne House] are eighteen and nineteen. And in our [Puerto Rican] community, we're adults. We're not teens." I offered, "Well, and they're also legal adults." Lourdes laughed:

Exactly! So that's the—that's one of the concerns, or pet peeve I have with the age group. That when we say [Millerston has] the highest teenage pregnancy rate, we're talking about girls that are between the ages of 17 and 19. And that a lot of 18- and 19-year-olds don't consider themselves teenagers, they consider themselves adults, and that way back when, in this country, um, there was a lot of students graduating at eighteen, getting married that June, and having babies at 19. And nobody saw that as an issue, or as a problem. But now all of a sudden this is a problem. And it's a problem because these girls are poor, and this country—or systems, or institutions—feel they are financially supporting these young women.

In this exchange Lourdes points out the discursive constructions of childbearing time, the normative proscriptions about appropriate fertility-timing behaviors, the instability of normative reproductive time, and how this is all connected to race and class. As Wanda Pillow puts it, "Teen mothers' bodies are marked and bear the marks of discursive, paradigmatic constructions of being 'out of time.'"[32] My exchange with Lourdes demonstrated this mark of being out of temporal sequence; as she explained, society deemed students at the Towne House "teen mothers" not so much because of their age as because of racialized ideas about poverty and welfare dependency.[33]

My conversation with Lourdes and the discussion at the MAMA group illustrate how teen childbearing disrupts "chrononormativity," or social patternings of experiences that conform to normative understandings of time.[34] Normative time follows a proscriptive, linear formula that adheres to dominant modes of fertility patterns, capital accumulation, longevity, and progress. In contrast, queer time "makes clear how respectability, and the notions of the normal on which it depends, may be upheld by a middle-class logic of reproductive temporality."[35] Viewing queer temporality through a queer of color lens reveals it to be a particular, white middle-class temporal logic that dictates fertility timing, living arrangements, or parenting styles.[36] In their failure to adhere to normative sexual and reproductive trajectories, as well as patterns of worker productivity and capital accumulation, racialized young mothers queer normative temporal arrangements.[37]

Like Lourdes, Towne House students also drew attention to raced and classed constructions of culturally sanctioned childbearing timing. For

example, Isabel used the nearby white, middle-class town of Hatherleigh
to demonstrate how race and class privilege mediated the pathology of
"teen" childbearing:

> For girls who live over here, in Millerston than girls who live in, let's say,
> Hatherleigh, I always say that those girls, it's a lot easier for them, a *lot*,
> because their parents end up with money. And so they have better environ-
> ments and they know that they don't have to worry about the things that we
> have to worry about, being in that we live in what people call the ghetto, and
> we have to fend for ourselves and do things for ourselves. I think it doesn't
> matter whether you're rich or poor. Teen girls—there's teen moms that are
> rich and pregnant; they just don't make a big deal out of it because they have
> money, so they can do whatever it is that they need to do. But when a girl
> who doesn't have anything gets pregnant and is on welfare, and everything,
> then everyone has a problem with teen pregnancy.

In other words, race and class privilege shape the temporal construction
of who is considered a "teen" parent, echoing Ferguson's understanding of
figures "outside the rational time of capital, nation, and family."[38] Isabel
continued: "I think that they [society] make it a big deal about us only
because they're taxpayers, and we're not, because we receive welfare. I
think that if you did a survey and went and knocked on everyone's door in
Hatherleigh, at least *half* or more of those people protesting against teen
moms have teen kids that are mothers." In Isabel's estimation, race and
class privilege afford young mothers a privacy that multiply marginalized
teen mothers do not have access to. Tucked away in white middle-class
suburbia, these teen mothers disrupt normative reproductive timing, but
that disruption is assuaged by their access to capital, their ability to avoid
public assistance, and their whiteness.[39]

Chrononormativity and its attendant discourses of race, class, gender,
and sexuality contribute to the pathologization and stigmatization of teen
motherhood. When I asked Cristina, a 20-year-old Latina mother to a toddler who was pregnant with her second child, why she thought society
judges young mothers, she referenced teen childbearing's disruption of
normative reproductive futures and socioeconomic mobility. "[Teen moms
get judged] 'cause of school and all that," she explained. "You know,
you're supposed to go straight to school, to finish school before we have
families. We live in our moms'—our parents'—home. What else? Our ages,

obviously. I don't know, they see teenagers as wild, that's why." In contrast, Marisol, a 21-year-old Latina mother to a toddler and an infant, internalized the notion that teen pregnancy is a problem because it forces young people to forgo a normative adolescence. As she explained, teen pregnancy is "difficult because you can't live your life." "You know what I mean?" she asked me. "I'm twenty-one, I don't go out to the clubs. I want to have fun but I can't. I got the responsibilities at home waiting for me right after school. Right after school I go pick [the kids] up, I have to go home, I cook, I clean, I give them a bath, then time to go to bed." This was a common example Towne House students used to discuss the ways that teen motherhood affected one's social life, particularly in relation to "going out." Towne House students lamented the loss of community and time for themselves brought on by motherhood, but also used this as a strategy to disidentify with "bad" teen mothers who did not conform to normative prescriptions about intensive mothering practices as a strategy of redemption.[40] For instance, Marisol criticized other young mothers who left their children with a grandparent every weekend to go out. She noted that this practice could be construed as a reason for social services to put teen parents under surveillance: "They can take your kids away for that." Indeed, disrupting chrononormative childbearing practices—whether having a baby before middle-class economic attainment, failing to devote all of one's time to intensive mothering practices, or simply being Black or brown—frequently precipitates involvement with the child welfare system.[41]

Interruptions to chrononormativity are at the heart of cultural anxieties about teen childbearing and are implicated in attempts to regulate the sexuality and reproduction of young economically marginalized women of color. As I show in the following two chapters, youth sexual health promotion discourses in Millerston linked sexuality and progress by positioning a reduction of the Latina teen birthrate as integral to the city's social and economic progress. Professional stakeholders located Millerston youth on a trajectory of progress in which having "hope" and avoiding pregnancy leads to a normative, heterosexual, middle-class family in the future. However, research demonstrates that structural factors such as racism, income inequality, and educational inequality (rather than simply having "hope") have the greatest impact on the futures of marginalized people.[42] Moreover, these chrononormative arrangements and prescriptions do not account for the messy, nonlinear realities of teen mothers. Pillow notes that teen mothers' failure to adhere to normative reproductive temporalities results in policy making in which their futures are not even imagined—the possibility, for instance, that teen mothers could envision a career beyond inflexible, low-wage service-sector employment.[43] Theorizing queer temporalities helps to explain how the social construction of "teen" motherhood is not so much about chronological age as about relationships to dominant modes of power. It also opens up a space in which to imagine radical futures for pregnant and parenting teens.

Mess

Social policy discourses and health promotion practice generally allow teen mothers to tell their stories in either of two ways: stories of redemption through hard work and individual self-sacrifice, or cautionary tales about the hardship of teen childbearing. As Ana Reyes Rivera pointed out, some teen parent advocates emphasize—sometimes to the point of romanticizing—the ways that motherhood can be a motivating force in a marginalized young person's life. Narratives of resilience and motivation are strategies for working against the deeply entrenched notion that teen pregnancy "ruins" a young person's life by instead positioning it as something that "saves" their life. These are strategies that young mothers use in their disidentifications with the pathology approach and are widely used by advocacy organizations like the Towne House and SOAP. Yet, although it might sully strategic narratives of resilience and individual success, it is important to make visible the messiness of young mothers' lives under intersecting systems of racism, classism, sexism, and so on. For Martin Manalansan, theorizing queer as "mess" is a strategy "for funking up and mobilizing new understandings of stories, values, objects, and space/time arrangements."[44] Mess highlights how the quotidian experiences of teen moms mess up normative social arrangements, sexual and reproductive practices, and the "neat normative configurations and patterns that seek to calcify lives and experiences."[45] Obscuring either the pleasures or the struggles of pregnant and parenting teens serves to reinforce a binary of prevention and redemption.[46] Theorizing the messiness of their stories neither pathologizes nor romanticizes the experience of teen mothers, but instead provides a way to imagine a politics in which their lives are neither wholly oppressive nor wholly liberating.

A community forum held in Millerston one spring illustrates the importance and potential of mess in young mothers' lives, as well as the danger in cleaning up their stories. The forum was the culmination of the MAMA group and the research project it grew out of. At the event, young mothers from the Towne House showcased the digital stories they had created in a panel format and responded to audience reactions. As I settled into my seat in the packed auditorium, I observed how infrequently such a wide range of constituents gathered together in one place. In addition to former and current Towne House students and staff, I noticed people from a variety of players in Millerston's youth sexual health promotion work, including PASH, SOAP, and various health and human service organizations. It was rare to see professional stakeholders who primarily worked in teen pregnancy *prevention* at a Towne House event. It was also rare to see children and babies at a Towne House event; as a policy, staff generally did not allow it. At this forum, fathers and grandparents soothed crying infants and chased around energetic toddlers while the Towne House students took the stage to present their work. Not accidentally, it was the annual National Day to Prevent Teen Pregnancy, and the week MASHPC held a series of teen pregnancy prevention events around the city. At this event, young people would tell a set of narratives very different from those presented at the teen pregnancy prevention rallies.

The Towne House executive director, a white woman in her fifties, spoke briefly before the students shared their digital stories. She stated that the students "had grown a lot in the 8 months since they made the stories," and repeatedly emphasized the stories were a "snapshot in time" of the students' lives. I had recently learned from a colleague that, elsewhere, the director had characterized the stories as "trafficking in tragedy." As the first story played, a narrative about navigating the teen parent shelter system, I shifted uncomfortably in my seat, turning the phrase over in my mind. I recognized that the Towne House, as a nonprofit organization in need of material, political, and financial support, needed to tell a particular narrative of young motherhood. I suspected that the director was worried that the messy realities of the narratives portrayed in the short films—of teen moms calling out abusive shelter staff, recounting tales of intimate partner violence, expressing ambivalence about motherhood, or admitting that they weren't always perfect mothers—would sully the reputation she and her staff had worked so hard to build. Students in the MAMA had reported that one of the reasons they enjoyed the group so much was that it afforded an opportunity to "tell it how it is." This was an opportunity they did not have in other Towne House courses. For the most part, staff encouraged or dictated that students' writing and art conform to a redemption-resilience narrative in which having a baby gave them the motivation to finish school, get off welfare, and become responsible citizens.

All around me I noticed service providers quietly dabbing their eyes with tissues. Their comments suggested the tears reflected not that they were sad, but rather that they were moved by the stories. One staff member from SOAP stood up, her voice trembling and her eyes teary, and remarked, "As someone who works with service providers, these stories show how much more work there is to do to prevent young moms from being shamed and stigmatized." PASH founder Jenny Díaz took the microphone and immediately got choked up. She acknowledged the strength she saw among the Towne House students and thanked them for bringing up the next generation. A Towne House student whom I didn't recognize stood up and thanked her peers for sharing their stories. "People gave me shit," she said, "but I know at the bottom of my heart that I'm a good mom." Watching the audience's visceral reactions, I couldn't stop asking myself, "What was so tragic about these stories?" They did not adhere to the normative prescriptions afforded to teen parent narratives, but their quotidian urgency spoke both to the fierceness of these young women *and* to the ways in which they suffered under the weight of shame and stigma.

The young-parent plenary at the SOAP conference, described at the beginning of this chapter, provides another useful instance for theorizing the necessity of mess in teen mothers' lives. The plenary began with the panelists scattered throughout the audience in a large conference banquet hall. One by one, they stood up, walked to the podium, and, with strong, steady voices, completed the prompt, "The last time I was shamed was when. . . ." Their statements included moments such as "when I was told I wouldn't go to college," "when I used my WIC vouchers,"[47] "when my coworker said I had accomplished a lot for having a kid at a young age," and "when I saw a video that said my son was more likely to be in jail." It was a powerful performance, and certainly piqued the audience's attention. As the panelists took a seat at the stage, I felt myself grow uneasy about what was about to happen next: were these young women speaking truth to power, or were they about to reproduce a well-worn narrative about resilience and redemption?

The panel consisted of five young women, none of whom appeared to be older than about 25, with carefully planned racial diversity: one Black woman, two Latinas, and two white women. They wore "business casual" attire—pant suits in muted colors—and spoke confidently and assertively while introducing themselves. A moderator asked questions such as, "Where or who would you be without stigma and shame?" and "How has being exposed to shame shaped the woman you are today?" In their responses, the young women reiterated, many times over, that they were professionals, educated, married, good parents, good students, religious, college graduates, business owners, and so on. Thinking back to the MAMA panel earlier that morning, when participants shared stories of having their food spit on in the teen parent shelter kitchen, of biological fathers who refused paternity, and of children mistakenly taken away by social services, I could not imagine Towne House students sitting on that stage. Tabitha and her classmates—who had already left the conference so they could pick up their children from the Towne House day care on time—wore low-cut T-shirts, big hoop earrings, and tight, ripped jeans.[48] At various points during our panel they cursed, cried, or refused to make eye contact with their audience. They were messy. They embodied Deborah Vargas's theorization of *lo sucio* as an analytic that exceeds racialized and sexualized normativity.[49] In contrast, the plenary panelists mobilized a tidy narrative of middle-class, heterosexual, Christian, hardworking, cultivated parenting in order to bolster the conference's theme of working to end shame and stigma. They were respectable teen moms, cleaned up to be the ambassadors of SOAP's campaign to end shame and stigma. And yet they also seemed to endorse stigma and shame as tactics necessary to clean up the mess of teen childbearing and produce tidy narratives.

The irony here is that the plenary panelists were insisting—intentionally or not—that shame and stigma shouldn't happen *because* of these respectable characteristics. What about all the other young moms, the many who don't have access to privilege, resources, and opportunities? What about the young moms who face considerable barriers to success, such as homelessness, food insecurity, violence from intimate partners and other family members, and their own or their family's struggles with substance abuse? Did they deserve stigma and shame? Is it only the married, devout, business-owning college graduates who shouldn't be stigmatized and shamed? I do not imagine that the plenary panelists or the SOAP staff would answer these questions in the affirmative. I do, however, want providers, scholars, and activists to consider the ramifications of neat, cleaned-up narratives. I want them to recognize that by playing into respectability politics, these narratives create a hierarchy of deserving and undeserving teen parents. I want all of us engaged in the lives of multiply marginalized young mothers to reflect on how the limited set of available narratives constrains how they envision their lives. I want professional stakeholders, researchers, policy makers, and cultural observers to analyze the limitations of policies and programs built around binary narratives of pathology and redemption. I want us all to sit with the discomfort of the complexities of young mothers' lives and acknowledge the ways in which teen motherhood is both liberating *and* oppressive.

Queer as mess involves "not a cleaning up but rather a spoiling and cluttering" of neat, easy narratives.[50] Rather than calcify the lives and experiences of marginalized teen mothers, I seek a messy method to spoil the neat, normative set of narratives circulating in policy, academic, and activist domains alike.[51] I resist "cleaning up" teen mothers' lives for inclusion into narratives of either prevention or redemption. According to Manalansan, messy queer knowledge is that which is uncomfortable, discomfiting, and untidy.[52] Undoubtedly, it is uncomfortable to advance an understanding of teen mothers' lives as simultaneously joyous *and* oppressive. This understanding goes against both health promoters' mobilization of teen pregnancy as a life-ruining social problem and advocates' narrative of teen pregnancy as a life-saving motivation. Nevertheless, theorizing mess is productive of imagining teen parenthood outside a binary of "good" or "bad," which can help policy makers and service providers begin to better meet the needs of marginalized young mothers.

WHAT DOES QUEER OF COLOR CRITIQUE TEACH US ABOUT RACIALIZED TEEN MOTHERS?

In thinking through what queer of color critique can teach us about teen mothers' stories, I return to Cathy Cohen's decisive 1997 essay, "Punks, Bulldaggers, and Welfare Queens." In this piece, Cohen argues for a political vision based on coalition among marginalized people, rather than basing political solidarity on shared identities. The practice of coalitional politics engages as the basis for advancing our collective liberation the shared marginal relationship to dominant power structures that normalize, legitimize, and privilege particular sexual and reproductive subjects. Cohen links the figures in her title by their relationship to dominant constructs of white, economically privileged, heteronormative sexuality. She cautions against frameworks that see oppression through a single lens and notes the dangers of working toward assimilation into dominant power structures. "Only by recognizing the link between the ideological, social, political, and economic marginalization of punks, bulldaggers, and welfare queens," she writes, "can we begin to develop political analyses and political strategies effective in confronting the linked yet varied sites of power in this country."[53] This vision of a coalitional politics is a key lesson that queer of color critique has to offer in theorizing the messiness of young mothers' lives. Like other sexual and reproductive subjects who strategically navigate hegemonic representations through disidentification, who disrupt normative patterns of time, and who mess up neat, binary stories of sexuality and reproduction, the lives of racialized teen mothers have important potential alongside those of the punks, the bulldaggers, and the welfare queens. What kinds of futures are possible when we organize around the shared relationship to power experienced by queers, teen moms, and all sexual and reproductive others?

Coalitional politics can inform the development and implementation of policies and practices that meet teen mothers' complex needs. The teen pregnancy prevention industrial complex understands teen mothers' needs as narrow and constrained: to prevent additional pregnancies and get off of welfare. Although at times it may uncritically reproduce narratives of redemption, the Towne House is a generative example of what affirming and supportive programs for teen mothers look like. However, the Towne House is a far distant outlier in its approach to education and social support services for young mothers. And even so, the school often relies on a tidy narrative of resilience and redemption. Understanding what teen mothers need through the lens of shared marginal relationship to power opens up the possibility of thinking about how racism, sexism, classism, and the like structure their lives simultaneously. In addition to providing affirming and supportive educational, social, and health services for teen parents, stakeholders can design policies and programs that take into account how intersecting systems of oppression affect these parents' ability to have the children they want and parent them with dignity and support. This vision would mean that teen moms are entitled to services that do not predicate access to support on conforming to a particular narrative of redemption or resilience. It would also encompass a commitment to incorporating critical consciousness into such services, whether in formal settings like the MAMA group or the more informal ways that educators like Lourdes Navarro pursued.

Queer of color critique teaches us to move beyond linear, binary understandings of teen mothers' lives and enables a capacious vision of liberation. We need policies and programs that support, rather than shame, teen parents by attending to their material needs even when they fail (or refuse) to conform to neat and tidy narratives. We also need to imagine a world in which, say, structural racism replaces teen pregnancy as an urgent social problem that service providers hold close to the heart. We need to imagine a world where teen mothers—indeed, all sexual and reproductive others—can be messy, without needing to clean up their stories to conform to normative representations and time lines. In the same way that activists have cautioned against the tidying up of queer and trans lives for assimilation into norms of domesticity and consumption,[54] I invite reproductive justice scholars and activists to take seriously what it would look like to queer our ideas about teen moms and their needs. In tandem with a reproductive justice framework, queer of color critique can be mobilized to advance a coalitional politics in which shared marginal relationship to power is the basis for collective liberation. I want to imagine a conference panel where young mothers can be respected without playing into respectability politics. I want teen moms on a panel to be able to share the messy realness of the systems they have to navigate, their struggles and ambivalences about motherhood, and their pleasures and desires. With their messy, disidentificatory, and time-disrupting stories in mind, I now zoom back out to consider how race and racialization function in Millerston's youth sexual health promotion work.

3 "It's their culture"

YOUTH SEXUAL HEALTH PROMOTION
AS A GENDERED RACIAL PROJECT

Early on in my fieldwork I attended a fund-raising event to benefit the Towne House at an elaborate banquet hall in Millerston's Heights neighborhood. As at many such events, the people and community that the organization served were largely absent. Attendees consisted primarily of faculty from the nearby colleges and universities along with representatives from local nonprofit organizations. I noticed that the walls were decorated with artwork created by Towne House students. After the almost entirely white audience took their seats at white-clothed tables preset with elaborately decorated, white-frosted cupcakes, Mayor Ryan Brown delivered brief, carefully scripted introductory remarks. He began by asserting that the Towne House is part of the "great city of Millerston." Brown then said that while politicians have historically "put people in boxes based on race, family formation, and sexual orientation," people have children in all different stages of life. As he often did while speaking at Towne House events, but not teen pregnancy prevention events, Mayor Brown shared that he was the son of a teen mom. Despite invoking race, Brown did not acknowledge either his whiteness or the particular racial framing of teen pregnancy in Millerston as a Latinx issue.

The well-known Latino author Junot Díaz was the event's keynote speaker, and along with the three Towne House students who introduced him, was one of the few people of color in attendance. The students nervously took turns reading their introductions from note cards. One shared that she liked how Díaz uses Spanglish in his writing, which she noted Towne House teachers did not allow. In contrast to the roomful of suits and at least one tuxedo, Díaz took the stage wearing jeans, a T-shirt, and an athletic jacket. He began his address by saying, "Next time you should structure it so the young sisters speak more," and noted that we often center the voices of those who have power, rather than those most affected by the issues at hand. Of all the speakers that evening, Díaz was the only one to explicitly name race or racism. Similarly, gender was both central and unremarked: although this was a fund raiser for an organization that aims to improve the lives of marginalized teen *mothers*, few speakers acknowledged how gendered inequalities structure young mothers' lives. Instead, the speakers and promotional materials emphasized vague slogans of hope and perseverance. Taken together, what this event centered (community outsiders, tokenized success stories) and what it silenced (discussion of white privilege, acknowledgement of race and gender inequalities) exemplify what I term a *gendered racial project*.

The concept of a gendered racial project is a strategy for naming and illustrating the processes by which race and gender interact to structure social meanings, experiences, and inequalities. These processes are so entrenched that we tend not to notice them in our communities, workplaces, and public policies. For example, by highlighting his story as a successful person raised in Millerston by a single mother, but failing to acknowledge his privilege as a white man, Mayor Brown elided the processes by which inequalities are raced *and* gendered. This elision obscures the lived experiences of race and gender inequalities and the signification of teen pregnancy as a Black and brown issue. Likewise, Junot Díaz's remark to let the "young sisters speak more" called out the event's failure to center Latina teen moms and highlighted the otherwise unremarked exclusion of the voices of pregnant and parenting teens. In a city where race and gender were implicated in a host of discourses, practices, and identities related to teen childbearing, this exclusion signaled the simultaneous ubiquity and silence of the Latina teen mother in Millerston. By

analyzing discourses of youth sexuality and reproduction in health promotion through the concept of a gendered racial project, I examine how
race and gender formations not only reveal but also reproduce inequalities. At the same time that health promotion efforts reveal disparities in
access to education or services, they also reproduce inequalities by failing
to attend to structural-level racism and sexism.

This chapter argues that youth sexual health promotion in Millerston
can be understood as a gendered racial project because it draws on
and reproduces deterministic notions of sexuality and reproduction in
ways that affect policy and practice. Youth sexual health promotion in
Millerston is always already about teen pregnancy *prevention*, and teen
pregnancy prevention is always already about *race*. I use the phrase
"always already" to signal the ways in which youth sexual health promotion is unthinkable without preventing teen pregnancy, and teen pregnancy is unthinkable without race. Although the projects, funding, coalitions, and committees in the city included the prevention of pregnancies
and STIs in their mission statements, their work focused almost entirely
on preventing pregnancy.[1] Although stakeholders called their work youth
sexual health *promotion*, it focused on what they wanted to prevent,
rather than what they wanted to promote.[2] Likewise, despite the central-
ity of race and gender to the teen pregnancy prevention industrial complex in Millerston, they are absent—but often implicated—elements of
discourse and practice. While race and gender were ever-present specters
haunting Millerston, committee meetings, local media, and participant
interviews rarely actually named them (much less racism or sexism as *systems* of oppression).

First, I describe the characteristics of youth sexual health promotion as
a gendered racial project. Next, I discuss the racialization of teen pregnancy in the United States and describe how race is "seen" and known in
Millerston. I then detail how Millerston's gendered racial project affects
stakeholders' understanding of youth sexuality and reproduction and the
types of programs they implement. Through this process, stakeholders
produce young Latinas' reproduction as a problem at the same time that
they shore up their own whiteness. The chapter concludes on a hopeful
note by commenting on how professional stakeholders can help plant the
seeds of racial justice in Millerston.

THEORIZING GENDERED RACIAL PROJECTS

According to Michael Omi and Howard Winant, racial projects describe "efforts to shape the ways in which human identities and social structures are racially signified, and the reciprocal ways that racial meaning becomes embedded in social structure."[3] Racial projects link signification and structure not only to shape policy and exercise political influence but also to organize everyday understandings about race, or to confirm "what everyone already knows."[4] Omi and Winant argue that "racial projects connect the meaning of race in particular discursive or ideological contexts and ways that social structures and everyday experiences are racially organized based upon that meaning."[5] Racial projects link the everyday experiences and meanings of race to the social and political contexts that elaborate ideas about "race." As one example, efforts to (re)biologize race through practicing race-based medicine or identifying genetic markers for "race" are part of a racial project in which the social signification of racial difference becomes embedded in biomedicine and thus the interactions between health care providers and racially marked patients.[6]

Racial projects are also gendered. The formation of racial meaning in society, the structure of racial inequalities, and the social experiences of people of color are intertwined with the signification, structural inequalities, and experiences related to gender. The concept of a gendered racial project recognizes the importance of gender in social processes related to racial signification and structure—without gender, such analyses are incomplete. Of course, sexuality, class, nation, ability, and many other social categories are important to racial formations; a gendered racial project analyzes the instances when gender is among the most salient.[7] A large and varied body of literature considers how gender is implicated in racial social formations, ranging from Korean women's emotional and body labor in beauty service work to the construction of how transgender women of color "do" gender.[8] Analyzing such examples as gendered racial projects links these disparate interactional and structural formations by explicitly naming and interrogating the ways in which the lived experiences of race and gender cannot be separated from the social signification of race and gender. Likewise, these lived experiences cannot be separated from the inequalities that hinge on that meaning. For example, gendered and raced ideas about Black or Latina women's reproductive health needs (e.g., pregnancy prevention upheld above anything else) are inseparable from the signification of women of color's fertility as excessive. Similarly, the raced and gendered inequalities built into accessing reproductive health care structure the individual experience of contraceptive use.[9] These experiences and inequalities reciprocally construct social ideas about race and gender that play out in health promotion policy and practice.

Gendered racial projects in Millerston consist of conflating the socially constructed, political concept of "race" with a deterministic Latino culture that prescribes the sexual and reproductive behaviors of young Latinas. As part of this project, health providers promote long-acting reversible contraceptives without a critical examination of their history in regulating the reproduction of women of color. Paying attention to the ways in which circulating discourses and individual health workers racialize teen pregnancy and teen mothers—that is, how these processes give racial meanings to teen mothers' existence, identities, and practices—is key to understanding how health promoters construct the "problem" and structure appropriate responses.

Youth sexual health promotion in Millerston exists alongside and intertwined with other historical and contemporary gendered racial projects related to reproduction, such as the politics of teen pregnancy and motherhood, punitive social policies related to welfare reform, and the regulation of Latina sexuality and reproduction. First, the racial project of producing "teen pregnancy" as a discursive construct and an object of social policy concern has a relatively short history.[10] The initial moral panic around *teen* pregnancy emerged in the late 1960s in response to increasing rates of unmarried sexual activity, pregnancies, and births among white middle-class young women. The emergence of teen pregnancy as an "epidemic" coincided with parents and professionals understanding it as a phenomenon that affected "our girls," that is, white young women.[11] Wanda Pillow argues that in this era teenage pregnancy prevention became a public policy issue in part so as to morally redeem white young women by rescuing them from the stigma of early pregnancies and their association with Blackness and brownness.[12] In other words, to have become a teen parent was to lose some of your access to whiteness and white privilege. By the mid-1990s, pregnant and parenting young women entered as subjects of policy debate surrounding welfare reform, with (particularly African American) teen mothers becoming virtually synonymous with "welfare mothers." Politicians, service providers, and the general public alike came to see pregnant adolescents as a group of undeserving, highly sexualized, and racialized young women who were a drain on taxpayer dollars. Likewise, they understood teen mothers to be producing children who were prone to poor educational performance, health problems, drug use, and incarceration and destined to become teen parents themselves. Public policy and health promotion discourses produced— and continue to produce—young mothers and their children as social and economic burdens, rather than a vulnerable group deserving of resources.

Second, white fears regarding the rapid growth of the Latinx population and the US panic about immigration have helped to shape a gendered racial project producing Latinas as "hypersexual" and "hyperfertile." As anthropologist Leo Chavez argues: "Latina reproduction and fertility have been a subject of not only public discourse but also of social science investigation and discourse. 'Latinas' exist and 'reproduction' exists, but 'Latina reproduction' as an object of a discourse produces a limited range of meanings, often focusing on their supposedly excessive reproduction, seemingly abundant or limitless fertility, and hypersexuality, all of which are seen as 'out of control' in relation to the supposed social norm."[13] Chavez contends that the pathologization of Latina sexuality and reproductive behavior is key to the "Latino Threat Narrative," or the idea that the shifting demographic makeup of the United States represents a threat to the "American way of life." Scholars and activists have noted the intensifying focus on Latina teens in pregnancy prevention discourses: the figure of the Black "welfare queen" is shifting toward that of a hyperfertile, opportunistic Latina.[14] For example, in her ethnographic work with Puerto Rican and Mexican communities in Chicago, Lorena García describes how health promotion discourses position young Latinas as "bad girls." They are always already pregnant or promiscuous, their bodies excessively reproductive, and their families strictly bound to a static, sexually silent Latino culture.[15] Likewise, Emily Mann demonstrates how health care providers frame young Latinas' sexual practices as potentially dangerous and out of line with normative scripts of reproduction. Providers prioritize the prevention of Latina teen pregnancy to the exclusion of addressing Latina patients' other sexual and reproductive health concerns.[16] In Millerston, although the teen birthrate among whites in the city is three times the statewide rate (36 births per 1,000 women ages 15–19 in Millerston, compared to 10.4 births per 1,000 statewide), policy and practice discourses frame teen pregnancy as an issue affecting young Latinas. As in the United States as a whole, teen pregnancy in Millerston is always already about race.

SEEING AND KNOWING RACE AND RACISM IN MILLERSTON

The ways professional stakeholders do (not) talk about race and racism in Millerston provide a good starting point for clarifying the parameters of teen pregnancy prevention as a gendered racial project. Race is not absent from health promotion discourse and practice in the city, but its presence is full of silences and lacks an analysis of power. Most often, service providers, educators, policy makers, and the media talk about race without actually talking about race. Recall my exchange with Hannah McNeil (described in chapter 1) in which she danced around the word *race* in attempting to describe the "deterioration" of her city. Hannah used coded terms such as *welfare* and *drug problems* to avoid ever actually naming race, much less racism. In doing so, she engaged in "dog whistle politics," the term legal scholar Ian Haney López uses to describe how racial code words like *inner city* or *at-risk* are "inaudible and easily denied in one range, yet stimulate strong reactions in another."[17] As Omi and Winant describe them, "code words like 'get tough on crime' and 'welfare handouts' reassert racist tropes of Black violence and laziness *without having to refer to race at all*" (emphasis added).[18] Through racial code words, health and human service providers, clinicians, and policy makers attribute racial meaning to youth sexuality and (potentially) pregnant teen bodies without ever explicitly invoking race. Indeed, *teen pregnancy* itself is a racial code word; its racial meaning is inaudible in that it literally refers to human reproduction in a certain age range, but it stimulates strong reactions by signifying a particular kind of pregnant teenager: one who is Black or brown, poor, single, uneducated, and probably not fit for parenting.

Stakeholders' race talk often refers to racial health disparities, specifically racial differences in teen birthrates. One year at the PASH Network annual community conference, Jenny Díaz delivered opening remarks in which she discussed how politics, race, and class "tie in" with health. She framed these in terms of "difficult conversations" that would lead to a "better understanding of the issues" and thus "better solutions." During a Q&A later that day, following another speech by Jenny in which she emphasized the high rates of teen birth among youth of color in Millerston and Carlsborough, an audience member challenged her on the use of "race" as a "risk factor" for teen pregnancy. The audience member, a Latina staff person at a provider training organization, began by emphasizing that the work was about "changing paradigms." She insisted, "We are talking about racial-ethnic health disparities, but race and ethnicity are not risk factors. We have these disparities because young people do not have opportunity or hope." Jenny responded that clinical medicine sees "race" as a risk factor and that she realized that she, as a Latina, shared that risk factor. "My ultimate goal," Jenny said, "is to get race off that list of risk factors. It doesn't matter you're purple, green, or blue, if you live in poverty."

This exchange illustrates a number of issues related to how racial discourses operate in Millerston. First, Jenny employed a colorblind approach that obscures racism by reducing racial inequality to economic inequality and homogenizing racial groups (we're all the same; it doesn't matter what "color" you are). Second, her remarks signal an understanding of race in biological and individual terms, rather than as a socially constructed, political category used in the service of maintaining white supremacy.[19] Note that Jenny did not argue against the understanding of race as a determinant of early pregnancy. Instead, both Jenny and the audience member minimized race by collapsing it into economic inequality. By framing race as a clinical "risk factor" or framing racial disparities as the result of a lack of "hope or opportunity," the conversation missed an opportunity to talk about the role of racism as a *system* of oppression that governs both individual experiences and population health outcomes.

Sometimes professional stakeholders did acknowledge the existence of racism in youth sexual health promotion, but more often they *almost* actually acknowledged it. Mayor Brown used this latter approach in a

MASHPC meeting when discussing the high rates of suspension at Millerston High School. "You have a Puerto Rican kid and a white kid," he said, "who do the same minor infraction, and only the Puerto Rican kid gets suspended." While racial disparities in suspension rates signal a form of institutionalized racism, Brown stopped just short of actually naming racism as the cause. Several months later, I asked the mayor about his thoughts on the racial politics of teen pregnancy in his city. He responded that it was a "heavy question" and that talking about race in the city was "loaded." "When people hear 'teen pregnancy,'" he said, "they assume it's happening in the Puerto Rican population. . . . I mean, I'm paraphrasing what other folks' perceptions are, mostly white folks, you know? And then you even hear it within the Puerto Rican population, too." Brown abruptly switched gears to highlight economic structures: "Just look at it, like economics, like income and property among these families as well, and the impact that that has on it. And there's economic opportunity again. So, you know, I think one of the best ways to prevent teen pregnancy is like, getting a good education and getting a good job." Note the absence of an acknowledgment of racial discrimination in employment, schooling, housing, and other administrative systems governing life chances. The remarks reduced teen pregnancy prevention to getting a good education and a good job, both of which are in short supply in Millerston. To draw on Brown's wording, when you've got a Puerto Rican kid and a white kid, and only the Puerto Rican kid is barred from fully benefiting from educational and occupational systems, something else is at issue: racial oppression.

Having sketched out the precarious dance around race in Millerston, I now expand on elements of youth sexual health promotion as a gendered racial project. Stakeholders produce and implement health promotion strategies that conflate the socially constructed political concept of race with an essentialized Latinx culture that structures young women's sexuality and reproduction. These discourses and practices also reproduce an ideology of colorblindness that enables the uncritical promotion of long-acting reversible contraception (LARC). Together, these elements erase the history of reproductive oppression experienced by women of color in the service of health promotion.

THE LATINO CULTURE NARRATIVE

Elizabeth Randolph, a white woman in her fifties, grew up in Carlsborough and began working for Continuum Health Services (CHS) in the late 1970s. When I spoke to her, Elizabeth managed all of the organization's reproductive health clinics in the county that encompasses Millerston. Because of her work, Elizabeth saw teen pregnancy mainly as a health problem, but thought that there was a cultural aspect to it as well.[20] Seated behind a large desk stacked with piles of papers and medical charts, she told me, "Not to sound racist at all, but it really is a Latino cultural issue. It just is not a bad thing if a kid gets pregnant. It's just much more socially acceptable within that community. Right or wrong, I don't know." Some Latina professionals also took up the cultural explanation for disproportionate rates of teen pregnancy in Millerston. Clarisa Ortiz, a Latina in her twenties who grew up in Millerston and coordinated the teen health programs at the Millerston Community Health Center, also used the phrase "it's a cultural thing" to explain the connection:

> I think because [the rate] is just so high here, and then when you look at the numbers, and the highest numbers are Latino, I have no choice but to make it more of a cultural thing. And not only that—not only like, a traditional Latino culture but also like, a Millerston culture, and when you walk around the streets of Millerston and you see that there's plenty of people, you know, saying that they're getting [welfare] assistance, and there are plenty of people who are kind of like, sometimes even gypping the system.

Clarisa linked high rates of teen birth to culture by virtue of the comparatively high rates of both Latinos and teen pregnancy in the city. In addition to a "traditional Latino culture," she extended this correlation to a "Millerston culture," which she describes as featuring visible dependency on welfare assistance. Clarisa understood the phenomenon of seeing others taking advantage of ("gypping")[21] the welfare system as a factor that fuels the teen pregnancy rate.

Hannah McNeil also connected high rates of teen pregnancy in Millerston to culture and emphasized the role of familial norms concerning early childbearing:

I think [teen pregnancy] is a cultural issue that is perpetuated, and because of the lack of education, I think that definitely has contributed to young people not having the understanding of what becoming a teen parent involves. And, unfortunately, because there is not that educational component as part of their upbringing, they tend to gravitate towards what they feel is the right thing to do. And because they have seen it, it's intergenerational. In order to change an intergenerational pattern, you have to be aware that there's a problem. And you have to *want* to change it. And I don't think that awareness, until now, has been there. So that's where we are helping. But without that awareness, I don't think that it could ever change.

Here Hannah identified a culture of teen childbearing as a deeply ingrained problem affecting generations of families (implied but not stated to be Latina mothers and their daughters). This problematic culture of teen childbearing positions whiteness and normative families as the default, neutral reproductive formation from which Hannah judges others. She saw a role for herself in teaching particular social groups how to change their family structures through "awareness." Her notion of awareness, however, is predicated on an individual behavior change model that fails to account for the structural inequalities that affect how people decide whether and when to have children.[22]

Although I seldom heard "racial inequalities" or "racism" mentioned in Millerston, stakeholders, committee reports, and news media regularly told a story about Latino "culture." This narrative equated race with an essentialized and deterministic Latino culture. It also homogenized "Latinos" as a singular group, rather than a large and heterogeneous group of people with disparate histories of (de)colonization and a range of geographic, linguistic, demographic, and cultural origins, not to mention sexual and reproductive practices. The narrative was not entirely uncontested, and professional stakeholders occasionally called into question the correlation between culture and teen birthrates. Nonetheless, the ubiquity and embeddedness of the narrative was notable, as was the breadth of health behaviors and outcomes that providers explained under the rubric of "It's their culture." The Latino culture narrative organized commonsense understandings of Puerto Ricans in Millerston and produced particular ideas about their sexual and reproductive attitudes and beliefs; for example, that Latinas do not use contraception or have abortions, that

Latinx families do not talk about sex, and that Latinx families encourage, condone, or accept teen pregnancy.

In calling for a more nuanced understanding of how Latinx people experience and negotiate sexuality and reproduction, I am not arguing that these experiences are unconstrained by power relations. Nor am I arguing that culture and family play no role in structuring reproductive beliefs and behaviors. Instead, I am calling attention to the ways the discursive production of "It's their culture" is raced, classed, and gendered, and how this discourse works both at the population level and through individual bodies.[23] Reifying Latino culture as the cause of teen pregnancy distracts us from the raced and gendered structural inequalities that are predictors of poor health and poverty. In addition, it limits the kinds of policies and programs that health promoters imagine and implement. In short, the Latino culture narrative works against a vision of reproductive justice. Even if there *were* a Latino culture in Millerston that dictated sexuality and reproduction, this fact would not justify the essentialization of this culture, the judgment of it as wrong or unhealthy, or the building of health promotion policy and practice around it.

"Latinos don't talk about sex"

The first element of the Latino culture narrative in Millerston is the notion that Latinx families and communities maintain a strict silence around sexuality and sexual health. Health educators and policy makers frequently posit that communication about sex and sexuality is key to preventing STIs and unintended pregnancies. Jessica Fields notes that proponents of both abstinence and comprehensive sexual health education rely on this "prophylactic of talk" to rationalize their objectives.[24] Yet neither group adequately accounts for the gender, sexual, and social inequalities that compromise both youth and adults' abilities to engage in effective communication about sexuality. A widespread belief among professional stakeholders that Latinxs simply don't talk about sex bolstered the prophylactic of talk in Millerston. Because they assumed sexual silence to be an essential part of Latino culture, stakeholders viewed increasing parental communication as an important objective of their work. "Rarely in a Latino family," Clarisa Ortiz suggested, "will you hear them talking to their kids about, you know, how to use a condom, why they should wait. It's more like, 'Don't have sex.' Why? 'Because I said so.'" Belief in the sexual silence of Puerto Rican families was so endemic that MASHPC members organized a series of "parent education" forums in the community with the goal of encouraging parents to talk to their children about sex. Few parents attended the sessions, which members attributed to poor timing, bad weather, and parents being distracted by a recent shooting in the community. While all of these factors were likely at play, stakeholders failed to understand that families might resent a group of mostly white strangers telling them how they ought to parent differently.

In addition, stakeholders failed to problematize the notion that something particular to Latinx families prevents them from having productive conversations about sexuality with their children.[25] As Lourdes Colón Cruz, the educational director at the Towne House, put it: "As a Latino person . . . the subliminal message that I've gotten from the dominant culture is, the reason why you're in this predicament [having a pregnant child] is because you don't talk about sexuality with your kids. And so, the innuendo there is *that the dominant culture does.*" Lourdes called attention to an implicit assumption embedded in the narrative of cultural silence: if Latinxs have difficulty talking about sexuality (theirs or their children's), non-Latinx people and non-Latinx families talk about it easily and openly. As Gloria González-López and Salvador Vidal-Ortiz argue, in addition to reinscribing an essential Latinx sexual culture and an absence of sexual silence among non-Latinxs, "sexual silence is not absolute but highly selective and that selectivity is not shaped by a so-called 'Latino culture' but by multiple forms of social inequality affecting other cultural groups as well."[26] Sexual silence is about power and inequality rather than "culture." It is not only Latinxs who are affected by social and cultural norms that, for instance, stigmatize sexual behaviors, socialize women as passive sexual subjects, prioritize men's pleasure, and pathologize sexually transmitted infections. These norms affect the conservations that *all* parents have with their children about sex.[27]

"Latinas don't have abortions or use contraception"

A second element of the Latino cultural narrative involves the belief that Latinxs are averse to using contraception and to terminating pregnancies.

Although she saw "the tide starting to turn in the population," Elizabeth Randolph believed that, in general, Latinas didn't "contracept because that was like a sin, because you know, you're Catholic."[28] Similarly, Clarisa Ortiz recounted, "It's a cultural thing. You know, for a white female, the mothers are more—like for me growing up [in the 1990s], for me it was like, only white people do that. Like white parents will get their child put on a birth control. We won't do that. But we're OK with them having kids at an early age." Mayor Brown wondered if the higher rates of teen birth among Latinas in Millerston were related to poverty or to "religious values within a certain community." "Anecdotally," he told me, "talking with families who are religious, obviously they don't believe in abortion. Many of the families I speak to, when a young woman gets pregnant, that's not a choice." Beth Emmerson, a white nurse in her fifties and regular MASHPC member, put it plainly: "In Millerston if you're Latina and you get pregnant, you are not going to have an abortion."

In working with young Latinas at the Towne House, however, I frequently heard examples of constrained choice and complicated decision making around abortion and contraception.[29] Despite the emphasis that public health and social policy discourses placed on contraceptive access for young mothers, I never once heard anyone express an unmet need for contraception. They did discuss the advantages and disadvantages of various methods, and shared their own experiences with one another. These conversations were grounded in the complicated social environment in which all users negotiate contraceptive choice—cost, side effects, provider influence, and so on. It was also not uncommon to hear a young woman rant about how abortion was evil and later admit that she'd had multiple abortions because "that was different." The notion that Latinas "don't have abortions" or "don't use contraception" is clearly much more complex than stakeholders in Millerston understood it to be.[30]

"Latino families promote teen pregnancy"

The third element of the Latino culture narrative circulating in Millerston posits that Latinas are more likely to become teen parents because Latino families promote teen pregnancy by failing to stigmatize early childbearing and by supporting their pregnant daughters. This element of the

Latino culture narrative derives from the Latinx cultural value of *familismo,* or respect and loyalty to and strong identification with the nuclear and extended family. Hannah McNeil saw family as playing a role in the high number of teen births in Millerston. She attributed it not to Puerto Rican culture specifically but rather to a Millerston Latino culture that she was knowledgeable about through focus group research:

> It's not, say, because you're Hispanic. Because there it's totally different. Like, in Puerto Rico, they don't have the problems that we have, as far as teen pregnancy. It's handled totally different within the family. In this particular Hispanic culture [in Millerston], it's not rewarded, but it's condoned. And, I mean, I don't think I'm generalizing, because I've been, like . . . well, I don't know. I've had enough focus groups. I've worked enough with focus groups with kids that have said their parents had them at 15. . . . So it's one of those kinds of things. And I think [the baby] only becomes part of the family, that it's an extended family, and it gives them support. And it's not like, you know, it's not looked upon in any way that it's going to prevent them from having goals.

In Hannah's estimation, the support that families in Millerston gave their pregnant daughters served to "condone" teen pregnancy. Although she argued that Puerto Rican culture on the island did not share the problem of teen pregnancy, Hannah connected Puerto Rican culture in Millerston to high teen birthrates.[31] Similarly, Beth Emmerson contradicted herself by invoking the cultural value of "Latino family" as a casual factor in high birthrates among young Latinas, after declaring that the cultural explanation was "hogwash":

> I even brought this up at the meeting this week at the Millerston Technical High School when the nurse there said, like, "Well, it's their culture. It's their culture to have babies." Come on. Whose culture is it to have babies?[32] It's not their culture to have babies. It just is an easy way to put it. It's their culture not to have an abortion. It's a culture for them to value family. When you talk about a Puerto Rican family, it's not the little nuclear family, it's blood relatives and it's also emotional relatives. So family, *familia,* is so much different to a Puerto Rican than to white people. It's their culture— they're not going to put up their babies for adoption. If they can't take care of their baby, they're going to give it to an aunt.

Thus, although Beth discounted the validity of culture as a causal factor in teen pregnancy, she nevertheless saw culture and the presence of extended family as an explanation for why Latinas don't have abortions or place their children for adoption.

Certainly, Latinxs may value family and consider family loyalty an important cultural value and practice. But assuming that valuing family is a causal factor in Latina teen pregnancy requires essentialist thinking that disregards the complexities of the meaning of family, the role of gender in the family, and the persistence of inequalities in the family. The internal logic structuring this part of the narrative assumes that (1) white parents uniformly condemn teen pregnancies in their families; (2) family stigma is a desirable teen pregnancy prevention strategy; and (3) there is something wrong or bad about families that nurture and support their children through challenging life experiences like unintended or early pregnancies. Moreover, as young mothers' narratives highlight in chapter 2, the assumption that Latinx families in Millerston are naturally supportive of their daughters' pregnancies obscures wide variations in family response and the structural inequalities that sometimes render extended families unable to provide financial or emotional support. Amy Lexington, the grants manager at SOAP, called out the problems with these assumptions: "When you talk to teen parents who are Latino, they're like, 'My parents were so mad!' . . . Everyone has this weird idea that white parents are really mad about teen pregnancy, but Latinos aren't. Families are all over the place, and it's this lack of respect and really othering Latinos in this area. I mean, it's just stupid." Indeed, it is quite "stupid"—not to mention contradictory and ineffective—to build health promotion policy and practice that disregard the influence of structural racism and its entanglements with gender and sexuality.

THE WORK OF THE LATINO CULTURE NARRATIVE

Empirical evidence suggests that Latinxs *do* value and practice communication about sexuality in their families, use contraception, have abortions, and hold a range of attitudes regarding teen pregnancy.[33] In a random-sample survey of adult Latinxs in California, California Latinas for Reproductive Justice found that 8 out of 10 respondents stated it is "extremely important" that parents talk to their children about sexuality-related issues, including continuing or terminating a pregnancy, sexual health and sexuality, and contraception.[34] Survey data also demonstrates that Latinxs are just as likely to use contraception and perhaps *more* likely to have an abortion than white women. Latinas who are at risk of unintended pregnancy (defined as having heterosexual intercourse within the past 3 months) use contraception in numbers similar to their white counterparts.[35] According to the National Latina Institute for Reproductive Health, the overwhelming majority of Latinas in the United States, including Catholic Latinas, use contraception at some point in their lives. Ninety-seven percent of Latinas who have ever had (heterosexual) sex have used contraception, and 96% of sexually active Catholic Latinas have used a contraceptive banned by the Vatican. The Latina Institute emphasizes that the issue is not that Latinas do not "believe in" contraception.[36] Rather, they often lack access to affordable contraceptive services due to factors that are also germane in Millerston, including health insurance coverage and the availability of clinics and competent providers.

California Latinas for Reproductive Justice found that female respondents ranked "access to contraception and birth control services" as an important service to have available in their communities. The organization also found that 52% of respondents personally knew someone who had an abortion, and more than 8 in 10 "strongly agreed" that every woman should have a right to decide for herself the number and spacing of her children.[37] "Hispanic" women accounted for 25% of the abortions that occurred in the United States in 2014.[38] Hispanic women in the United States have abortions at twice the rate of white, non-Hispanic women.[39] The abortion rate among Hispanic teenagers is similar, with a rate of 15.3 per 1,000 women ages 15–19, compared to 8.5 per 1,000 white women ages 15–19.[40] Some Latinas are more likely than others to have an abortion, with Puerto Rican women more likely than Mexican American or Cuban American women.[41] Latinxs hold a range of beliefs regarding the acceptability and legality of abortion. A 2011 national poll of registered Latino voters found that 74% of respondents agree that "a woman has a right to make her own personal, private decisions about abortions without politicians interfering." Nearly three out of four respondents (73%) agreed that "we should not judge someone who feels they are not ready to be a parent," and about two-thirds (61%) agreed that "the amount of money a woman has or does not have should not determine whether she can have an abortion when she needs one."[42]

Because data on contraceptive use and abortion are not collected and reported at the city level, and because my research cannot speak to family and youth attitudes in Millerston regarding these matters, I cannot unequivocally state that the elements of the Latino culture narrative are completely unfounded. Yet the extent to which the narrative accurately reflects whether young Puerto Rican women in Millerston do or do not use contraception, have abortions, talk about sex with their families, or receive support in the event of an unplanned pregnancy doesn't actually matter. Either way, the Latino culture narrative is doing the work it is meant to do: sustaining the gendered racial project of youth sexual health promotion in Millerston. Amy Lexington trenchantly called attention to this process when she told me:

> This concept that, and I've heard even [health and human service] providers say this, the concept that it's a cultural thing, that it's something wrong with their culture. [But] it's not a problem among Latino culture. Although there are cultural elements that, I think, contribute to early pregnancy and parenthood, it's not, like, a problem with the culture. And what happens is people say this, or they kind of hint at it, and what happens is it lets people off the hook because it becomes this kind of normalized, naturalized thing. That's, like, "Well, that's just the way they are, so we can't do anything about it." Which is absolutely not the way it is.

Amy conceded that there were cultural elements that contribute to early parenthood, but she took to task health and human services providers for relying on the culture narrative to "let themselves off the hook" for their responsibility in naturalizing inequalities. Conflating race with culture allowed stakeholders to promote individual behavior change strategies to reduce racial health disparities in the city, strategies anchored in conforming to white middle-class childbearing norms. This conflation also allowed stakeholders to position young Latinas in need of saving and to escape responsibility for their collusion in maintaining the structures of white supremacy. Through this process, youth sexual health promotion affirmed the neutrality of whiteness and white middle-class reproduction. Preventing teen pregnancy thus becomes a way to protect young women from losing access to whiteness and white privilege. In short, the Latino culture narrative circulating in Millerston obscured how ideas about racial difference are key organizing principles of youth sexual health promotion. I now turn to a specific component of the youth sexual health promotion strategy in the city—long-acting reversible contraceptives—to illustrate how colorblindness functions in youth sexual health promotion as a gendered racial project.

COLORBLINDNESS: WHAT'S NOT TO LARC?

Eduardo Bonilla-Silva calls attention to the shifting forms of racial domination in the United States that have heralded a so-called post-racial, colorblind era.[43] He details how racial discourses and practices have become increasingly covert as whites invoke claims of "reverse racism," and as Jim Crow era practices, such as housing segregation, have not disappeared but have merely been rearticulated in ways less obvious to most white people.[44] Central to this post-racial era is an ideology of colorblindness, which is a rejection of the concept of "race" itself in the service of repudiating the existence of racism as a system of oppression.[45] As Omi and Winant have articulated this ideology:

> Those advocating a colorblind view of race assert that the goals of the civil rights movement have been substantially achieved, that overt forms of racial discrimination are a thing of the past, and that the US is in the midst of a successful transition to a "post-racial" society. From a colorblind standpoint, any hints of race consciousness are tainted by racism. Thus it is suggested that the most effective anti-racist gesture, policy, or practice is simply to ignore race.[46]

Colorblindness performs a sort of trick by distracting us with the notion that "we're all the same" and making institutional and structural inequalities harder to recognize. Michelle Alexander cites one prominent example of this distraction by illuminating the ways in which the war on drugs and mass incarceration have become a "new Jim Crow" that disenfranchises Black men. For instance, although laws prohibit explicit discrimination based on race in educational settings, the school-to-prison pipeline nonetheless bars young men of color from educational and occupational attainment.[47]

In a parallel to reproductive health care, today providers seldom explicitly sterilize women without their consent,[48] but instead implicitly control their reproduction through the type of care they provide. An ideology of colorblindness enables the uncritical and ubiquitous promotion of long-acting reversible contraception (LARC). LARC includes methods such as Depo Provera ("the shot"), intrauterine devices (IUDs), and subdermal contraceptive implants (Implanon or Nexaplon). These methods are extremely effective in preventing pregnancies, with efficacy rates similar to those for surgical sterilization (fewer than 1 out of 100 users each year will experience a pregnancy). Clinicians and researchers distinguish efficacy rates for contraceptive technologies in terms of "typical use" and "perfect use." Because LARC is a "set it and forget it" method, there is little room for user error (such as forgetting to take a pill each day), so typical use is nearly the same as perfect use. LARC is a provider-controlled method that a user cannot easily discontinue, even when faced with undesirable side effects or adverse health complications. These contraceptives also make it more difficult for a user to switch methods or to stop using contraception altogether.[49]

The significant increase in funding and the number of community health projects and professional guidelines that promote LARC illustrate the current enthusiasm for it among health care providers in the United States. The "Contraceptive Choice Project," a $20 million demonstration project in St. Louis that began in 2007 and enrolled nearly 10,000 women, is the most notable of such projects.[50] In 2014 the American Academy of Pediatrics revised its policy statement on contraception for adolescents to promote LARC as a first-line contraceptive choice for young people.[51] The CDC reports that LARC use among teens ages 15–19 years old at Title X family-planning clinics increased 1,500% from 2005 to 2013, from 0.4% to 7.1%.[52] The enthusiasm for LARC stems in large part from its stated potential to reduce unintended and teen pregnancies, framed in terms of "reducing the burden" to taxpayers. Scholarly and news media accounts of the promise of LARC foreground its potential to reduce teen births and thus public assistance expenditures.[53] The neoliberal logic underlying this framing essentially shifts the burden for reducing poverty from the state to the bodies of individual poor women.[54] Poor women are literally bearing responsibility for the disappeared social safety net by accepting a particular kind of medication, one that has a long and pernicious history.

Reproductive justice activists and scholars have pointed to the lack of a race and class analysis that contributes to an uncritical promotion of LARC and inhibits reproductive autonomy by promoting "LARC first" to "risky" women, that is, women who are young, economically marginalized, or of color.[55] As Anu Gómez, Liza Fuentes, and Amy Allina explain, "LARC promotion must expand—not restrict—contraceptive options for all women, particularly for women whose racial, ethnic, or class identities have made them targets of forced sterilization and of policies aiming to restrict their fertility."[56] Activists and scholars emphasize that no particular contraceptive method is necessarily oppressive or emancipatory, and argue that people should have access to LARC methods if they desire them. To be sure, there are barriers to obtaining LARC, such as prohibitive cost and lack of availability. People at risk for pregnancy may desire long-acting reversible methods for a variety of reasons, including efficacy and convenience. Nevertheless, just as professional stakeholders in Millerston use the Latino culture narrative to evade responsibility for structural racism and economic inequality in the city, "narrowing the scope of possibilities for family planning innovation to promote a particular class of technologies," Gómez, Fuentes, and Allina argue, "allows the widespread social inequalities that underlie unintended pregnancy to be invisible."[57]

Scholars and activists have extensively documented the histories of reproductive coercion aimed at poor women, disabled women, and women of color. These practices include coerced sterilization of economically marginalized and disabled women facilitated by state eugenics boards in the early twentieth century. More recently, various legislative actions have attempted to require recipients of public assistance to accept a LARC method, and judges have compelled women to undergo sterilization or accept LARC as a condition of a reduced prison sentence.[58] Coercive contraception practices have a long history among Puerto Rican women in particular, on both the island and the mainland.[59] As I discuss below, this situation has important implications for teen pregnancy prevention in Millerston. Although today the government rarely outright sterilizes people against their will,[60] in the "post-racial" era subtler forms of contraceptive coercion are common. For example, researchers have found evidence of "soft eugenics,"[61] such as racial discrimination in family planning settings, including a greater likelihood that physicians and educators will counsel Black and Latina women to restrict their childbearing than they will white women.[62] Likewise, research has demonstrated that women of color experience intimidating recommendations of sterilization and LARC methods that are both explicit and implicit.[63]

Enthusiasm for LARC promotion in Millerston mirrors trends nationally. Increasing the number of teens using LARC methods was an objective of the multisite Teens Count project, which coordinated much of the community-based youth sexual health promotion in the city during the time of my fieldwork. One strategy that Teens Count used to reduce teen pregnancy was to encourage clinics to implement the Centers for Disease Control and Prevention's (CDC) best practices for "Contraceptive and Reproductive Health Services for Teens." These best practices include guidelines that health care providers promote LARC to a teen at every clinic visit (regardless of the reason for the visit) and provide "quick start" insertion during that same visit, and that clinics train more providers in insertion technique.[64] Some professional stakeholders expressed concern about the uncritical and widespread promotion of LARC to young people in Millerston. Their concerns were overshadowed, however, by the recommendations of funding agencies and the objectives of larger health promotion projects, such as the Teens Count initiative, in which they participated.

In her role coordinating teen health promotion at the Millerston Community Health Center, Clarisa Ortiz administered a CDC grant that aimed to increase the number of providers trained to insert LARC devices and the number of young people using them. Clarisa explained to me this new initiative's evolution and purpose:

CLARISA: I guess there were these conversations happening amongst the bigwigs, that you know, if clinics were able to have more LARC available, there would be a higher rate of less pregnancies amongst adolescents, amongst young adults, yada yada. So they wanted to put this theory to the test.

CHRIS: OK.

CLARISA: So we are a pilot clinic that was chosen for this grant to see if we have more doctors trained in LARC insertion, and more LARC available, instead of having patients come in, set up an appointment, and have to wait till their first period, you use the quick-start method and have it just—less barriers and more education and more doctors available, and more youth put on LARCs, then you would see a decrease in the pregnancy rates.

CHRIS: So is part of it also promoting certain types of contraceptives, or just training the providers on how to use them?

CLARISA: Yeah. Promoting and training both. So we're going to get doctors trained, having just more staff ready to do the work, instead of just relying on one or two individuals.

Although Clarisa could not provide process or outcome data describing her clinic's initiative, the Teens Count project reported that its clinic partners had implemented twenty-nine out of the CDC's thirty-seven best practices for working with youth, including quick-start insertion of IUDs.

Teens Count also reported that from 2010 to 2012 the percentage of women ages 12–19 using a LARC method who visited a clinic in the greater Millerston area increased two and a half times. When a presenter announced this finding at a coalition "collective impact" meeting in winter 2014, attendees from health and human service organizations across Millerston rose from their seats and literally cheered at the news, using the noisemakers and kazoos provided (discussed in chapter 1). My thoughts at this moment echoed my reaction to a middle- or upper-class white woman declaring that preventing teen pregnancies among economically marginalized women of color is an issue "close to the heart" (described in the introduction). It was disconcerting to witness a group of majority-white, middle-aged, and class-privileged service providers from outside the community "cheer" at this new version of a practice that policy makers and health care providers have historically used to limit the childbearing of marginalized peoples based on their perceived unfitness as reproducers. It is an ostensibly post-racial, colorblind society that allows professionals with race and class privilege to celebrate this announcement.

In line with existing research, professionals in Millerston often failed to understand the myriad reasons why a young woman might not desire a long-acting contraceptive method.[65] Emily Lambert, a white social worker in her forties who coordinated primary- and secondary-school teen pregnancy prevention programs through a large health and human services provider, shared a story about a woman in one of her organization's teen parent support programs whom she characterized as lacking a sense of responsibility:

> She has three kids, she's 24, she's pregnant with her fourth, and talking to her about birth control, [she says she] doesn't need it [and] doesn't want it, but she doesn't want any more kids, because her hands are full, and she doesn't have a job. Sooooo work with me here because I'm thinking if you use birth control, then you wouldn't have that other child that you're saying you don't want, but you don't want to use birth control . . . so this whole "how do I understand that kind of thought process and get through to you" is very frustrating. . . . There's all these reasons they don't want something inserted into their body—they don't want to gain weight [sarcastically]— there's all these things, but in my head those are just excuses, right? I mean you're going to gain weight if you get pregnant so what's an extra ten pounds if you gain weight this way? It's not like you're an exercise freak anyway, you know, it's just I think they're just excuses.

Emily's minimization of contraceptive side effects is notable given the evidence that these side effects have considerable social weight and meaning and are often a key reason for discontinuance.[66] Clarisa Ortiz shared a similar story that she described more than once as "crazy":

> We had an adolescent who got the [IUD] inserted, didn't like it, went to the emergency department at the hospital, told the people, "Take it out!" Instead of them conferring with her PCP [primary care provider], or telling her to go back to the PCP to have that done, because we did the procedure, they took it out. And then, the patient came back, and she was like, "I want it back. 'Cause, you know, I don't want to get pregnant."

Both Emily's and Clarisa's remarks illustrate an inability to view contraception as a negotiated, embodied practice situated in a social context. Their comments also express the responsibility that service providers feel they have to encourage marginalized young women to use LARC. Here we can see how professional stakeholders' desire to reduce the teen birthrate takes precedence over the needs of the contraceptive users themselves.[67]

No one, especially young, economically marginalized women of color, utilize contraceptive technologies outside a social context that produces and regulates bodies and sexualities. Like users of all kinds of medications, contraceptive users must balance the risk of pregnancy with a host of potential side effects, including long-term health implications, cost, ease of use and discontinuance, their partners' expectations, and the social meanings attached to particular methods. Is it really so "crazy" to be ambivalent about such a complicated health care decision?

Colorblindness also enabled the uncritical promotion of LARC in Millerston by obscuring the of history of coercive sterilization directed at Puerto Rican women and the use of Puerto Rico as a site for developing modern contraceptive technologies. In her longitudinal ethnographic work on sterilization among Puerto Rican women in Brooklyn, Iris López illustrates the nuances of this history and argues that it is a mistake to assume that Puerto Rican women, then or now, have been either passive victims of contraceptive coercion or completely autonomous actors in their reproductive decisions. Rather, a complex interplay of historical, political, and economic factors structures their relationship to, and high rates of, sterilization and LARC.[68] Migration experiences, economic changes on the island, their social support systems or lack thereof, relationships to their husbands and children, awareness of gender inequalities, and lack of access to quality housing, jobs, education, and good health care services all play a role in Puerto Rican women's experiences with sterilization and LARC.[69] When health care providers and educators disregard this history, they fail to consider how the history of reproductive coercion and constrained choice might affect the contraceptive decisions of young Latinas in Millerston. Under a guise of colorblindness, providers ignore, and in some ways repeat, histories of contraceptive coercion.

Ana Reyes Rivera, a Latina sexual health educator in her twenties who grew up in Millerston, became interested in this topic because her grandmother who raised her never talked about sex and sexuality. "For a long time," Ana said, "I thought it was maybe because my mom had me at such a young age, and she was afraid if she talked to me about sex I would end up pregnant." Yet, as she grew older, Ana realized her grandmother's "sexual silence" stemmed from her experience of coercive contraception:

My aunt actually explained that my grandmother had an IUD put in around the time that birth controls were being tested in Puerto Rico. And she didn't really understand. She did want to have some form of birth control, but she didn't understand how long the IUD was going to work, and how it actually worked. So after that I became really interested in the testing—the birth control testing in Puerto Rico—and then I thought, I never asked her, but then I thought, like maybe it has to do something with that, that's why she doesn't talk about sex and birth control.

This realization prompted Ana to become interested in her family's experience with sex, birth control, and pregnancy. Her aunt, who had her first child at 17, while still living on the island, was later pressed into having a tubal ligation and eventually a hysterectomy. Ana told me: "She explained to me that having her kids at an early age was a blessing in her eyes, because if she would have waited, till like a 30, 35-year-old age, she wouldn't have been able to have kids, because by 30 she already had a hysterectomy." Like the women in López's research, Ana has a family history that complicates the elements of the Latino culture narrative that interpret Latinas' reluctance to use contraception or have abortions as the result of religious or family values.

The moment at the annual PASH Network conference when an audience member called out Jenny Díaz on her use of *race* as a risk factor created a brief opportunity to discuss issues related to coercive and constrained contraception. The conference included a screening of the controversial documentary *La Operación,* which some observers have criticized for its reductionist depiction of sterilization coercion.[70] The day after the screening, Jenny Díaz interrupted a keynote speaker, an original member of the Our Bodies, Ourselves collective, to share an anecdote from the time she was in medical school and attended a young patient who didn't know that she had been sterilized. Jenny stated that having a baby at a younger age becomes a norm when women know sterilization is a possible part of their future, and added that it is important to "have this conversation about what has happened to mothers, grandmothers, and how it affects the young women we serve." As the director of the PASH Network and a person heavily involved with the Teens Count initiative, Jenny indirectly promoted LARC use but was equivocal about it when we spoke privately in her office. Her equivocations about LARC were similar to her ambiguous statements about whether teen pregnancy was a "problem." Aside from this brief moment at the conference, however, conversations about the history and implications of coercive contraceptive and sterilization practices, or about the social and political inequalities that affect contraceptive choices, were absent from youth sexual health promotion in Millerston.

Ana wasn't the only stakeholder in Millerston who mentioned the complexities of contraception. Kristina Myers, a white nurse practitioner in her fifties who served students at Millerston High's Teen Clinic, was an outspoken advocate of offering contraceptive access through the school clinic. This was a proposition that the school administration vocally opposed. In one tense MASHPC meeting, Kristina addressed the Millerston superintendent of schools, stating, "I'm not allowed to do what I've been doing for 25 years, which is to help women have babies and not have babies [when they want to]." Privately, she told me:

> I'm not saying that if a girl came into my office and I could put in, you know, a long-acting reversible method of contraception that would give her three years of not having a baby, that that's how you solve teen pregnancy. I mean I think it's—you have to help with kids' self-esteem, and you have to offer them opportunities, and they have to go to a school where there isn't like a policeman sort of, you know, standing guard.

Kristina was clear that although she saw contraceptive access as an important part of women's reproductive autonomy (even proclaiming in the MASHPC meeting that it was an important part of her identity as a feminist, the only time I heard this word used in all of my years working in Millerston), she did not see LARC as a magic bullet for preventing teen pregnancy. Instead, she named the policing and militarization of schools with a large population of students of color as a problem that limited young people's ability to thrive.

Similarly, as a grant writer and project manager, Amy Lexington dealt closely with funding agencies and acknowledged that the "power structure in Puerto Rico, you know, colluding with the US government to sterilize women" had an effect on the field of reproductive health work that professional stakeholders had not adequately dealt with. "The CDC is very much promoting IUDs and the contraceptive implants," she told me, "and we really have been doing some soul searching about what does this mean . . . there's a real push to get more IUDs and implants in young people and it can be really sticky." Nevertheless, Ana, Kristina, and Amy's resistance to the gendered racial project in Millerston bumped up against the powerful structures of the teen pregnancy prevention industrial complex. Each of them was limited by the missions of the organizations they worked for, the requirements of the grants that funded their jobs, and the overwhelming signification of teen pregnancy as an urgent social problem. Revealingly, by the time I concluded fieldwork, all of them had moved on to jobs outside youth sexual health promotion.

For the most part, a commitment to the colorblind ideology was endemic to Millerston's youth sexual health promotion work. This commitment allowed professional stakeholders to minimize the side effects of contraceptive technologies, to elide racial discrimination in health care, and to disregard the history of reproductive control aimed at women of color. In particular, colorblindness empowered stakeholders to promote individual behavior change and abdicate responsibility for structural inequalities. If overt racism is a thing of the past and we are really "all the same," as the colorblind perspective purports, then the promotion of particular contraceptive technologies can be seen as race neutral. Thus, health care providers and educators can disregard the implications of historical and current coercive practices. Moreover, as Omi and Winant argue, neoliberalism has both "overlapped with and required colorblindness."[71] Because the pathology approach to teen pregnancy understands it to be a "burden" on taxpayers, neoliberal logic urges health promoters to privatize the burden of inequality by placing it on the individual bodies of young, economically marginalized women of color.[72] These young women then take on responsibility for inequalities by using a LARC method. This is the fallacy of LARC: the notion that persuading a population to use a particular contraceptive method could singlehandedly end unintended pregnancies (and thus poverty) elides the fact that poverty creates unintended pregnancies, rather than the other way around.[73] This notion is an example of what I call *causal fantasies*, which I explore in the following chapter.

THE IMPLICATIONS OF MILLERSTON'S GENDERED
RACIAL PROJECT

The gendered racial project of youth sexual health promotion in Millerston organized everyday understandings of race in the city into an essentialized and deterministic "Latino culture," and structured health promotion efforts according to a particular understanding of young Latinas' sexuality and reproduction. Combined with a post-racial colorblind ideology that obscures histories of reproductive oppression, the culture narrative both produced and constrained the sexual subjectivity of young Latinas in Millerston. What's more, stakeholders collapsed inequality into "culture," as Amy Lexington put it, in order to "get themselves off the hook" and abdicate responsibility for structural inequality. Individual health promotion strategies, such as acceptance of long-acting provider-controlled contraception, cannot possibly account for the racial and economic inequalities that contribute to higher rates of unintended pregnancies among economically marginalized women of color. As Laura Briggs argues, "If Puerto Rican folks are poor, it can't have anything to do with the United States or colonialism. If Puerto Rican poverty is caused by something about Puerto Ricans themselves, then they need the United States to help them."[74] The same is true in Millerston: by individualizing and privatizing sexual health, stakeholders were able to reproduce the institutionalization of health promotion. Youth sexual health promotion aimed at changing individual behaviors cannot eliminate the effects of colonialism and reproductive oppression or provide adequate education and employment opportunities in a racist society under late capitalism. But it can provide lessons about how Latinxs can talk to their kids about sex and encourage young women to choose birth control methods that cannot be easily stopped without the aid of a health care provider. Advocating that young people just need hope, opportunity, and an IUD to escape the effects of a race-, class-, and gender-stratified society means that there is always a role for benevolent outsiders.

Although health promotion work in Millerston rendered whiteness invisible, interrogating it is key to a critical public health practice. This interrogation is particularly important in a place where white people develop and implement a good deal of the health promotion that targets people of color, as is the case in public health generally. The invisibility of whiteness in Millerston took many forms, ranging from the unacknowledged white privilege held by most of the professionals in the TPPIC to the disproportionately high white teen birthrates in comparison to other cities and the state overall. Most notably, whiteness was invisible in the colorblind approach to sexual health that collapsed racial and economic inequalities and promoted long-acting provider-controlled contraceptives. As Omi and Winant explain, in the neoliberal project of "reinforced social inequality in a U.S. rid of its welfare state, with all the redistributive dimensions of social rights finally repudiated, it would be necessary not to only to oppose demands for racial justice and racial democracy; it would be necessary to take race off the table."[75] By taking race "off the table" in Millerston through the invisibility of whiteness, the TPPIC obscured the racial politics of majority-white people who regulated the sexuality and reproduction of youth of color, shored up the whiteness of professional stakeholders, and maintained a system of stratified reproduction.

To conclude on a more hopeful note, I offer that seeds of racial justice have been planted in Millerston and in youth sexual health work more generally. Though disparate and nascent, voices are calling for a reproductive justice framework in Millerston. Kristina Myers named our colonial relationship to Puerto Rico and argued that a racial justice lens was important to her work. Amy Lexington critiqued the CDC's (and Millerston's) promotion of LARC methods above all others. Jenny Díaz acknowledged, albeit briefly and contradictorily, that the history of reproductive oppression aimed at women of color mattered in youth sexual health promotion work. Lourdes Colón Cruz gestured toward the possibility of racial justice when she told me, "I think that racism is a powerful tool against poor and marginalized people—that the seeds of racism have been planted so, so well that it's been internalized in poor communities and we have begun to believe that the stereotypical comments, views, and attitudes are real." However, these dissenting voices are often drowned out in the dominant discourses of the teen pregnancy prevention industrial complex. Key to the germination of these seeds is engaging with the raced intersections of class, gender, and sexuality, as well as naming the history of reproductive control experienced by women of color. Shifting youth sexual health promotion to a reproductive justice framework means moving from a focus on distributing condoms and "hope" to a broader analysis of racial, economic, cultural, and structural constraints on power. In this book's conclusion, I detail specific strategies that youth sexual health promotion in Millerston and elsewhere might employ to move toward a reproductive justice framework and integrate principles of racial justice into their work. First, I turn to an examination of how stakeholders take up and deploy notions of choice and scientific discourses of sexuality in Millerston.

4 Sex, Science, and What Teens Do When It's Dark Outside

At a particularly memorable MASHPC meeting, Millerston's superintendent of schools, David Moreno, joined the regular crowd of health and human service providers assembled in the computer lab of the Millerston Youth Center.[1] The meeting was unusually tense and confrontational, with a lot of big personalities grappling for floor time. As we waited for the superintendent to arrive, Jenny Díaz apologized that she was going to show a PowerPoint presentation that most of the attendees had already seen multiple times. This slideshow consisted of graphics depicting the teen birthrate in Millerston over time along with a summary of the work conducted under the auspices of the PASH Network, the Teens Count initiative, and MASHPC. Jenny shared that she had recently attended a meeting with the superintendent during which she had felt as if she was part of an inspirational movie similar to *Lean On Me*, in which a fictional failing urban high school is turned around through the work of a maverick principal. "I'd never left a meeting feeling like that," she remarked.

When the superintendent arrived, Jenny launched into her well-worn PowerPoint presentation. It began with graphic representations of the Millerston teen birthrate in relation to the state as a whole and to the overall US rate. The graphics Jenny used to illustrate the different rates consisted of a silhouette of a pregnant woman with a ponytail—presumably meant to represent a teenager.[2] The graphics were sized to represent places with lower to higher rates, so that the Millerston pregnant teen silhouette was the largest. Jenny went on to describe the various programs and grants at work in the area, including her PASH coalition and the Teens Count grant. The slides graphically represented these projects as a watering can that was watering a tree titled "Teen Pregnancy Prevention." As she often did during her presentations, Jenny acted as a cheerleader for MASPHC by emphasizing that all the hard work members were doing to transform youth sexual health in Millerston was paying off. She noted that the teen birthrate in the city had declined in recent years. "You guys made that 14% drop in the teen birthrate happen in Millerston!" she exclaimed. "And we want the teen birth to go down for the next year, the next five years, and forever after that." The superintendent spoke up at this point to offer that he didn't think comprehensive sex education in the schools was doing what it was supposed to, and that it might even be doing the opposite. "We are focused on results and we are not seeing them," he said. "Kids are having kids and they are leaving the schools. Kids having kids is a tragedy, and education is the future of the community."

MASHPC members bristled at the idea that their work was not producing results. In response to David's comments, tensions arose between the superintendent and various members over the relative efficacy of contraception access in the schools, sex education curricula, and parent engagement. Some members, such as Kristina Myers, argued forcefully for contraceptive access in the high school teen clinics. David did not seem convinced that this was desirable or feasible, but he did wonder aloud if this was the "fundamental change" that the Millerston public schools needed. Jenny struggled to gain control of the discussion as members raised their voices and became noticeably agitated. "The fundamental change you're talking about," she said, frustration evident in her voice, "is a landscape of opportunity," and she asserted that young people will use birth control if they know they have a good job in the future. At this comment, Beth Emmerson used the tension in the room to redirect the conversation to her research, which involved focus groups she conducted with nonparenting youth in Millerston about their perceptions of teen pregnancy in the community. She emphasized that these teens had goals for themselves and thus didn't allow themselves to be home without parental supervision for more than twenty minutes. It was early December, and daylight savings time had recently ended, meaning that the sun set in the Northeast as early as 4 PM. Beth practically shouted, "What are you going to do when it's 5 o'clock and it's dark out?!" Her argument that the lack of daylight in the winter months was a factor in teens having unprotected sex, and thus babies, seemed to resonate with the rest of the group as they murmured and nodded their heads affirmatively.

This meeting helps frame how discourses of science and sexuality play out in Millerston's youth sexual health promotion work. Jenny's presentation to the superintendents used epidemic and eradication language to talk about teen pregnancy—as if it were polio or the guinea worm, something we should (and could) eliminate altogether. Her statement that the work of professional stakeholders in Millerston caused the 14% drop in the teen birthrate was curious. As someone trained in academic public health, Jenny had likely learned about epidemiologic and statistical measurement of causality and knew that there were too many confounding variables to state so categorically that MASHPC's work *caused* the decline in the teen birthrate. Likewise, in asserting that "kids having kids" caused students to drop out of high school, David eclipsed an established body of literature showing that most teen parents drop out of school *before* having children and that teens who leave school after having a baby do so because of the school's inability or refusal to meet their needs.[3] Similarly, as a nurse researcher who had studied teen childbearing, Beth was probably familiar with the research documenting the determinants of unintended pregnancy. Her assertion that an early sunset was making young people have sex (not because sex is pleasurable or has important social meanings attached to it) and that all teen sex inevitably led to pregnancy and thus babies (because teens are irresponsible with contraception and Latinas don't have abortions) implied a convoluted understanding of sexuality, desire, agency, and reproductive health decision making.

This chapter uses feminist science studies and critical sexualities scholarship to analyze how professional stakeholders in Millerston take up and deploy discourses of sex and science. These discourses work to align youth sexual health promotion policies and practices with a notion of linear progress from nonnormative (young, single, poor) reproduction to normative (older, two-parent, middle-class) reproduction. First, I describe how youth sexuality in Millerston is premised on notions of responsibility and choice while producing a particular set of silences. I call this *responsible silence* to signal the conflicting demands it makes of young people. Despite the well-documented evidence that poverty is a main determinant of unintended pregnancy, stakeholders understood it in terms of individual choice and responsibility.[4] At the same time, responsible silences concealed pleasure, desire, abortion, and LGBTQ youth. Next, I draw on feminist science studies to demonstrate how causality and evidence were understood in Millerston's teen pregnancy prevention industrial complex. I describe how policy makers and service providers utilized *causal fantasies* that permitted them to validate certain kinds of knowledge and types of evidence while ignoring others. These causal fantasies took the form of magical thinking about the causes and consequences of teen pregnancy, attributing declining teen birthrates directly to their work, and disregarding evidence concerning the equivocal outcomes of teen childbearing. At the same time, stakeholders promoted evidence-based sexual health education as a solution to teen pregnancy. Their selective use of scientific knowledge permitted them to confirm and legitimize taken for granted assumptions and to elide the politics of racially and economically privileged professionals regulating the sexuality of economically marginalized youth of color. The chapter concludes by considering how notions of social, economic, and scientific progress are integral to the relationship of sex and science in Millerston.

PRODUCING YOUTH SEXUALITY IN MILLERSTON

Social science scholars of sexualities have shaped our understanding of sex and sexuality as not merely natural, biological processes or categories but also forms of socially and politically produced knowledge. This work illustrates how "sexual meanings, identities, and categories [are] intersubjectively negotiated social and historical products—that sexuality [is], in a word, constructed."[5] As Breanne Fahs and Sara McClelland explain, critical sexualities studies is both a subfield of study and a lens, or a "way of looking" at sexuality that attends to the collision of sex and power.[6] Critical sexualities scholars have directed our attention to the ways sexuality is not simply an individual private act or identity but also a form of social power that creates meaning and is organized by its intersections with race, class, gender, ability, nation, and so on.[7]

The notion of sexuality as a discourse that produces individuals, populations, bodies, and fields of study is of course indebted to Foucault, who marked the "incitement to discourse" producing sexuality as an object and technique of knowledge. This sexual incitement to discourse produces a "multiplication of discourses concerning sex in the field of exercise of power itself: an institutional incitement to speak about it, and to do so more and more; a determination on the part of the agencies of power to hear it spoken about, and to cause *it* to speak through explicit articulation and endless accumulated detail" (emphasis in original).[8] Foucault's "repressive hypothesis" is useful for understanding how youth sexual health promotion manages to obscure sex and sexuality while attempting to change individual behaviors around it. Foucault identifies a paradox in the idea that society has repressed sexuality, particularly since the nineteenth century.[9] At the same time that social institutions and actors have been "silent" about sex, they have simultaneously produced it as a core feature of human identity and the subject of ever-expanding discourses.[10] Power does not ignore sexuality but rather creates social and political meanings about sex through an incitement to speak about it. In Millerston, this power produced a limited way of understanding sexuality that featured both silence *and* constant talk about youth sexual behavior. It produced teens as particular kinds of sexual subjects, ones who are always "at risk," who are devoid of pleasure and desire, who lack agency but at the same time are unconstrained by social inequalities. Although discourses of sexuality produce teen sexual subjectivity as nonagentic, health promotion practice calls upon them to engage in practices of the self, such as abstinence from (presumedly heterosexual) sexual activity or compulsory contraceptive use in the name of decreasing teen pregnancy rates, bolstering the neoliberal state, and creating normative families.

Millerston's participation in activities for the National Day to Prevent Teen Pregnancy set the stage for elucidating how discourses of sexuality operated in the city. The National Day occurs every year in May during National Teen Pregnancy Prevention Month. The National Campaign to

Prevent Teen and Unplanned Pregnancy coordinates the National Day, and activities take place in cities and towns across the United States. Every May, Millerston participates in National Day activities with a series of events sponsored by city government and community-based organizations. They hang a banner from City Hall to a building across the street announcing that May is the National Month to Prevent Teen Pregnancy. I joined National Day activities for the first time in 2012 by attending a resource fair and reception that rain forced inside City Hall instead of on the building's lawn. As they do each year, organizers titled the event "You Have Choices / ¡Tienes Opciones!" Area agencies such as the Boys & Girls Club, Girls Inc., Continuum Health Services, the Millerston Community Health Center, and the PASH Network crowded their displays and tables into the City Hall basement. For the most part, white women from these organizations staffed the tables. The youth in attendance were almost entirely Latinx; both groups sported T-shirts and buttons with the "You Have Choices / ¡Tienes Opciones!" logo. Youth-produced teen pregnancy prevention posters lined the walls and featured slogans such as "Stay a teen," "Avoid crotch rot," "You'll have no freedom as a teen parent," "No more parties, no more movies," and "Would you rather buy condoms or diapers?" Mayor Ryan Brown began the speakers' portion of the event by announcing that he "wants a healthy future for the city of Millerston" and that "the future of Millerston depends on resolving this issue," that is, teen pregnancy. "As all of you know," he said, "teen pregnancy does have an economic and social impact on our city." He then expressed his desire for all city youth to go to college and have a nice house and a good job. The next speaker was a Latina woman who was in her mid-thirties and who had had her first child at 17. She was the only self-identified teen parent in attendance,[11] and became noticeably teary-eyed as she told the audience the only narrative that could be allowed in that space: "Getting pregnant young meant I couldn't do everything I wanted to. Having a child at a young age can drastically change your life, and not always for the best."

I was unable to attend the 2013 National Day events, but news media coverage indicated a sunny day that allowed the activities to be held on the lawn outside City Hall. Colorful lawn signs emblazoned with "You Have Choices / ¡Tienes Opciones!" decorated the area, leading the newspaper to caption its photo: "The message to young people about having sex and getting pregnant or making a smart decision was clear on a sign outside Millerston City Hall on Wednesday." Referring to the teen birthrate, the article quoted Hannah McNeil as saying, "We may be number one in the state, but our rates are dropping and continue to drop." A young woman, identified as a freshman at Millerston High, told the reporter that a lot of pregnancies happen because guys talk insecure girls into having sex. "Guys can say anything to girls these days to get what they want," she said.

In the leadup to the 2014 National Day, MASHPC members lobbied successfully to have the event held at the city's two high schools in order to "reach the youth where they are." On the day of the event, the gymnasium was filled with students, though they were required to be there as part of the regular school day. Adults and some students wore "You Have Choices / ¡Tienes Opciones!" T-shirts, and the banner from City Hall was displayed behind a makeshift podium. A health teacher introduced the events by thanking Hannah McNeil and the members of MASHPC, whom she described as a group of people who "work to increase options for you" and "help you make correct choices." David Moreno spoke first. "The statistics on teen pregnancy in Millerston are very concerning to me," he said. "We are number one in the state on teen pregnancy, which is not a good statistic." He noted that "choices have consequences," and that while not studying for a test may result in a poor grade, "today we are talking about choices that have lifelong consequences. This is about your own life, your own future. Making good choices is very, very important." David continued on to say that he did not want to be number one in the state anymore: "I don't think we are making the right choices at this point. So I want you to be thinking about the serious message that it's not a good idea to engage in irresponsible sex without having thought out 'What is the consequence of that?'" Next, assistant superintendent Mark Rowan awarded students for the best essay response to the prompts "Think from the perspective of a baby, to think how your chances and your life would be affected if you're the baby of a teen parent"; and "What is the journey of becoming a teen parent and what are the effects of becoming a young mother or father and how does it influence the rest of your life?"[12] He announced the winners and awarded prizes including candy, movie tickets, and amusement park season passes.

Next up was the inspirational speaker whom Hannah McNeil had invited. A Black man in his thirties wearing an oversized tracksuit, he did a nice job drumming up excitement in the otherwise uninterested group of students. He showed the students a short film projected onto the far wall of the gymnasium. It is worth describing at length:

A white teen boy and girl are making out on a couch, and the boy pressures the girl to "bring it to the next level." She says she's not ready and the next scene shows her crying outside a large suburban house while melodramatic music plays. "One week later," we see the boy walking down the hallway at school with a new girl, who brushes by the first girlfriend. Cutting back to the couch, the new girlfriend tells the boy, "It's amazing how comfortable I am with you; I feel like I could do anything with you." They start to kiss and the shot fades, leading us to believe they had sex. "Four weeks later" we see a shot of a pregnancy test, and the girl pulls out her cell phone to call the boyfriend, who is sleeping. She tells him she has "bad news"—she's pregnant. "What?!" he replies, as if he had never considered this possibility. He says he "has to go" and hangs up on her. The melodramatic music continues to play as she encounters him at school two weeks later. She asks to talk about the pregnancy, but he says it's not a good time. "You don't understand," she says, "we have to talk about it." "No, *you* don't understand!" he replies. "I had a life, I had dreams, that's all gone now. I wanted to go to college, I wanted a good career—you ruined that." He points his finger in her face and begins to walk away. She retorts, "I ruined your life!? You're not the one who has to carry a baby for 9 months. Are you gonna be sick for half that time? Are your friends and family gonna talk about you every time you turn your back? At least you get to finish high school—I won't get to finish my senior year!" He just walks away, and she calls after him: "What about our baby!" Solemnly he replies, "I just wish we would have waited." "Yeah," she says, "me too." The screen turns to black-and-white and then reveals the text "Nearly one million young girls become pregnant each year."

It would be easy to write off the video shown during the assembly as histrionic and hyperbolic. To do so, however, would be to overlook how it represents dominant and disciplining understandings of youth sexuality in the United States. The video, like youth sexual health promotion more generally, reduces "sex" to a very specific behavior. This behavior, heterosexual, penetrative vaginal sex, has an inevitable consequence—pregnancy—and pregnancy inevitably ruins lives. As other scholars of youth sexualities have observed in their work on similar representations, the video positions boys as sexual aggressors and girls as defenders of purity.[13] In this reductive view of sexuality, women's pleasure does not exist; in the video, for example, it is not even considered that the girl might experience desire or pleasure from her relationship. Moreover, since sex is unfathomable outside heterosexual, procreative sex, there are no sexual practices that young people may engage in that have a lower (or nonexistent) risk of pregnancy. Sex is inevitably dangerous and guaranteed to end badly; in the story, contraception was not part of the picture, as the young woman had sex once and became pregnant. Carrying the pregnancy to term and raising the baby is the only option available in this scenario—abortion and adoption do not exist. Likewise, dropping out of school is inevitable. The film also does not challenge the intensely gendered messages. Girls who don't give in to sex will be publicly ostracized, but if they do have sex, their lives are over. Boys are jerks who cannot take responsibility for their actions, and girls "ruin" boys' lives by getting themselves pregnant. The gendered messages may very well have resonated with the high school students, but did not challenge the realities of hegemonic masculinity among high school boys that arguably contribute to negative sexual health outcomes.[14] What's more, the white middle-class setting and protagonists in the film speak little to the material realities of young people in Millerston and other economically marginalized communities of color.

After the video finished playing, the inspirational speaker told the students, "A lot of times, we go out and have sex and don't think about the consequences. I'm not here to tell you not to have sex. I'm telling you about the consequences of your actions. If you choose to have sex unprotected: disease, babies, etcetera. I know myself, personally, I'm a single father; I don't like it, because I'm raising children by myself." Then, abruptly switching gears, he tore off his tracksuit with a flourish to reveal a suit and tie underneath. "I made some bad choices, but I was able to turn it around." He shared success stories of other young Black men he knew who had made the "correct choices" and now had jobs as a chef or a DJ. The speaker then invited some students down from the bleachers and engaged them in awkward and forced conversations about "the choices they want to make in their lives." Then, without commentary, he blasted music from the gym's sound system to play a clip from Beyoncé's then popular song "Partition." The event wrapped up when organizers distributed "You Have Choices / ¡Tienes Opciones!" buttons, bracelets, and cards with links to the "You Have Choices" website, and the health teacher delivered closing remarks. "A very powerful message for us here at Millerston High today," she told the students. "The choices we make lead us into our future, each one of us, the many choices we have in our lives, the decisions that we make, makes us the people that we are today and leads us to the people we're going to be in the future."

Responsible Silences

At a certain point in my fieldwork I began to realize that I had spent a considerable amount of time in meetings, conference rooms, community events, car rides, classrooms, clinics, and living rooms listening to people discuss "sexual health" and "sexuality" without ever actually talking about *sex*. In the same way that stakeholders talked about race but rarely actually named it, they also continually talked about sexuality without ever acknowledging the material realities of sex or the bodies of sexual actors. The preoccupation with young people's sexual activity in Millerston was almost entirely divorced from the fact of sex itself. While there was ample talk of "responsible" sex that included condoms and birth control, there was no discussion of desire, pleasure, or consent. There was also no discussion about the health of LGBTQ youth or about abortion. In what would come as no surprise to Foucault, sex was everywhere and nowhere at once. Sexuality was ostensibly always at the table, though stakeholders almost never actually mentioned sex: it was glossed over, absent, and assumed through a process of responsible silence. As Beth Emerson alluded in the confrontational MASHPC meeting, we all know what teens are doing when it's 5 o'clock and dark out.

Responsible silences around pleasure, LGBTQ youth, and abortion are related because they all work to avoid something—sexual desire, sexual diversity and fluidity, abortion stigma, and so on. Likewise, these responsible silences construct sexual pleasure, queer sex, and abortion as outside responsible sexuality, and therefore something that should not be spoken about. To take pleasure and desire first: discussions of these were missing not only in National Day events but in youth sexual promotion work in the city overall. As other scholars have noted, these discussions are not just absent but are missing in specific ways that conceal race, gender, and class inequalities and make the absence of pleasure appear to be an individual-level problem.[15] Scholars have long documented and critiqued the lack of pleasure and desire in sexual health education; this absence is certainly germane to Millerston.[16] It was rare to hear professional stakeholders in Millerston talk about young women as owning desire and pleasure or name the missing component of desire in sex education.[17] Although they emphasized sexual *responsibility,* they were silent about sexual *subjectivity.* If stakeholders did mention desire or pleasure, it was only during one-on-one interviews. For example, Ana Reyes Rivera, who was particularly insightful about the politics of her work as a health educator, rhetorically asked me, "Is it really sex ed if we're not talking about pleasure?" However, that teens, and girls in particular, might desire sex and experience pleasure from it while also doing it "safely" (defined narrowly as not becoming pregnant) was not part of the conversation at the National Day events or in the TPPIC more generally.

The inclusion of Beyoncé's song "Partition" at the assembly is an interesting example of the erasure of pleasure and desire that illustrates how sex in Millerston was everywhere and nowhere at once. In contrast to the way the event framed sex as dangerous and did not acknowledge how it could be pleasurable or fun, the song from Beyoncé's eponymously titled 2013 album positions women's sexuality as agentic,[18] overtly refers to sexual acts, and demonstrates women's desire. The song's explicit lyrics describe a sexual encounter between Beyoncé and (presumably) her spouse, Jay-Z, that occurs in the backseat of limousine. Beyoncé asks the driver to roll up the partition separating the passenger and driver areas of the vehicle so that no one sees her "on her knees," likely performing oral sex on Jay-Z. The pair are so turned on, Beyoncé sings, that they may not even make it to the club. Going at it in the backseat, her mascara is running, her lipstick is smudged, and her clothing is ripped and covered in her partner's ejaculation. Again, Foucault would not be surprised that an event whose purpose was to warn young people about the dangers of sex and admonish them to make the "correct," responsible choices also included music describing oral sex, ejaculation, rippled blouses, smudged lipstick, ass-grabbing, and dirty talk. Sex is everywhere and nowhere at once.

Second, youth sexual health promotion efforts in Millerston were almost entirely silent about the sexual and reproductive health of LGBTQ youth. The comprehensive curricula in use in the public schools did not include content for queer or trans youth, project activities rarely collected data on them, and organizational mission statements did not identify them as target populations. Not only were there no LGBTQ-specific youth sexual health promotion efforts in the TPPIC, but stakeholders rarely even acknowledged their existence.[19] Ana Reyes Rivera verbally changed "boyfriend" and "girlfriend" to "partner" when delivering comprehensive sex education curricula as part of her job. Melissa Campbell, the director of youth and young parent services at a community-based nonprofit, was the only professional stakeholder I spoke to who shared that she was not heterosexual. Melissa referenced the research showing that queer youth actually have *higher* rates of unintended pregnancy than their heterosexual counterparts.[20] Nevertheless, for all the passion about lowering high rates of teen pregnancy and STIs in the city, there was seldom any mention of the sexual health of LGBTQ youth. This absence was curious given that research generally positions LGBTQ youth as an "at-risk" population with regard to sexual health behaviors and outcomes.[21] In one Teens Count meeting, a member of the project's external evaluation team read statistics on the 928 youth served by project activities, noting that they were 32% male, 68% female, and 1% transgender. It was not clear if this 1% consisted of trans masculine, trans feminine, or nonbinary youth, and the presenter stumbled over the word "transgender" as if she'd never seen it before, referring to it as "1% . . . gender served." Beyond these brief examples, there were no other mentions of the sexual health of queer or transgender youth in Millerston, nor were there educational efforts tailored to their needs, identities, or bodies.

Third, stakeholders' silences around abortion were notable given the element of the Latino culture narrative that assumed sexual silence on the part of Latinx families contributed to teen pregnancy. The silence surrounding abortion was not merely an assumption on the part of white providers that "Latinas don't have abortions"; it also reflected the pervasive stigma attached to abortion and its construction as something that should be "safe, legal, and rare."[22] The fact that legislative restrictions on abortion services, especially for minors, have expanded exponentially in recent years is implicated in this silence. Professional stakeholders, organizations, and health promotion projects did not include abortion as part of a strategy to reduce the teen birthrate in Millerston. They did not include abortion as part of their efforts to increase access to health services for youth. They did not include abortion providers in the resource lists they distributed to youth. Sex education curricula did not include information about abortion. Of course, given that Ana Reyes Rivera went off script in her delivery of sex education curricula, it is possible that other individual stakeholders in Millerston spoke to youth about abortion. Formally, however, abortion was absent from youth sexual health promotion efforts in the city.[23]

Although they did not include abortion access as part of "youth sexual health," stakeholders relied heavily on the framework of "choice." Choice rhetoric invoked responsible behaviors while remaining silent about the full range of sexual and reproductive options. This framing occurred most notably through the campaign "You Have Choices / ¡Tienes Opciones!" which featured posters, lawn signs, T-shirts, buttons, and health resource cards emblazoned with the slogan, and through the implementation of a curriculum titled "Making Proud Choices." When I interviewed Elizabeth Randolph of Continuum Health Services, she explained, "Our mantra's always been around choice and your choice." I asked if she meant that was her mantra or the organization's. "Both," she replied. "I mean, people who work for us generally have a—you know—certainly we're not advocates of teen pregnancy. We want to make people aware of their choices and make educated decisions for themselves." Here Elizabeth mentioned that many of her staff would consider themselves "pro-choice" in the liberal feminist notion of the freedom to choose abortion. Yet she also felt compelled to point out that they were "certainly" not supportive of the choice to become pregnant at a young age. While discussing inequalities in the city with Mayor Brown, I mentioned the emphasis on "choice" at the high school rally and asked his thoughts on promoting choice in a situation of marked socioeconomic inequalities. In a sudden shift from his acknowledgment earlier in our conversation of the constraints on socioeconomic mobility faced by people in his city, he responded: "I mean, I think they do have choices. You can be poor and you can be going to the public schools and you can do well in your pathway out of poverty for your family or for yourself. Obviously, it's to finish school and hopefully go on to college." Despite acknowledging that myriad social and economic inequalities affected city residents, Brown framed solutions in terms of individual personal responsibility, rather than political transformation and redistribution of social goods.

This use of "choice" rhetoric is noteworthy for two reasons. First, youth sexual promoters were not promoting increased access to *all* sexual and reproductive choices; only certain choices were valid and acceptable. The choices to intentionally parent at a young age, not use contraception, or engage in "irresponsible" sex were not among the choices they promoted. Second, paradoxically, neither was the choice to have an abortion, which is the most common use of the word "choice" surrounding sexual and reproductive health. The ubiquitous "You Have Choices / ¡Tienes Opciones!" slogan was contradictory given that not all young people— especially economically marginalized youth of color—have "choices" in a city replete with structural violence. Many youth in Millerston and elsewhere did not have access to quality health care, freedom from violence, good schools, meaningful employment opportunities, and so on. The rhetoric of "choice" appeals to neoliberal logic—we are, ostensibly, freely choosing autonomous actors in the private marketplace of choices—but conceals the fact that many young people in communities like Millerston don't have such choices. This rhetoric shifts the responsibility away from the state to the self-governing neoliberal actor whom health promotion discourses invite to make (particular, acceptable) choices. Yet simply telling youth that they have choices does not make it so. The invited inspirational speaker at the National Day rally illustrated this shift—and its raced and classed meanings—when he asked the students, referring to the whiter, wealthy Heights neighborhood of the city, "I understand that uptown is where the people that got money live? You know what separates y'all from uptown, right? The choices you make. That's it." Thus, race and class inequalities remain silent while sexual health outcomes are reduced to solely a result of responsibility and "the choices you make."

ENTANGLEMENTS OF SCIENTIFIC EVIDENCE IN MILLERSTON

Discourses and practices of public health science rely on these responsible silences to privilege certain kinds of "truth": pleasure is irrelevant to sexual health, LGBTQ youth don't get pregnant or get someone else pregnant, and abortion must be avoided personally and politically. Both silences and science also work to muddy the relationship between agency and structure by reducing health outcomes to individual behavioral factors. Turning to feminist science studies can help us to understand the ways science produces particular knowledges, truths, and bodies, rather than viewing it as an apolitical, value-free process of truth.[24] This framework mobilizes a critique of scientific practices and discourses by analyzing biological determinism, notions of objectivity and value neutrality, and the production of scientific knowledge, particularly as they relate to gender, sexuality, race, dis/ability, and so on. As Laura Mamo and Jennifer Fishman note, feminist science studies links theory and practice while theorizing and imagining how things could be otherwise.[25] Scholars in this tradition have studied knowledges and technologies related to the feminist health movement, the "naturalness" of monogamy, epidemiological and lay knowledge about cardiovascular disease, and lesbian pregnancy, among many others.[26]

There is relatively little work in the public health sciences that "turns the gaze inward" to analyze the field's epistemological, ontological, and methodological commitments, making it apt for a critique through the lens of feminist science studies.[27] The dominant paradigm in health promotion is positivist, reflecting both the biomedical origins of public health and the social science objectives of legitimating the study of society by utilizing the scientific method.[28] The positivist tradition in health promotion holds an epistemology "based on the concept of disease as something that can be 'treated' objectively, separate from [an] individual's experiences of the material reality of their everyday lives."[29] Critics note that the influence of positivism in public health research and practice has resulted in work that pays only lip service to the field's stated goal of social justice, fails to analyze power, marginalizes qualitative and interpretive research, and neglects lay expertise.[30] In addition, the push toward evidence-based medicine has heavily influenced the public health sciences. Evidence-based medicine posits that a scientifically rigorous approach to clinical decision making is at all times superior to the "unsystematic and 'intuitive' methods of individual clinical practice."[31] Applied to public health, evidence-based practice is "the development, implementation, and evaluation of effective programs and policies in public health through application of principles of scientific reasoning."[32] The push for evidenced-based sexual health education curricula, at the federal level and in Millerston, is one example of evidence-based public health.

In Millerston, individual stakeholders, organizations, and coalitions understood science to be value-free and politically neutral and, as such, used it as a strategy for legitimizing youth sexual health promotion. This strategy was both a response to abstinence-only advocates and a selling point to policy makers and community members who viewed sex education as too politically charged. As Beth Emmerson explained at one PASH Network meeting, touting the scientific efficacy of evidenced-based sex education was a way to distance it from the "dirty sex" stuff. Jenny Díaz put it like this: "I'm just saying, 'This is how your body works. I believe this is based on biology.'" In the Millerston High teen pregnancy prevention video, one health teacher characterized the comprehensive sex education curricula used in the school as just "trying to get the facts across." In the same video, Hannah McNeil offered a scientific argument for school-based sex education: "It's so important because knowledge is power. And without the knowledge about sexual health, they are apt to make poor choices. By undergoing these science, evidenced-based programs which are proven to reduce the incidence of teen pregnancy, then I think that there's no question as to the benefit of students being exposed to it." These comments reflect how the presumed neutrality of scientific sexual "facts" masks the inherently political nature of both sexuality and science. Science was a rational way to justify interventions ranging from distributing condoms in schools to preventing teen pregnancy in order to decrease the high school dropout rate. In what follows, I draw on feminist science studies to analyze the production of scientific knowledge in the TPPIC and consider its entanglements with evidence-based public health. Michelle Murphy defines entanglements as "attachments of material, technical, and social relations across divergent and even antagonistic terrains of politics."[33] Through their entanglements with evidence-based public health, stakeholders in Millerston both mobilized and repudiated scientific notions of causality, data, significance, and evidence.

Causal Fantasies

One way stakeholders were entangled with evidence-based public health involved what I call *causal fantasies*. This concept draws on the notion of magical thinking, an unsubstantiated belief that phenomena are related in a cause and effect way, and on the legacy of scientific racism, the practice of using empirical evidence to justify the inferiority of certain racial groups.[34] Causal fantasies and scientific racism bear many similarities, but the former is more varied and complex in its construction and uses. Causal fantasies may rely on racism, but also many other forms of oppression (often simultaneously). They establish fantastical causal relationships, sometimes based on scientific discourses, other times not, that distract from the reproduction of inequality. Causal fantasies overpower existing and demonstrable causal relationships that conflict with the worldviews of those who hold them. In addition, causal fantasies are strategies that establish cause-effect relationships in order to support particular goals. They validate certain kinds of knowledge and scientific evidence while ignoring others, specifically to promote individual-level solutions to structural-level problems.[35]

Causal fantasies enabled the TPPIC to codify taken for granted truths while reproducing the structure of its own internal coherence. For example, stakeholders overlooked the equivocal data on outcomes of teen childbearing (and certainly the evidence showing *better* outcomes) as well as research showing that most teen parents drop out of school before becoming pregnant (rather than the widespread belief that teen pregnancy causes school dropout). At the same time, they employed causal fantasies that enabled them to naturalize claims about causality and youth sexual health. The most prominent of these consisted of stories in which taken for granted truths and assumptions were made into undisputed facts. This sort of magical thinking about the causes of teen pregnancy conveniently ignored science *while also relying on it* to legitimize particular truths. Causal fantasies variously attributed teen pregnancy to an early sunset, not having a movie theater in town, experiencing a lack of love, school suspensions, and not going on LARC. They also enabled stakeholders to assert spurious claims about the causal relationship between their work and declining teen birthrates in Millerston.

The magic recipe of sex education, contraception, and "hope" was key to causal fantasies in that it was the primary policy and practice strategy in the city. Again, this was the case despite the large body of research suggesting that structural factors have much stronger explanatory power for teen births.[36] Most stakeholders acknowledged, or at least alluded to, the social and economic inequalities that affected teen pregnancy in Millerston. Yet they nonetheless focused their efforts (and their self-congratulation) on increasing the uptake of evidence-based sex education curricula in the public schools and in community-based organizations and increasing the number of teens on long-acting contraception.

A session on "holistic approaches to teen pregnancy prevention" at one year's PASH Network annual conference illustrated how causal fantasies focused on individual-level solutions to structural-level problems. The facilitators stressed that teen pregnancy was the "symptom of a larger problem" and that macro-level solutions, such as factors in the policy environment, "protected" youth from teen pregnancy. In a brainstorm on structural factors for addressing teen pregnancy in the community, the audience offered "inspire hope," "mentoring," "show youth other options," "good experiences," "college tours," "believe in young people," "be part of the process of change," and "provide parameters and expectations"—all individual-level strategies. Jenny Díaz echoed this causal fantasy in the MASHPC meeting when she stressed to the superintendent the importance of contraceptive access: "Young people will use contraception if they know they have a good job in the future." On the whole, stakeholders spoke quixotically about "giving" the young people in Millerston "access to hope and opportunity," but failed to translate this goal into actionable policies or programming. In this way, causal fantasies disregard structural oppression—you can't "create" hope and opportunity, especially in an era of immense wealth disparities, a disappearing (or already dismantled) social safety net, and vastly altered economic structures. Sitting through lessons on recognizing the symptoms of chlamydia and gonorrhea or having an IUD inserted cannot create opportunities for meaningful employment, extend access to quality, affordable education or health care, or guarantee freedom from interpersonal and state violence.[37]

Despite equivocal research on the outcomes of teen parenting, stakeholders mobilized a causal fantasy in which teen parenting is always already bad for the parents, their children, the community, and the city itself. As I discuss in the introduction, the commonly held belief that teen pregnancy and parenting are wholly detrimental does not hold up under scrutiny. In addition to reversing the causal relationship of teen pregnancy and school dropout, stakeholders' entanglements with evidence-based public health frequently muddled the relationship between poverty, inequality, and teen pregnancy.[38] Whereas a growing body of research indicates that poverty and inequality are key contributors to teen pregnancy rates, stakeholders largely saw it the other way around.[39] They often attributed inequalities in Millerston related to employment, income, and opportunity to the rate of teen pregnancy and parenting in the city. As Clarisa Ortiz put it, teen pregnancy was "obviously expensive" and "really downgrading our city." Mayor Brown echoed this sentiment at his National Day remarks when he stated that "teen pregnancy does have an economic and social impact on our city." During the course of my fieldwork, I heard teen moms blamed for practically all of what ailed the city—at times it seemed as though pregnant teenagers were to blame for the decline of manufacturing itself. Stakeholders not only clung to research that amplified or distorted the negative effects of teen childbearing but also ignored qualitative research conducted with young parents. Qualitative research findings on experiences and outcomes of young parents are more positive than population and economic-based studies but are suppressed "not only because such studies may pose a challenge to the official orthodoxy regarding teenage mothers, but also [because they] reflect a common perception that qualitative research is less rigorous and accurate."[40]

The ways that stakeholders understood and mobilized data is central to causal fantasies and their entanglements with evidence-based public health more generally. In another causal fantasy, stakeholders ascribed the decline in teen birthrates in Millerston directly to the bold battle against teen pregnancy and STIs they were waging, as Jenny Díaz emphasized in the meeting described at the beginning of this chapter. After a long delay in releasing data for the years 2011 and 2012, in the fall of 2014 the state department of public health finally released vital statistics data showing that the teen birthrate in Millerston had fallen from 83.6 births per 1,000 women ages 15–19 in 2010, to 68.3 per 1,000 in 2011, and to 57.1 per

1,000 in 2012. This decline represented a 32% drop from 2010 to 2012. At the MASHPC meeting following the data release, members celebrated the 32% decrease as a direct result of the committee's work. Furthermore, they attributed the decline specifically to Hannah McNeil's leadership of the committee, prompting the city to officially proclaim that date as "Hannah McNeil Day" in Millerston. Although the activities of MASHPC and the partners of the Teens Count initiative likely had some degree of impact on teen pregnancy in the city, there is no way to establish a direct causal effect, much less the *magnitude* of that effect. Teen birthrates had been on the decline in Millerston, the state, and the country for many years. In the same period that the 32% drop in Millerston occurred, teen births fell 18% in the state overall and 14% in the United States as a whole.[41] In fact, during this period, the rate dropped in all but two of the 25 cities in the state with the highest teen birthrates. Moreover, the Millerston rate decreased 28% from 2008 to 2010, *preceding* the Teens Count initiative, and thus was similar to the 2010–12 decrease attributed to stakeholders' work.

A number of factors influence teen birthrates at the population level, including shifting fertility patterns more generally, and the age at first birth has steadily increased for women in all racial and ethnic groups.[42] Teen birthrates are also influenced by a variety of changes such as increased health care access under the Affordable Care Act, changes in the economy, changes in norms around condom use and safer sex, and easy access to sexual health information via the internet.[43] The lack of research at the city level to explain teen birthrate decreases allowed stakeholders to create stories that fit their narrative of progress—that is, to imagine a direct causation between their work and the changing rates. The work of the Teens Count initiative may very well be *correlated* with the 32% drop in the teen birthrate, but it is not a necessary or sufficient *causal* explanation. To fully explain the drop, we would need to look to other, intervening variables that affect the teen birthrate, data that do not exist at the city level. In a peculiar entanglement with evidence-based public health, stakeholders' causal fantasies attributed the decline in Millerston's teen birthrate directly to their work despite the lack of data suggesting correlation, or for that matter, causation. The outcome data that MASHPC and Teens Count collected on their efforts were limited to process-based metrics such as the number of teens who participated in evidence-based sexual health curricula, the number of teens who visited a partner clinic in the previous year, the number of staffed trained, and the number of condoms distributed. This sort of data cannot demonstrate that stakeholders' work caused the decline in the teen birthrate, nor does it demonstrate the quality of the clinical services provided, the efficacy of the educational content, or even youth perceptions of hope and opportunity.

Stakeholders often touted the importance of "being grounded in the data," and one facilitator at a *Teens Count* meeting proclaimed that "if it can't be measured, it's not on the agenda." Yet they failed to recognize how data construct what is and can be known about youth sexuality and reproduction in Millerston. For example, there was a constant conflation of and slippage between "teen birth" and "teen pregnancy" rates. These slippages worked as a tactic of data massaging that made abortion and the complicated social experience of resolving an unintended pregnancy invisible.[44] Even Jenny Díaz, who clearly valued data and often spoke in numbers, frequently exhibited this slippage, as she did when describing the Teens Count project at a partner meeting: "The purpose of the initiative is to reduce teen birth—er, um—teen pregnancy." That stakeholders conflated teen pregnancy and teen birth was indicative of the silence surrounding abortion among policy makers and service providers, who did not view abortion access as part of a strategy for reducing the teen birthrate. In addition, although stakeholders spoke almost constantly about the declining rates in Millerston, they were always careful to note that there was still a problem in the city, namely, racial disparities. While I do not disagree that racial and ethnic disparities in teen birthrates exist and are meaningful, the emphasis on racial disparities was in part a discursive move. That is, the emphasis on racial disparities ensured the perpetuation of the TPPIC even as national, state, and local teen birthrates were dropping. As a teen parent said in the Millerston High–produced teen pregnancy prevention video, "The teen pregnancy rate in Millerston is decreasing, but everyone agrees that it is still much too high." Yet a discussion of or action plan to address the structural causes of racism that exacerbated these disparate rates was absent from the focus on racial disparities in teen pregnancy rates.

Making Proud Science

Stakeholders were deeply entangled in tensions and debates surrounding the science of sexual health education. Although they disregarded evidence regarding the equivocal outcomes of teen childbearing, qualitative research with young parents, and evidence complicating the causality of teen pregnancy, stakeholders highly valued and promoted "scientific" or "evidence-based" comprehensive sexual health education (CSE). In 2010, a 7–3 vote among members of the school committee had approved an expanded sexual health education curriculum allowing for the implementation of CSE in the Millerston public schools. Stakeholders regarded this vote as one of the major victories they had seen in the city, as they understood CSE as a key factor in reducing teen pregnancy in the city. Like other proponents of "scientifically based" or "comprehensive" sex education, they positioned the superiority of the approach in contrast to its much-maligned (in public health circles, at least) predecessor "abstinence only until marriage" (AOUM) instruction.

As a policy strategy, AOUM was birthed by the 1996 welfare reform act, which decimated the safety net for poor women and their children. Welfare reform funneled billions of dollars into programs that taught young people that "abstinence from sexual activity is the only certain way to avoid out-of-wedlock pregnancy, sexually transmitted diseases, and other associated health problems" and that "a mutually faithful monogamous relationship in the context of marriage is the expected standard of sexual activity."[45] Conversely, comprehensive sex education consists of programs that "include age-appropriate, medically accurate information on a broad set of topics related to sexuality including human development, relationships, decision-making, abstinence, contraception, and disease prevention."[46] "Scientifically based" refers to curricula that have undergone rigorous evaluations and been found to have statistically relevant outcomes on metrics such as delaying the onset of intercourse and increasing condom or contraceptive use.[47]

In addition to reducing the incidence of teen pregnancy and STIs, outcomes measured by CSE experimental or quasi-experimental evaluations prioritize behavior such as "reducing the frequency of sex," "reducing the number of sexual partners," and "using condoms or birth control," as well as attitudes such as "perceived efficacy of condoms in preventing pregnancy," "condom hedonistic beliefs," and "perception of severity of pregnancy and childbearing."[48] The science of CSE thus includes only certain types of research and particular ways of knowing about the world. For example, "scientific" outcomes of CSE do not measure knowledge about pleasure or inequality, or behaviors such as affirmative consent or navigating sexual stigma.[49] As Jessica Fields reminds us, there is much to critique about comprehensive approaches as well: simply basing them in "science" does not mean that they avoid reproducing ideas about sex as inevitably risky and dangerous, disregarding pleasure and desire, positioning young women as defenders of sexual purity, erasing queer and transgender youth, or relying on racist tropes about the pathological nature of reproduction among women of color.[50]

Two of the scientifically based comprehensive curricula used in Millerston, "Making Proud Choices" and "¡Cuídate!" reveal their value-laden assumptions even in their names. "Making Proud Choices," a program designed for urban African American youth ages 11–13, acknowledges that abstinence is the "best choice," but also "emphasizes the importance of condoms to reduce the risk of pregnancy and STIs, including HIV, if participants choose to have sex."[51] In addition to the fact that, as a small city with a population that's half Latinx, Millerston does not at all match the target population for this intervention, the curriculum continues the trope of proper choices in an environment full of unacknowledged constraints. "Making Proud Choices" positions sex as risky and dangerous: the first half of the curriculum focuses on the "consequences of sex," framed as disease and pregnancy. The latter half focuses on strategies for preventing STDs and pregnancy through "refusal and negotiation skills." "Making Proud Choices" also includes a theme of "protecting the family and community" as a motivation for practicing safer sex. The creators position this theme as a way to shift the "traditional exclusive focus on individualistic HIV/AIDS knowledge and individualistic attitudes toward risky behavior."[52] Yet the burden of protecting the family and community falls on the individual teens themselves, without an acknowledgement of the myriad structural factors, such as poverty, racism, homophobia, and sexism, that contribute to HIV transmission.[53] The curriculum attributes high rates of STIs and teen pregnancy to young people's inability to "express their sexual feelings in a responsible or accountable way." Similar to the National Day events in Millerston, "Making Proud Choices" frames "sexual responsibility" in terms of choosing abstinence or using condoms.

Table 1   *"Making Proud Choices" curriculum*

Module 1	Getting to Know You and Steps to Making Your Dreams Come True
Module 2	The Consequences of Sex: HIV Infections
Module 3	Attitudes about Sex, HIV, and Condoms Use
Module 4	Strategies for Preventing HIV Infection: Stop, Think, and Act
Module 5	The Consequences of Sex: STDs
Module 6	The Consequences of Sex: Pregnancy
Module 7	Developing Condom Use and Negotiation Skills
Module 8	Enhancing Refusal and Negotiation Skills

SOURCE: "Making Proud Choices!" ETR, accessed June 10, 2020, https://www.etr.org/ebi /programs/making-proud-choices/.

Stakeholders loved "¡Cuídate!" or "Take Care of Yourself!" for its specifically Latino-focused approach.[54] According to its creators, "¡Cuídate!" is a "cultural and theory-based HIV sexual risk-reduction program designed specifically for Latino youth."[55] Similar to "Making Proud Choices," the curriculum stresses abstinence and condom use. Program goals include "highlight[ing] cultural values that support safer sex practices and refram[ing] cultural values that are perceived as barriers to safer sex."[56] The curriculum reframes the Latino cultural value of machismo— as the creators define it, an emphasis on men's power through strength and control in decision making—to represent the values of caring and taking responsibility for yourself and others. Put another way, the curriculum tells men that they can refocus hegemonic masculinity into appropriate caretaking behaviors. Similarly, the curriculum reframes the cultural value of *marianismo*—which, according to the creators, expects women to stay virgins until marriage, have children, and be devoted to their husbands—to "encourage young women to consider condom use and refusal of sex as ways of protecting themselves."[57] Put another way, the curriculum tells women to comply with compulsory heterosexuality and to deny their own desires as a protection strategy. The designers acknowledge the heterogeneity of "Latino" culture and Latinos themselves, but nonetheless offer a curriculum based on presumed shared cultural values that does not challenge, but reframes, sexism and heterosexism through a focus on individual behaviors in the form of condom use and refusal of sex. In addition to flattening culture and disregarding the impact of social and political inequalities, the curriculum focuses on the most conventional or stereotypical Latinx cultural values (i.e., family, masculinity, respect) and fails to incorporate other values also prominent in Latinx cultures (i.e., anticolonialism, economic justice) that could have considerable impact on sexual health.

Millerston youth who participated in these scientifically based curricula most likely learned some important knowledge and skills. But as Jessica Fields argues, we ought to consider not only what sex education might *prevent* but also what it *promotes*. In "asking more" of sex education, Fields redirects our attention to the generative capacity it has to shape the social, collective, and individual experiences of sexuality. What would sex education in Millerston look like if it confronted the legacy of coercive sterilization among Puerto Rican women, the regulation of poor women's fertility cloaked in fears of the welfare queen, and the promotion of long-acting contraceptives to young women of color? What would it look like if it acknowledged all young people's desire and pleasure, the persistence of rape culture, and the needs of queer and transgender youth? What would it look like if sex education in Millerston were reframed with Michelle Fine's notion of "thick desire" in mind, which understands sexuality for all people across age, gender, or sexual orientation "within a larger context of social and interpersonal structures that enable a person to engage in the political act of wanting"?[58] What would it mean to theorize policy making and programming "not merely from a perspective of minimal loss, but from a perspective that sees [young people] as entitled to desire in all of its forms; entitled to publicly funded enabling conditions across racial, ethnic, class, sexual, geographic, and disability lines"?[59] In other words, rather than cloaking sex in science so as to make it appear apolitical, what would happen if sexuality in Millerston was understood as constituted by and mediated by social, economic, and political factors?

THE PROGRESS OF SEX AND SCIENCE

At one Teens Count meeting, the facilitator called us back to our seats following a small group activity by exclaiming, "Why are we here? Because we're making tremendous progress!!" He also told us that the "shared indicators" of success found in our "common agenda" were the "holy grail" of progress. These shared indicators included metrics like "number of youth reached by evidence-based curricula" and "number of condoms" distributed. As I observed these meetings, I often found myself wondering how many of those students saw their lives, bodies, and desires reflected in the lessons they sat through. I wondered how many of those condoms were actually used, how many were used correctly, and how many young people gained the skills to effectively negotiate condom use in consensual, pleasurable sexual activity. I wondered how the entanglements with evidence-based public health limited what we know and do not know about youth sexuality in Millerston.

The marriage of sex and science in Millerston does work similar to that done by the Latino culture narrative and the ideology of colorblindness described in chapter 3: it both produces and constrains what is and can be known about youth sexuality. The deployment of sexual and scientific discourses in Millerston is ultimately about notions of progress, and these discourses are mutually constitutive. Progress links sexuality to science through positioning a reduction of the teen birthrate as integral to the social and economic progress of the city, as illustrated by Mayor Brown's National Day comments: the youth in the city will make progress by having "hope," by not being pregnant, and going on to have a normative, heterosexual, middle-class life course. In this way, wrapping sex in science not only makes it appear asocial and apolitical but also reproduces the teen pregnancy prevention industrial complex itself. It enables stakeholders to extol the importance of structural factors impacting the health of young people in Millerston while continuing to focus their efforts on individual behavior change strategies and self-congratulation.

I follow Sara McClelland and Michelle Fine in arguing for a "critical sexuality science" that "suspends the 'givens' of adolescent sexualities." This science would not hide inequality in the language of "giving" hope and opportunity but would instead acknowledge the embodiment of "sexual subjectivities situated in larger yearnings for a life of economic, intellectual, and civic possibilities."[60] In asking for more, a critical sexuality science dares to interrogate that which is always already assumed. It does not merely aim to prevent certain outcomes but instead promotes agentic sexuality for all people while centering the voices and experiences of those most marginalized by interlocking systems of racism, classism, ableism, heterosexism, and transphobia. The productive power of a feminist critical sexuality science lies in its potential to fully respond to the complexities of sex in a world marked by power imbalances.

Conclusion

Around the time I concluded fieldwork in Millerston, I presented findings from my research at a conference panel on abortion, contraception, and sexuality. I shared my initial theorization of the teen pregnancy prevention industrial complex and an analysis of how sexual and scientific discourses operated in the city. There was a decent-size audience for a morning session, and I got a few chuckles with my use of a Foucault meme to illustrate the simultaneous obsession with and absence of sexuality in Millerston.[1] My copanelists were reproductive justice scholars whose work I was familiar with, and the Q&A session was lively and productive. One audience member perceptively inquired about the cognitive dissonance that allowed stakeholders to emphasize the social determinants of health while focusing their efforts on modifying individual behaviors. In response to this question, one of my copanelists turned to me and said, "I mean, I used to collaborate with some of these organizations in Millerston, and I've got to say that it's progress that they even *acknowledge* social structural factors!"

My copanelist's comment was not an uncommon response to my research. Nevertheless, given that a reproductive justice framework and vision pushes back against individual understandings of health and rights, it was surprising to hear this comment from someone engaged in RJ research. I would agree that *acknowledging* structural determinants of health is certainly better than pretending they don't exist. However, I am reluctant to frame the work of the teen pregnancy prevention industrial complex in Millerston as a form of progress. The progress frame implies linear improvement toward a predetermined end and lacks a nuanced analysis of gender, race, and sexuality. It also invokes a constrained vision of sexual and reproductive health politics that limits how we imagine the purpose of our work. While it was probably better that stakeholders in Millerston knew, at least theoretically, that social factors like race and poverty affected people's health, that awareness did not impact how they actually conducted their work. It is easy to critique social structures while nonetheless continuing on with your day-to-day work in ways that do not incorporate those critiques. Moreover, as *Distributing Condoms and Hope* demonstrates, eliding the structural determinants of health, social, and economic inequalities only serves to further reproduce them.

Although I reject the notion of the field as a place "out there" that you "return" from when fieldwork ends, it was around the time of this conference that I shifted from active data collection in Millerston to focusing on the analytic and writing aspects of this project. For the first time in seven years, I was not working in Millerston in some capacity. With this distance, I found myself thinking of youth sexual health promotion work in Millerston as the sort of montage that ended each season of HBO's acclaimed series *The Wire*. Set in Baltimore, the series is notable for its trenchant examination of how social, political, and economic institutions, including law enforcement, the criminal justice system, the school system, public health, and the media, fail both the urban poor and the professionals charged with serving them. According to Anmol Chaddha and William Julius Wilson, *The Wire* illustrates how "individuals' decisions and behavior are often shaped by—and indeed limited by—social, political, and economic forces beyond their control."[2] The montage that ends each of the five seasons follows the partial resolution of major cases and minor subplots but nonetheless depicts "business as usual" continuing within the city: cops continue to bust drug dealers, some drug dealers go to prison while new ones take over their corners, some addicts get clean while others pick up a habit, and public servants continue to struggle to do right by the people they serve.

Of course, Millerston is not Baltimore, but the dynamics of the teen pregnancy prevention industrial complex bear some similarities to the idiosyncrasies of law enforcement and the drug trade depicted in the show: there are not distinct "good guys" and "bad guys" (everyone is both); people are muddling through, doing the best they can within the constraints they must work under; and the more things change, the more they stay the same. Shortly after I transitioned away from active fieldwork in Millerston, some of the characters and circumstances in the city shifted, but the work of the teen pregnancy prevention industrial complex carried on as usual. The culmination of my data collection coincided with several major changes in the city. Jenny Díaz left her position as executive director of the PASH Network and moved out of state. Hannah McNeil retired from the Millerston Board of Health and moved to a whiter, more affluent neighboring town. The Millerston public school district was placed under state receivership for being "chronically underperforming," and David Moreno was ousted as superintendent. The Statewide Organization on Adolescent Pregnancy (SOAP) closed its doors, while the Towne House expanded its services to include postsecondary education. Many of the individual stakeholders I interviewed took new jobs outside Millerston. Most notably, the 5-year $1.1 million Teens Count project ended, and the collection of initiatives associated with it carried on loosely and without funding. The more things changed in Millerston, the more they stayed the same.

RACE AND REPRODUCTION IN HEALTH PROMOTION

With this montage in mind, I step back from the details of next season's "plot" to consider the implications of neoliberalism, whiteness, and public health labor in Millerston. Viewing youth sexual health promotion through these lenses helps us to think more complexly about notions of hope and progress. Next, I offer practical steps for working toward reproductive justice in Millerston through a reproductive justice framework, vision, and movement. These steps include promoting thick desire, listening to pregnant and parenting youth, turning the public health gaze inward, and partnering with organizations working for racial and reproductive justice. Finally, using the notion of "educated hope," I argue for a reframing of hope as a mode of critique that imagines and demands something more of health promotion.

In tracing discourses on youth sexuality and reproduction, this book emphasizes that the politics of race, reproduction, gender, sexuality, and science both produce and constrain how we understand and how we engage in community health work. Activating a critique of the teen pregnancy prevention industrial complex provides a rubric for making sense of dispersed forms of power in health promotion. The TPPIC has both material and discursive effects. For instance, the gendered racial projects of the Latino culture narrative and the colorblind approach to LARC promotion demonstrate how gender and race formations have concrete implications for health promotion as well as the social meanings of race and gender. Gendered racial projects play out simultaneously through discourses, such as the racialization of teen pregnancy, and through interactions, such as when a medical provider pressures a young Latina to accept a LARC method. Likewise, particular mobilizations of scientific knowledge invoke responsible silences and causal fantasies that play out both discursively and practically. Building a movie theater in downtown Millerston is likely to have little effect on the sexual and reproductive health of marginalized youth in the city, just as evidence-based curricula that erase desire, pleasure, abortion, and LGBTQ people are unlikely to teach them skills with which to navigate sexuality in an unequal world. Pregnant and parenting teens are caught up in these processes, but rarely on their own terms. Looking toward their messy narratives and thinking queerly about their lives are strategies to push back against the pathologization-romanticization binary *and* to craft policies that meet their needs. Before outlining specific strategies for working toward reproductive justice, I turn to neoliberalism, whiteness, and labor to summarize the effects of race and reproduction in youth sexual health promotion.

THE TWILIGHT OF HEALTH DISPARITIES?

Neoliberal logics organize and sustain the teen pregnancy prevention industrial complex on multiple levels.[3] The economic logics of neoliberalism that promote free trade policies and privatization helped to decimate the manufacturing industry and contribute to an upward redistribution of wealth and resources. These changes are felt throughout the world, and acutely in Millerston, as the manufacturing economy disappeared without an adequate replacement and as the government has continually reduced or restricted public assistance benefits. Meanwhile, the cultural logics of neoliberalism promote personal responsibility and "choice" and thus privatize the effects of systemic inequalities onto individuals.[4] As countless scholars have shown, neoliberal logics now structure much of social and political life, ranging from the experiences of gender, sexuality, and bodies to health promotion and schooling.[5]

The rhetoric of "choice" used by the TPPIC in Millerston, most explicitly in the ubiquitous "You Have Choices / ¡Tienes Opciones!" slogan, and the promotion of individual behavior change (e.g., using LARC) for remedying systemic inequality (e.g., racial health disparities) are hallmarks of cultural neoliberalism. The ineffectiveness and ethical implications of promoting individual behaviors to address structural problems form a widely acknowledged, yet seemingly intractable problem in health promotion.[6] Neoliberal logic enables, bolsters, and sustains this tension. Such logic allows the TPPIC to foreground high teen birthrates, low high school graduation rates, and high numbers of families living in poverty—all consequences of inequality—but privatize responsibility for these inequalities by distributing condoms and promoting empty notions of hope. Further, neoliberal logics allow the TPPIC to portray young people in Millerston as freely choosing, autonomous actors who are unconstrained by power relationships and material realities: they "choose" to (not) become teen parents, (not) go to college, (not) be single parents, (not) be poor, and so on. As a result, stakeholders are able to consolidate the need for their professional roles in health promotion and obscure their social, racial, and economic privilege, thus maintaining the structural violence that created a need for their intervention in the first place.

THE INVISIBILITY OF PUBLIC HEALTH WHITENESS

Neoliberalism and colorblindness often work in tandem.[7] A few of the professional stakeholders I spoke to did notice that the public health professionals in Millerston were overwhelmingly white,[8] and some did acknowledge their own whiteness. For example, Kristina Myers—who stood out among my respondents as employing a racial justice framework—stated, "I feel funny saying this because, um, you know, I'm a privileged white person, so who am I to sort of think that I understand a culture?" Emily Lambert acknowledged, "I'll always be a white lady, and I think I need to be aware of that when I'm talking to a lower-class Latino woman [sic]." Similarly, Beth Emmerson told me, "We don't need white people coming in there and saying, 'This is what we think you need,'"—an ironic statement considering that was precisely what MASHPC (the Millerston Adolescent Sexual Health Promotion Committee) did. Although Kristina named white privilege, the statements from Emily and Beth merely illustrate an acknowledgment of the fact of their whiteness itself, without showing an understanding of its unearned, invisible social benefits. None of these respondents included actionable steps in their statements or analysis. Racial justice activists and educators argue that this trend toward "acknowledging" white privilege is usually to the benefit of the white person attempting to assuage their guilt, as Mia McKenzie explains: "What I find is that most of the time when people acknowledge their privilege, they feel really special about it, really glad that something so significant just happened, and then they just go ahead and do whatever they wanted to do anyway, privilege firmly in place. The truth is that acknowledging your privilege means a whole lot of nothing much if you don't do anything to actively push back against it."[9] McKenzie was writing with a particular audience in mind, one that already sees themselves as allies to people of color. For some white professionals in the TPPIC, acknowledging white privilege might be an important first step in making whiteness visible in Millerston and transforming the youth sexual health promotion industry. Making visible the whiteness in the TPPIC must occur in tandem with an interrogation of how professionals benefit from the existence of the complex itself. In addition, as McKenzie highlights, acknowledging and making whiteness visible must be followed by specific, material changes in the framing, development, and implementation of youth sexual health promotion, as discussed below.

A JOBS PROGRAM FOR THE MIDDLE CLASS

Like other scholar-activists who work toward liberation for teen and young parents, critics often challenge me about whether I am "promoting" teen pregnancy. This is a trick question, as it implies only one "correct" answer. The question speaks to the need, as I demonstrate in chapter 2, for a nonbinary way of thinking about teen childbearing that refocuses attention on the messy experiences of teen pregnancy and parenting. In addition, the question helps to elide the ways in which public health professionals and researchers benefit from the pathologization of teen sexuality and reproduction. There's a saying in health promotion that we are "trying to work ourselves out of a job." Ostensibly, once we fix the public health problem at hand, there will no longer be a need for our work and we will move onto a new issue. As I discuss in chapter 2, stakeholders differed in their opinions as to whether teen pregnancy was here to stay, whether it was a problem or not, and so on. However, the fact that the rates can never get "low enough" to liberate teen pregnancy from being a public health problem speaks to the ways in which the TPPIC is structurally invested in *not* working itself out of existence. Rather, the TPPIC guarantees the existence of a sort of jobs program for the middle class, ensuring that there will always be work for (mainly white) middle-class women in preventing pregnancies among economically marginalized youth of color. Here I am not making a rational actor argument that professionals disingenuously engage in this work to fulfill their own self-interests. Rather, I am pointing out that sustaining middle-class jobs (in the form of midlevel human service, clinical, and educational providers) is one noteworthy effect of the youth sexual health promotion industry.

My copanelist at the conference was not the first person to defend stakeholders from my critique of their failure to attend to structural-level problems while promoting individual behavior change. I want to consider what this tension between agency (stakeholders' intentions) and structure (the factors impacting their work) reveals about public health work and the potential of a critical public health practice. A common and, I believe, oversimplified response to my analysis of the TPPIC is to emphasize the very real constraints that policy makers and service providers face in their work.

This response argues that professionals might very well understand and prefer to work on structural-level issues, such as eliminating racism and poverty, but are constrained by the setup of the nonprofit industrial complex.[10] In other words, there is little "professional work" in dismantling racism, and there is a surplus of "teen pregnancy prevention" jobs in programs targeting communities of color. Tackling systemic social problems like racism and economic inequality is much more difficult to implement, measure, and justify to funders than distributing condoms and talking about hope.

Of course, stakeholders *do* face constraints in their work, but nonetheless make decisions about language, framing, programs, participants, communication, and so on that help reproduce teen pregnancy as a pathology plaguing economically marginalized women of color. It is not an accident that teen pregnancy prevention stigmatizes and shames young mothers, and it is not an accident that health promoters push certain contraceptive technologies over others. That they face constraints on their work does not require their collusion in reproducing the very structures that construct the TPPIC in the first place, including the industry of middle-class health promotion jobs. A truly liberatory, critical public health practice would start with the health issues that communities identify for themselves—a sentiment that many people working in health promotion express but do not follow.[11] If they did, there would not be a teen pregnancy prevention industrial complex in Millerston.

TOWARD REPRODUCTIVE JUSTICE IN MILLERSTON

I want to imagine what reproductive justice could look like in Millerston and anyplace else where health promotion plays out in a neoliberal landscape dominated by white, middle-class professionals—that is, the vast majority of public health research and policy making. Working toward reproductive justice in Millerston must include a framework that shifts the way we understand youth sexuality and reproduction away from a narrow view of simply preventing teen pregnancy toward a vision in which young people have the tools, resources, and support they need to make a range of sexual and reproductive health decisions. This shift must include action that works in solidarity with liberatory social movements. I first offer four action steps that stakeholders can use to work toward applying reproductive justice principles to youth sexual health promotion in Millerston and elsewhere. However, in the spirit of this book's critique, I also offer a call to abolish the teen pregnancy prevention industrial complex itself.

1. Promote Thick Desire Rather than Prevent Teen Pregnancy

A reproductive justice framework requires fostering the conditions under which people can exercise a full range of reproductive options, including contraception, abortion, and parenting. Preventing unintended pregnancy is part of reproductive justice, but not as a narrow focus on preventing teen pregnancy regardless of an individual's desires and choices. One strategy that health promoters can use in working toward reproductive justice is to frame their work in terms of "thick desire."[12] Rather than considering the work in terms of what they want to *prevent*, health promoters could cast it in terms of what they want to *promote*.[13] Instead of merely preventing pregnancy, this reframing would define the goals of contraceptive access and school-based sex education in terms of promoting young people's ability to have the economic, social, and political power and resources to make decisions about their bodies, sexuality, and reproduction. Promoting thick desire might very well include expanding access to LARC or implementing comprehensive sex education curricula, but it would do so with the objective of promoting agentic sexuality for young people rather than merely preventing them from getting pregnant.[14] The goal is thick desire, not simply reducing the teen birthrate. At the same time, teen birthrates would likely be lower when teens experience thick desire.

Promoting thick desire also involves grounding sexuality and reproduction in their social, economic, and political contexts. For example, sexual health education curricula might include lessons about the history of contraceptive coercion. Community health coalitions might include training for youth and adults on political advocacy and engagement alongside the basics of contraceptive efficacy and STI transmission. Policy makers might contextualize Millerston's economic problems as consequences of the history of racism and forced migration, rather than blaming them on high teen birthrates. Reframing teen pregnancy prevention in terms of thick desire goes beyond access to contraception, abortion, and sex education to also including support and dignity for young parents, freedom from sexual shame and stigma, access to quality education and meaningful employment, and freedom from state violence. This shift in how we understand the goals and objectives of youth sexual health promotion doesn't necessarily change every aspect of the day-to-day work, but it greatly transforms how we understand the work's purpose and how we frame it for ourselves and others.

2. Listen to Pregnant and Parenting Youth

Promoting youth sexual health cannot come at the expense of the dignity and well-being of pregnant and parenting youth. Stigmatizing and shaming young parents as a strategy of pregnancy prevention damages their dignity and well-being, as does forcing young parents into a binary narrative of "You ruined your life" or "You redeemed yourself." Health promotion has long relied on stigmatizing undesirable health outcomes ranging from obesity to lung cancer to HIV as a strategy for motivating people to change their individual behaviors: eat more vegetables, quit smoking, use a condom.[15] Health promoters must take a hard look not only at the ethics of shaming and stigmatizing teen parents as a prevention technique, but also at its deleterious effects on young parents and their children. When young parents see those posters of sad-looking toddlers lamenting that they're supposedly more likely to go to prison because their mom was less than 20 years old when she gave birth, they know the toddlers are meant to be their children. This does nothing to help improve their life chances.

As evidenced by stakeholders' reactions to the Towne House students' stories at various conferences and community forums, there is a transformative power in listening to teen parents. This power lies in not only crafting policies and programs that meet their complex needs but also allowing them the space to be messy and imperfect. Listening to pregnant and parenting youth means helping to create such spaces, and not just inviting youth to speak at prevention events about how difficult their lives are. Listening also involves supporting their efforts to be affirmed as parents, but also as students, activists, friends, lovers, and community members. Stakeholders in youth sexual health promotion should familiarize themselves with qualitative research that paints a more robust picture of the lives of teen parents, should create opportunities for teen parents to share their stories with a variety of constituents in ways that are empowering, and should push back against negative portrayals of young parents in health promotion efforts. This work might include reading and citing research that illuminates the struggles *and* joys of teen parenting, implementing storytelling workshops similar to the MAMA group, and refusing to distribute prevention materials that stigmatize teen parents.

3. Turn the Gaze Inward

I invite public health professionals to engage in the uncomfortable reflexivity of considering how power and privilege operate in our work and the field overall. Instead of focusing on eliminating health disparities by "working ourselves out of a job," perhaps we should consider whether we are the right person for the job in the first place. Turning the gaze inward involves not only an examination of racial, economic, and social privilege but also taking actionable steps to redistribute power in community-based public health. Examining our privilege involves health promoters looking around the table to notice who is there and who is not. It also includes observing the ways in which people with privilege and power are defining health problems and their solutions on behalf of those who are marginalized and oppressed. Coming to terms with power in public health requires analysis and action that is uncomfortable and challenging.

Turning the gaze inward also requires us to make significant changes in the ways we develop and implement health promotion programs. For example, we must respond to the health needs that are identified by the communities most affected, rather than the health needs that funding agencies or research entities identify. This might mean that health promoters in Millerston prioritize, say, ending police brutality over preventing teen pregnancy. In addition, turning the gaze inward means that privileged public health professionals reorganize their roles so as to function as allies to those burdened by health inequalities. Instead of serving as decision makers or frontline providers, they can use their skills and resources to support the work of those most affected. For example, stakeholders might use their expertise and professional connections to secure grant funding for a project designed by the community, and then step back to serve as a supportive resource to the project instead of leading it themselves. An important part of reorganizing community health efforts in this way is to develop and support the leadership of multiply marginalized stakeholders. There are long-standing and robust traditions in the public health sciences, such as critical public health and community-based participatory research, that take seriously the workings of power in health promotion.[16] There is much to be learned from these traditions in Millerston and elsewhere.

4. Partner with Organizations Working for Reproductive and Racial Justice

Alongside frameworks and visions that critically analyze power and privilege, there are abundant opportunities for stakeholders to partner with and learn from groups that are already doing the work of racial and reproductive justice. These collaborations could be as simple as one-time trainings or as involved as longer-term partnerships. It may take some time before youth sexual health promotion in a city such as Millerston could be fully integrated into movements for social justice; meanwhile, a training on, for instance, dismantling white privilege or communicating about abortion with diverse communities could go a long way.

In one generative collaboration, white stakeholders in places like Millerston could connect with organizations and projects that focus on white people's role in dismantling racism. Rather than leaving the responsibility with people of color, groups such as White People Challenging Racism: Moving from Talk to Action engage white people to do the work of undermining white supremacy.[17] The group accomplishes this work through community organizing, education, and movement building. Participating in such activities could be transformative in helping stakeholders to analyze white privilege and how it affects the framing and implementation of health promotion in economically marginalized communities of color. Similarly, youth sexual health promotion stakeholders, organizations, and coalitions could partner with national-level reproductive justice organizations for technical assistance, capacity building, and training. For example, initiatives like Teens Count could incorporate trainings on the practical implementation of RJ principles from SisterSong: Women of Color Reproductive Justice Collective as part of their work.[18] Instead of facilitating top-down parent education forums or hosting teen

pregnancy prevention rallies, committees like MASPHC could invite the
National Latina Institute for Reproductive Health to conduct leadership
development institutes for Latinas in the community.[19] Finally, coalitions
such as the PASH Network could develop a strategic vision with the assistance of consultants such as the Center for Advancing Innovative Policy
(CAIP), which focuses on base-building, strategic alliances, and collaborative visioning.[20] Working with CAIP could help coalitions in Millerston
develop policies that truly address the connections between "hope" in late
capitalism and sexual and reproductive health outcomes.

EDUCATED HOPE AS A MODE OF CRITIQUE:
TOWARD AN ABOLITIONIST PERSPECTIVE

Some readers may dismiss these recommendations as utopian foolishness
ungrounded in the everyday realities of public health work. However, following José Esteban Muñoz's incitement to engage in critique to "stave off the
failures of imagination," I offer them to ignite a conversation about the politics of race, reproduction, and science in community-based public health.[21] I
also want to go beyond these steps focused on reforming existing youth sexual health promotion efforts and toward abolishing the teen pregnancy prevention industrial complex itself.[22] In imagining the abolition of the TPPIC,
Muñoz's theorization of "educated hope" resonates with me. Muñoz charac-
terizes educated hope as a practice not of announcing the way things *ought*
to be, but instead imagining how they *could* be.[23] He argues that to practice
educated hope is to advance a critique with the "the goal of enacting a world,
the actual creation of that goal and the actual movement towards that goal."[24]
Educated hope is a mode of critique that works toward a utopic vision without eliding the messiness of the path toward that vision—the means are just
as important as the ends. At the same time that we turn the gaze inward or
partner with reproductive justice organizations, we must also work to build
a truly liberatory public health practice. This work must involve abolishing
the teen pregnancy prevention industrial complex. In its place, rather than
preventing pregnancies among economically marginalized youth of color,
public health work in places like Millerston would focus on racial and economic justice as strategies for improving community health.

I offer this notion of educated hope as a strategy for Millerston, and for health promotion more generally, to move toward an abolitionist politics.[25] Muñoz acknowledges that hope is risky. Nevertheless, he asserts that "if the point is to change the world we must risk hope."[26] Hoping for an abolitionist public health politics might seem particularly risky when the violence of reproductive injustice and racial capitalism manifests in both extraordinary and quotidian ways.[27] In this political moment it may feel impractical to hope for a youth sexual health promotion that it is anti-racist, is LGBTQ-inclusive, supports teen parents, and expands choice to include the right to prevent pregnancy *and* to parent our children with dignity and respect. Yet it is moments like these, when everything seems broken, that we can hope for and build something more, something different. Mobilizing educated hope as a mode of critique is a strategy for enacting the world we want to live in.

I hope that we can dismantle the teen pregnancy prevention industrial complex. I hope that young people in Millerston and elsewhere can access contraception that fits their individual health and social needs. I hope that they can learn about racial justice alongside learning about how to put on a condom. I hope that they learn how sex can be fun, pleasurable, and safe. I hope that LGBTQ people can see their lives, identities, and bodies affirmed in sexual health promotion. I hope that teen moms can be fabulous and messy without being shamed, stigmatized, or used as warning signs to others. I hope that privileged public health professionals will focus on work in communities they are a part of. I hope that when working in communities they are not a part of, they use their privilege as a strategy for leveraging resources to address the health issues that communities define for themselves. I hope that the leadership of multiply marginalized public health professionals can be centered and nurtured. I hope for a sexual health promotion that dares to interrogate that which is always already assumed. I hope for a sexual health promotion that does not merely aim to prevent certain outcomes but instead promotes agentic sexuality for all people. I hope for a critical public health theory and practice that centers the voices and experiences of those most marginalized by interlocking systems of racism, classism, ableism, heterosexism, and transphobia. This is the kind of educated hope I want to distribute.

Organizations and Projects in Millerston

Continuum Health Services (CHS)	The main provider of sexual and reproductive health services in the region, CHS provides family planning and HIV/AIDS services throughout its many locations. In addition to providing clinical services, CHS engages in policy and advocacy work surrounding sexual and reproductive health.
Millerston Adolescent Sexual Health Promotion Committee (MASHPC)	Group composed of representatives from city government, health clinics, and social service organizations whose mission is to "develop community-based, multi-faceted approaches to decrease teen pregnancy and sexually transmitted infections (STIs) in Millerston." MASHPC originated in a municipal committee on economic development.
Millerston Community Health Center (MCHC)	Millerston's federally qualified community health center, MCHC provides primary care, dental care, health education, and case management services and is the major medical provider in the city.

Moms Are Majorly Awesome (MAMA)	A youth engagement group at the Towne House that focuses on strategizing how to use digital stories for strategic communication about teen pregnancy and parenting.
Promoting Adolescent Sexual Health (PASH) Network	Umbrella organization formed by Jenny Díaz that consists of community partnership organizations in the greater Millerston-Carlsborough area. PASH serves as a visible organizing presence in the region with the goal of using "research, advocacy, and community education and collaboration to influence policy and practice in adolescent sexual health." The network administers grants, organizes trainings, structures coalition work, and holds an annual sexual health conference.
Statewide Organization on Adolescent Pregnancy (SOAP)	Policy advocacy and provider-training organization working in communities across the state. SOAP mobilizes communities around both teen pregnancy prevention and support for young parents.
Teens Count	Project in Millerston and Carlsborough funded by the Centers for Disease Control and Prevention. Teens Count is a project of PASH and SOAP whose goal is to reduce teen birthrates in these cities by 10% in 5 years through community mobilization, clinical coordination, evidence-based programming, and stakeholder education.
The Towne House	Millerston's community-based, alternative education, high school equivalency program for pregnant and parenting young women. The Towne House provides extensive wraparound services to students, including child care, transportation, health care, counseling, and college preparation. The program is nationally recognized for its excellence in the humanities and arts and for its high graduation and college placement rates.

Methodological Notes

When describing my work to colleagues across various academic fields, I often characterize myself as "disciplinarily promiscuous." I was trained as an interdisciplinary social scientist in a public health department that focused on critical and humanistic approaches. Methodologically, I tend to hang out with sociologists, and my theoretical frameworks derive from the overlapping, interdisciplinary fields of gender and sexuality studies, critical race studies, queer studies, and science and technology studies. Because of this disciplinary promiscuity, my methods borrow, adapt, and push against several traditions in social research, most notably ethnography and discursive methods. I think of the research in this book as "ethnographic," rather than as "an ethnography," and as "discursive," rather than as "a discourse analysis." Each of these latter terms strikes me as too stable, bounded, and specific to do justice to the promiscuous, feminist, critical approach I take in *Distributing Condoms and Hope*.

An important component of critical social science research is that it does not separate epistemology from methodology. That is, it does not decouple what we believe can be known about the world (and who knows it) from the strategies we use to study it. Joey Sprague argues that what differentiates critical research from "uncritical" research is not the particular methods used (e.g., statistical modeling or participant observation), but rather how the researcher uses the methods, both technically and politically.[1] Therefore, we must pay attention to the kinds of questions we ask, the analytic frames we use to interpret findings, and the ways we communicate the results of research.[2] At the heart of critical research is a commitment to uncovering the reproduction of inequality and working toward social transformation and emancipation, a commitment that is at the heart of this book. In what follows, I consider the methodological approach and specific research methods in *Distributing Condoms and Hope* in terms of what it means to do critical, feminist, and disciplinarily promiscuous research in community health.

Because I had been an employee in community-based organizations in Millerston for several years prior to beginning an official research project, it was relatively easy to gain "entry" into the "field." I began networking with organizations such as the PASH Network and SOAP after shifting my focus away from the Towne House to Millerston's youth sexual health promotion efforts more broadly. I reached out to Jenny Díaz for permission to begin attending MASHPC meetings and then became active in events related to the Teens Count project. When conducting participant observation in youth sexual health promotion settings, I identified myself as a graduate student in public health who was interested in responses to teen pregnancy in Millerston. Only at the Towne House did I identify myself as a teen parent. Negotiating the tensions of my identity as a teen parent and my political commitments to reproductive justice meant that I often remained quiet when I observed racial microaggressions, magical thinking (see chapters 3 and 4, respectively), and so on. Often my interlocutors assumed, simply because of my status as a graduate student in a public health department, that I believed teen pregnancy was an urgent social and health problem. This assumption speaks to the durability of "teen pregnancy as a problem" in public health and social policy discourses. While I was never dishonest about my views on sexual and reproductive politics, I also did not insert them into conversations where they were inappropriate or disingenuous.

Rather than a "sample," the fifteen professional stakeholders I interviewed are best conceived of as a selection of key informants. Since many of the professional stakeholders I interviewed knew me from attendance at community events and coalition meetings, for the most part I simply sent them an email or spoke to them after a meeting to request an interview. I contacted most participants directly to ask for an interview, and occasionally participants referred me to a colleague for an interview. Interviews took place wherever it was most convenient for the participant, and most interviewees chose to conduct the interview at their place of employment. Only one key informant, a staff coordinator of the health education program in the Millerston public schools, refused to be interviewed, citing that they no longer worked for the district.

I informed participants that the purpose of my study was to gain a better understanding of how public health and social policy stakeholders in the greater Millerston area make sense of teen pregnancy and parenting and how to best develop programs and policies related to youth sexuality. I was careful to explain that I was interested in hearing their beliefs about what was happening in Millerston and what to do about it, as opposed to hearing commonsense understandings or positions articulated by their organizations. Interviews began by inviting the participant to tell me about the work they do in the community, how they came to do it, and what they liked and disliked about it. I asked what they believed to be the most important issues facing Millerston and then asked specific questions related to teen pregnancy that sought to elucidate their views on problem constructions; race, class, and gender; the sexual health needs of young people; and the best way to approach policy and practice. I audio-recorded all interviews with a digital recording device and wrote up brief field notes after each interview that focused on contextual information, initial impressions, ideas for future interviews, and emergent findings. A paid research assistant transcribed all interviews verbatim. Although I subscribe to the school of thought that views transcription as an important part of the analytic process and believes that the interviewer is the ideal person to do the transcription, repetitive strain injuries in my hands and wrists prevented me from doing the transcription myself. To compensate for this, I read and reread the transcripts several times over in order to familiarize myself with the data.

I sustained my connection to the Towne House through a variety of side research projects in collaboration with other researchers. In the first of these, I interviewed students at the Towne House about their perceptions of health and social justice, their perspectives on teen pregnancy in Millerston and more generally, and how they thought their interactions with service providers helped or hindered their success. Students were recruited by presenting the project in Towne House classrooms and inviting students to participate in an in-depth interview in a private space at the school. A few years later, after I began conducting research on youth sexual health promotion in the city more broadly, I returned to the Towne House as a research assistant on a larger project that used storytelling to push back against negative representations of young mothers. This project enabled me to spend more time at the Towne House facilitating the MAMA group and interviewing additional students. I interviewed twenty-six students in total. In the state where the Towne House is located, parents less than 18-years-old are considered emancipated minors and therefore do not need their parents' permission to participate in research. All of the human-subjects research conducted with professional stakeholders and Towne House students was approved by the institutional review board at the University of Massachusetts Amherst.

I had to negotiate a range of positionalities and identities in my varied research settings, ranging from interviews with professional stakeholders to those with young parents, from participant observation at the Towne House to attendance at MASHPC meetings. As I describe in the introduction and chapter 2, I navigated my "insider"-"outsider" status as a graduate student alongside my (sometimes disclosed) status as a former pregnant teen. Sometimes people read me as Latinx, and other times people read me as white. Sometimes they read me as one of them; other times they read me as an outsider. Mediating all of this, and rarely spoken about or acknowledged, was my queer gender and sexuality. As I discuss in chapter 4, queer people were mostly absent from youth sexual health promotion in Millerston, and most students and staff at the Towne House assumed everyone there was straight (though, of course, that was not the case). At the time of my research, the vast majority of people I interacted with read me as a woman and, because I had a kid, as heterosexual. This was the case despite my stereotypical markers of queerness, such as an asymmetrical short haircut. Often the people I interacted with mapped on to me the identities that best reflected their own positionalities and their preexisting beliefs about who I was and what I was up to. My professional, mixed-race, teen parent, gender, and queer positions meant that I was a sort of fieldwork chameleon. In part, I facilitated this chameleon-like status through frequent code-switching. In settings where I interviewed or observed professional stakeholders, I dressed in neat pants and a button-down shirt or cardigan (a look I call "professor-lite"). Conversely, when working with Towne House students, I wore the same uniform I've worn since high school: jeans and a T-shirt or hoodie. In settings with professional stakeholders I would generally cover up my tattoos or hide my piercings, but with young people I was more likely to let them show. This was a less a strategic choice to establish rapport with young people than it was simply that I loathe dressing up and take any opportunity to avoid doing so. Similarly, when surrounded by professionals, I worked to clean up my "potty mouth" and speak in proper English, though I did not always do this once I had established rapport with Towne House students. Again, this was less a strategic choice than an opportunity to disengage from the exhausting performance of the middle-class, normatively raced and gendered behavior expected of people in professional situations. Nevertheless, my queerness, affect, and insider- or outsiderness undoubtedly affected my interactions with professionals and young people alike.

I spent countless hours conducting participant observations at MASPHC meetings, Teens Count events, PASH Networks events, the Towne House, and other sites. During these observations, I took handwritten field notes following the guidelines described by Emerson, Fretz, and Shaw.[3] In writing these field notes, I focused on a variety of elements, including initial impressions, a sense of what seemed significant or unexpected, what those in the setting experienced as significant or important, how routine actions in the particular setting took place, and sensory details including visual, oral, aural, and spatial observations. I aimed to "show" rather than simply "tell" what was happening in interactions. Depending on the setting, my balance of "participant" versus "observer" dictated the level of detail I was able to capture. For example, in MASHPC meetings, I sat in mainly as an observer, whereas at conferences or community forums, where I might also be presenting or facilitating, I took as detailed notes as were possible. I would often audio-record oral notes as I drove home from an event and later type notes from those recordings. I believe that fieldworkers are never detached, neutral observers, and so I took care to make notes on my own positionality and interactions within the setting. At the end of the day, I would type my handwritten notes with the perspective that writing field notes is a construction or filter, rather than a mirror, of reality. As Emerson, Fretz, and Shaw note, "'Doing' and 'writing' should not be seen as separate and distinct activities, but, rather, as dialectically related, interdependent, and mutually constitutive activities."[4] Thus, my in-process analytic writing not only described the people and places I observed but also asked questions, made comparisons, noted what was present and what was missing, made connections to the research questions, and noted any emergent findings.

Fieldwork and analysis were not distinct or separate processes of my research, but rather overlapped and informed each other. Indeed, writing field notes, poring over archival materials, and conducting interviews were all interpretive tasks. During data collection, I kept notes and wrote brief memos on emergent themes and ideas. Sometimes this occurred by sitting down at the computer to type in a stream-of-consciousness fashion; at other times I would jot down notes to myself on Post-its and type them up later. Concurrent data collection and analysis enabled me to pursue new lines of inquiry through theoretical sampling and seek out additional interview participants, observation settings, or archival documents that would inform my developing ideas.[5] Prior to formal analysis, I organized all of my data into a series of three-ring binders, one each for interview transcripts, participant observation notes, health education materials, and archival documents. I followed the principle of saturation to guide me in knowing when I had collected "enough" data. Saturation refers to the "building of rich data within the process of inquiry" by focusing on the comprehensiveness of data and common characteristics among sites and participants.[6] Saturation is less about having "heard it all before" and more about having built a rigorous theoretical argument from one's data. I recognized saturation in my data when I had constructed a 360-degree view of youth sexual health promotion in Millerston that encompassed perspectives from a wide variety of interlocutors.

The procedure I used for analyzing my interviews, participant observations, and archival materials was guided by a constructivist grounded-theory approach to coding and was followed by situational analysis mapping. According to Kathy Charmaz, a constructivist approach to grounded theory assumes that neither data nor theories are separate from the observer.[7] Rather, researchers construct theories grounded in data "through our past and present involvements and interactions with people, perspectives, and research practices."[8] I used open coding techniques for all interviews and participant observation notes, as well as for most of the archival materials (where it made sense to do so). Following Charmaz, I highlighted processes in the data using gerunds and looked for in vivo codes that represented respondents' understanding of situations and processes. Generally, these codes were in the form of quotes. I developed codes inductively from the data while keeping in mind my research questions; existing theories on race, sexuality, risk, and the body; and emerging theories and ideas. I developed codes with an eye to making them fit the data, rather than making the data fit the codes.

After open coding all materials, I began focused coding by going back through the materials and selecting codes with the most relevance to my research questions. I typed up all of these codes, copied them onto Post-it notes, used large sheets of butcher paper to organize the Post-its, and then refined them into focused codes and subcodes by moving the Post-its around. I compared codes against one another to identify both similarities and differences in the data while also keeping in mind the importance of what did not appear in the data—what was silenced or missing. Next, I wrote a codebook in which each code and subcode was described in narrative format.[9] The main codes included Race and Racism; Conceptualizing Millerston; Telling Social and Political Stories; Public Health Discourses and Epistemologies; Sex and Sexuality; and Doing the Work. Once the codebook was completed, I imported the text of the interviews and field notes into MAXQDA version 11. Finally, once the materials were coded in the software program, I ran reports on individual codes in order to collate excerpts and prepare for situational mapping exercises.

Adele Clarke's "situational analysis" extends traditional grounded theory strategies in qualitative inquiry by pulling them around the postmodern turn. In this approach, interview and ethnographic data are analyzed alongside existing narrative, visual, and historical discourse materials to constitute the "situation *per se* as the ultimate unit of analysis."[10] In my case, the "situation" was that of youth sexual health promotion in Millerston. Clarke argues that situational analysis can "deeply situate research projects individually, collectively, organizationally, institutionally, temporally, geographically, materially, discursively, culturally, symbolically, visually, and historically" by comprehending the elements and relations of the situation.[11] According to Clarke, situational analysis is valuable for examining how discourses produce identities and subjectivities, power-knowledge, ideologies, and forms of social control.[12] Situational analysis can make possible a more complete construction of the situation, including how the situation of inquiry creates and legitimizes particular discourses.[13] The approach addresses multiple discourses related to the situation of inquiry, not merely the master discourses at work, thereby allowing the analyst to "turn up the volume" on lesser-but-still-present discourses, less-but-still-present participants: the quiet, the silent, and the silenced.[14]

Practically speaking, situational analysis allowed me to analyze a large volume of data from a variety of sources simultaneously. Theoretically, situational analysis was an ideal choice for an analytic strategy in that it acknowledges that research and interpretation are always already political and that analysts must move beyond the knowing subject to examine salient discourses within the situation of inquiry.[15] As I discuss in the introduction, I do not discount the importance of "voice" in social science research, particularly among historically marginalized groups. However, I also want to complicate the notion of "giving voice" and the possibility of a presocial knower divorced from their discursive context. Clarke also argues that the objective of situational analysis is to "capture complexities," rather than aim for simplifications, which is key to my critical inquiry into teen pregnancy. Youth sexuality research suffers from oversimplification on the part of scholars across the political and ideological spectrum, and *Distributing Condoms and Hope* is an attempt to capture the messiness inherent in how we make sense of the discursive productions of reproduction, sexuality, politics, and health promotion.

Situational analysis uses analytic mapping exercises as a way of "moving in and around the data." The resulting maps are not intended as final analytic products but rather help the researcher to "open up" the data. As visual representations of data, Clarke suggests that maps "help to rupture some of our normal ways of working and allow us to see things fresh."[16] Maps work as discursive devices to make assemblages and connections, illustrate spatial and temporal narratives, and allow for unmapping and remapping of ideas. The mapping exercises in my analysis proceeded as follows. After spending time with my data through constructing the codebook, reviewing emergent findings memos, and studying my code reports, I descriptively laid out the most important *human and nonhuman, material, and symbolic-discursive* elements in the situation of concern in the research.[17] Clarke advises that these elements are to be understood as broadly conceived and framed by the analyst, who inquires: *Who and what are in the broader situation? Who and what matters in this situation? What elements "make a difference" in this situation?* I laid out these elements into a "messy map," which simply consists of a large sheet of paper with these elements arranged in no particular fashion.

After examining the messy map, I then organized the identified elements into an "ordered/working map" according to their discursive domain. These include individual and collective elements or actors; political, economic, temporal, symbolic, and spatial elements; and related visual, historical, and narrative discourses (see table 2). Reviewing the "ordered/working map" allowed me to identify how elements of the situation work within and through various discourses. In particular, situational analysis highlighted the ways in which youth sexual health promotion is always already about teen pregnancy prevention and teen pregnancy is always already about race; the silence and invisibility of teen parents; how race and sexuality were continuously invoked without ever actually naming racism or sex; and how the selective uptake of scientific discourses affected stakeholder knowledge and practice. Significantly, situational analysis made visible the workings of the teen pregnancy prevention industrial complex and allowed me to simultaneously analyze the overall discourses and effects of the situation alongside the individual actors within it.

By way of a conclusion, I return to the practice of uncomfortable reflexivity that I discuss in the introduction. Part of this practice is dealing with the partial and incompleteness of data and the messiness of producing knowledge, as well as engaging with the limitations and absences in my analysis. Critics may be quick to point out that my closeness to the topic of teen childbearing prevents me from conducting a neutral, objective analysis. They may question whether I "got it right" given my social positionalities and political commitments. Some may even dismiss it as "me-search." To obviate, or at least temper, these critiques, I'll offer that they are

Table 2 Ordered situational map

Individual human elements/ actors	Pregnant and parenting teens Teens who are not pregnant or parenting Clinicians Teachers and health educators Social workers Policy makers
Collective human elements/ actors	SOAP MASHPC Community-based organizations The Towne House PASH Network Teens Count
Discursive constructions of individual and/or collective human actors	Moral panic "We're just trying to help this population" Youth as lacking hope What everyone already knows "We just don't want to be #1" The "problem" Funding
Political/economic elements	Neoliberalism City government Institutional racism Structural violence Catholicism
Temporal elements	Declining teen birthrate in US and Millerston "Back in the '90s" Changing norms around age at first birth Decline in manufacturing/economic changes in city Post-Fordist economies Migration (forced and economic)
Major issues/debates (usually contested)	Contraceptive access in schools Prevention strategies and tactics Nature of the problem
Nonhuman elements/actants	Safe(r) sex LARC Evidence-based curricula Condoms

	Health education materials
	Millerston High pregnancy prevention film
	Funding and grants
Implicated/silent actors/ actants	Pregnant and parenting teens
	LGBTQ youth
	To some extent all teens are silent, esp. the "bad ones"
Discursive constructions of nonhuman actants	Abortion as a sin
	Contraception as easy/safe/compulsory
	Health education as "comprehensive" and "scientifically based"
	Contraception and sex ed curricula as apolitical
Sociocultural elements/ symbolic elements	Young women as sexual gatekeepers
	Actual sex
	Race and racism
	Latinx "culture"
	Heteronormative, phallocentric sexuality
	Causal fantasies
	Youth sexual health promotion as always already about teen pregnancy
	Teen pregnancy as always already about race
	Talking about sexuality without ever actually talking about sex
	Talking about race without ever actually talking about race
	National Day to Prevent Teen Pregnancy
Spatial elements	Millerston neighborhoods (Heights, Canals, etc.)
	Two Millerstons
	Two valleys
	Puerto Rican migration
	Daily white migration to work in city
Related discourses (historical, visual, or narrative)	Latino family/culture narrative
	Health disparities
	Opportunity/hope/progress
	Headless pregnant teens
Other key elements	(Lack of) reproductive justice framework
	Sexuality and families as sites for the reproduction of empire

SOURCE: Adapted from Clarke 2005.

partially correct. This is the case not because I was hopelessly embedded in my topic and could not see beyond it but because *the production of knowledge is always already political.* It is never detached or neutral. This is as true for me as it is for researchers who view sexual health promotion through a colorblind lens or who understand preventing teen pregnancy to be an urgent social problem. Likewise, criticizing research as "navel-gazing" or "me-search" too narrowly focused on one's on social positionalities—and therefore lacking objectivity and validity—is never a critique lobbed at people in positions of power studying other people in positions of power. That is, white men studying other white men is never dismissed as "me-search."[18] Producing knowledge is always messy, and I invite us all to sit with that discomfort.

Notes

1. All names of places, people, projects, and organizations are pseudonyms.

2. All data referenced is from the time of my study, 2012 to 2015.

3. The long history of economically privileged white women's participation or complicity in regulating the lives of economically marginalized people or communities of color spans professions including social work, nursing, and health education. For instance, Susan M. Ryan (2003) details how antebellum benevolence toward Black and Indigenous people "provided Americans with ways of understanding, describing, and constructing their racial and national identities" (5). Similarly, Regina Kunzel (1995) analyzes how evangelical women in the maternity home movement of the early twentieth century drew on traditions of female benevolence in order to redeem and reclaim unmarried mothers. In Puerto Rico during the same time period, liberal health promoters sought to reform motherhood through a "soft eugenics," focused on imparting advice to poor women in order to curb their reproduction as well as strengthen the nation (Briggs 2002, 90).

4. The terms scholars and activists use to refer to the colonized peoples of the Caribbean and Latin America without using language that is androcentric or erases gender-nonconforming individuals is an area of contention. Using the masculine *Latino* to refer to a group of people of a variety of genders is problematic, prompting the neologisms *Latin@* and *Latinx*. While it is imperfect, I use

173

Latinx for the following reasons. First, unlike *Latin@*, it is inclusive of people with a nonbinary gender and has the benefit of a clear pronunciation (La-teen-ex). Second, *Latinx* is quickly becoming the most common term used by intersectional scholars calling attention to and working against racialized and gendered oppressions (Scharrón–Del Río and Aja 2015). I use the term *Latinx* to refer to hypothetical or unknown groups of people, whereas I use *Latina* where it is appropriate for groups that are all women. When I use the term *Latino,* as in the "Latino culture narrative," I do so intentionally to signal that I am talking about a discursive construction—one that is not necessarily concerned with addressing gender essentialism or gender-based oppression. When referring to secondary research or data, I use the term that appears in the original text or interview, usually *Latino* or *Hispanic.*

5. For coverage of stigmatizing campaigns and push back from teen parent advocates see Bayetti Flores 2011; King 2013; Malone 2013; Rankin 2014; Schroder 2013; and Zoila-Pérez 2011. For academic analyses of these and other campaigns, see Daniel 2017 and Vinson 2018.

6. A 2005 landmark report from the Bay Area organization Asian Communities for Reproductive Justice (now Forward Together) defined reproductive justice as "the complete physical, mental, spiritual, political, economic, and social well-being of [all people], and will be achieved when [all people] have the economic, social, and political power and resources to make healthy decisions about [their] bodies, sexuality, and reproduction for [themselves], their families and communities in all areas of [their] lives." For additional foundational texts on reproductive justice (RJ), see Luna and Luker 2013; Ross 2006; Ross and Solinger 2015; Silliman et al. 2004.

7. As the Black Lives Matter movement has made strikingly clear, reproductive justice involves being able to raise Black and brown children without fear that police can gun them down with impunity.

8. The linking of *sexual* and *health* is a relatively recent phenomenon in public health research and practice, and a phrase whose semiotic and semantic uses scholars have sought to unpack. The World Health Organization (WHO) first issued a definition of sexual health in 1975; the most recent iteration reads, "Sexual health is a state of physical, mental and social well-being in relation to sexuality. It requires a positive and respectful approach to sexuality and sexual relationships, as well as the possibility of having pleasurable and safe sexual experiences, free of coercion, discrimination and violence" (WHO 2019). In everyday use, however, the term is far from standardized and evokes a wide range of bodies, affects, and social problems. It is sometimes subsumed under or used interchangeably with *reproductive health.*

Steven Epstein and Laura Mamo (2017) have observed an explosion in the term's use in journal articles, newspapers, and websites beginning in the early to mid-1990s. They argue that a salient function of linking *sex* to *health* is to sanitize and legitimize the former: "health" protects researchers, medical providers, and health promoters from the stigma and controversy of sexuality. Likewise, sexual health operates in a series of social problem niches, two of which are prominent in *Distributing Condoms and Hope*. In the niche "controlling population growth and promoting procreative autonomy," sexuality is reduced to heteronormative reproduction, and health is understood as control over one's reproduction. Here the absence of health is unintended pregnancy and the way to avoid ill health is to regulate reproduction. Similarly, in the niche "containing the threats of irresponsible behavior," *sexuality* invokes a morally charged social practice, and the meaning of *health* connotes social betterment. Here, sexual and social anarchy characterize the absence of health, and sex education is a strategy for avoiding it. See also Epstein 2018. Throughout the text I use *youth sexual health promotion* as this was the term in circulation in Millerston during the time of my fieldwork.

9. Foucault 1980, 119.

10. Feminist journalists and academics (Bhatia 2013; North 2012) have criticized Kristof for fashioning himself as an emancipator of oppressed women worldwide (Kristof and WuDunn 2010).

11. This widely cited statistic comes from data, analyzed by the National Campaign to Prevent Teen and Unplanned Pregnancy, that measures the cumulative risk of pregnancy before the age of 20 by adding together the yearly pregnancy rates of women ages 14–19, a technique that is not the standard epidemiological measure of cumulative risk. For information on calculating cumulative risk, see Rothman, Greenland, and Lash 2008.

12. Kristof 2014.

13. Fraser and Gordon 1994.

14. Martin et al. 2017.

15. World Bank 2015.

16. Alford and Hauser 2011.

17. Alford and Hauser 2011. There is also debate about the usefulness of contrasting teen pregnancy rates in the United States with peer countries in Western Europe. The two regions are considerably different in terms of cultural attitudes about youth sexuality, access to universal health care, and the presence or absence of a social safety net, all of which render the inequalities related to early childbearing more or less severe. See, for example, Schalet 2011.

18. The teenage *pregnancy* rate is composed of all pregnancies, including births, abortions, and miscarriages. The teen *birth* rate is the generally used indicator for discussing teen pregnancy in the United States and thus I will use it through this book unless otherwise specified.

19. Kost and Henshaw 2014.

20. Kost and Henshaw 2014.

21. Kost and Henshaw 2014.

22. Wilson and Huntington 2006.

23. See Solomon-Fears 2016. In August 2017, the Trump administration quietly defunded TPP grantees by ending their current grants in June 2018, rather than 2020. In early 2018, the administration began to signal its intention to begin shifting federal dollars back into abstinence-only approaches by redesigning the criteria for funding under the TPP. Then, in the spring of 2018, in response to series of successful lawsuits brought by organizations slated to receive funding, the Department of Health and Human services announced it would continue funding recipients for the following year.

24. As of this writing the Trump administration is also in the process of attempting to make changes to the Title X family planning program, such as implementing a "gag rule" that would bar clinics who receive Title X funds from providing or even referring patients to abortion services.

25. Bonell 2004; Hoffman 2008; Klein 2005; Kost and Henshaw 2014; Penman-Aguilar et al. 2013; Rich-Edwards 2002; Scally 2002; Sisson 2012.

26. Hoffman 2008. Notably, the report does not explicitly illustrate its research methods and does not indicate if the results are statistically significant.

The National Campaign is a nongovernmental organization funded through private and public sources that produces a variety of fact sheets and data briefs about the "costs and consequences" of teenage childbearing and offers educational resources to teens, parents, and policy makers, among other activities. Although the organization changed its name in December 2017 to Power to Decide: The Campaign to Prevent Unplanned Pregnancy, I refer to it here by its name at the time of my fieldwork. As I describe elsewhere (Barcelos 2014), the National Campaign is an exemplar for understanding the politics of teen pregnancy prevention in the United States.

27. National Campaign to Prevent Teen and Unplanned Pregnancy 2016.

28. For one of the first critiques of the social construction of teen pregnancy in the United States, see Luker 1997. For an early examination of the politics of teen pregnancy, see Ward 1995. These works are among those published in the 1990s that inaugurated a new generation of social science critiques on teen childbearing. Although they called attention to the social processes whereby teen childbearing was constructed as a social problem, they nonetheless took a realist approach that understood it to be, in fact, a problem.

29. Geronimus 2003, 887.

30. Geronimus 1996; Geronimus 1997; Geronimus 2003; Geronimus 2004.

31. Fessler 2003; Furstenberg 2003; Furstenberg 2016; Lawlor and Shaw 2002; Rich-Edwards 2002.

32. Geronimus 2003; Rich-Edwards 2002.

33. Furstenberg 2003; Furstenberg 2016; Geronimus 2003; Geronimus and Korenman 1993.

34. For example, by comparing sisters—one is a teen mother and one is not—or by comparing young women who had a miscarriage as a teenager to those who carried the pregnancy to term.

35. Most teen births pose low medical risk. Although there are modest risks of low birth weight and preterm delivery for very young teens (those under 16 years of age) (Cunnington 2001; Kramer and Lancaster 2010), the vast majority of teen births in the United States occur to older teens (Martin et al. 2017). Some researchers have even found young maternal age to be a protective factor against low birth weight and infant mortality in economically marginalized communities (Rich-Edwards et al. 2003; Geronimus 1996 and 2001). Geronimus (2003) suggests that early childbearing, particularly among urban, African American young women living in poverty, may be an adaptive strategy to alter fertility-timing norms to respond to shortened health and life expectancies (this is known as the "weathering hypothesis").

36. Fessler 2003; Geronimus 1996; Geronimus 1997; Geronimus 2003; Hotz, McElroy, and Sanders 2005; Sisson 2012. A large majority of research on teen childbearing is quantitative. Wilson and Huntington (2006) suggest that qualitative research on this topic is inhibited by the dominance of economic- and population-based studies on teen pregnancy and parenting for two reasons: qualitative findings are generally more positive (and thus challenge dominant ways of knowing about adolescent childbearing), and qualitative inquiry is thought not to be real "research." Moreover, Wilson and Huntington consider whether the reliance on scientific discourse—and its attendant assumptions of value neutrality and truth-telling—limits *what is* and *can be known* about teen pregnancy.

37. For example, Hotz, McElroy, and Sanders (2005) report findings that contradict the common assumption that having a child young results in decreased lifetime earnings. They find that early childbearing results in *increased* earnings over time: teen mothers would have earned an average of 31% less per year if they had delayed their childbearing. See also Erdmans and Black 2015; Kearney and Levine 2012.

38. As an example, one of the goals of welfare "reform" in the United States was to reduce teen childbearing and poverty by restricting access to cash assistance. Yet empirical research suggests that in many cases welfare reform exacerbated the inequalities it purported to address. See Edin and Shaefer 2016; Danziger 2010; Furstenberg 2016; Hao and Cherlin 2004; Kalil and Danziger 2000.

39. See, especially, Hoffman 2008; Hoffman and Maynard 2008. This body of research uses stigmatizing and pejorative language such as "kids having kids" (Hoffman and Maynard 2008) and "the devastating consequences of teen pregnancy and parenthood" (Candie's Foundation 2015). The pathology approach generally understands the determinants of teen pregnancy to be individual behaviors and attitudes such as "intentions toward abstinence or condom use"

(Kaye, Suellentrop, and Sloup 2009). It employs a variety of prevention strategies ranging from prevention campaigns that shame teen parents to policies that restrict their access to welfare assistance. In the pathology approach, improving the lives of teen mothers and their children is a means to the ends of benefiting their children, reducing taxpayer burden, or reining in presumed sexual promiscuity. This approach sometimes acknowledges, but does not emphasize, socioeconomic or racial inequalities in the distribution and determinants of teen childbearing. The pathology approach lacks a historicized understanding of sexuality, fertility, race, and adolescence.

40. The *reform* approach also understands teen childbearing as a social problem but differs in its conceptualization of causal mechanisms, consequences, and prevention strategies. Research in this vein posits poverty as a key determinant of teenage pregnancy and pushes for structural social change as the primary policy strategy to reduce teen childbearing (instead of punitive policies or demonizing teen mothers). Here the "problem" is not so much teen childbearing itself as the social conditions that make some young people more likely to be teen parents and create disadvantages for those who do. Correspondingly, this research frames determinants of teen pregnancy in terms of stratification (economically marginalized women and women of color are more likely to be teen parents) and frames consequences in terms of the inequality of outcomes for teen mothers (teen mothers face stigma and a lack of supportive services) (Sisson 2012). Although the reform approach seeks to address structural issues, it tends to focus on individual-level solutions such as comprehensive sexual health education programs and contraceptive access (Advocates for Youth 2008; Kirby 2007). Advocates of this approach argue that the focus on abstinence-based sex education not only exacerbates teen pregnancy rates but also denies young people a positive and healthy sexuality (Santelli et al. 2006). Key to the reform approach is a notion of "prevention as social justice" and "social change as a means of prevention" (Sisson 2012). In other words, teen pregnancy is something that we ought to prevent, not because it is inherently pathological, but because there is a need to reform our frameworks and strategies in order to redress inequalities.

41. The *critical* approach deconstructs the problem of adolescent childbearing and imagines radically different approaches to programming and policy making. Likewise, critical research emphasizes how the production and circulation of knowledge about teen childbearing affects policy and practice. Wanda Pillow's work is an exemplar of the critical approach (Pillow 2003a; Pillow 2004; Pillow 2006a; Pillow 2006b). She extends her ethnographic work in a school-based teen parent program with a feminist genealogical analysis of how educational policy discursively positions teen mothers. Pillow seeks to "trace not only *what is said* about teen mothers, but how teen mothers *are said* and what this means for the development and implementation of educational policy affecting school-age mothers" (2004, 8; emphasis added). The critical approach aims not

to reform teen pregnancy prevention efforts but instead to challenge what is and can be known about teen childbearing, thus illuminating the need to radically transform policies and programs.

42. Most research on youth sexual health promotion has examined how gender, race, class, and sexuality play out through school-based sex education, rather than through community-based public health. See Bay-Cheng 2003; Connell and Elliot 2009; Elia and Tokunaga 2015; Fine and McClelland 2006, Irvine, 2004.

43. Bowleg 2017; Buchanan 2000; Lupton 2015; Metzel and Kirkland 2010; Petersen and Lupton 1996.

44. For discussions of social determinants of health, see CSDH 2008; Marmot 2005, and Marmot 2007. The emphasis on social psychological theories of health behavior change demonstrates the field's reliance on individual strategies for addressing structural-level problems. For example, the foreword to the fourth edition of the widely used textbook *Health Behavior and Health Education* states, "Health behavior change is our greatest hope for reducing the burden of preventable disease and death around the world." This statement is surprising given the large body of literature documenting the degree to which social and economic inequality contributes to and exacerbates poor health. For a critique of the reliance on individual behavior change strategies as the cornerstone of community health promotion, see Buchanan 2000.

45. Thompson and Kumar 2011.

46. To take a historical example, we can attribute dramatic declines in mortality rates during the late nineteenth and early twentieth centuries not to individual health behaviors or any health education campaign but rather to macro-level social changes such as improved sanitation, the enactment of labor laws, and expansion of social programs. See CSDH 2008; Hofrichter 2003, Wilkinson and Marmot 2003.

47. Green and Labonte 2007, Nettleton and Bunton 1995, Petersen and Lupton 1996.

48. All economic, educational, and health data are based on state and federal government estimates from the time of my fieldwork in 2012–15.

49. Prior to 2002 Millerston had alternated between the first and second spot since the late 1980s.

50. Ventura, Hamilton, and Mathews 2014.

51. The state department of public health data do not disaggregate "Black, non-Hispanic" and "white, non-Hispanic."

52. This was before the Food and Drug Administration enabled nationwide access to emergency contraception without a prescription.

53. Pillow and Mayo 2007.

54. Clarke 2005, xxviii. See also Clarke, Friese, and Washburn 2015.

55. A. Gubrium, Hill, and Flicker 2014.

56. Collins 2000.

57. Naples 2004, 373.

58. Hesse-Biber 2007.

59. Sprague 2005.

60. Pillow 2003b, 188.

61. For a useful discussion of the messiness of vulnerability as an ethnographic practice, see Meadow 2018.

62. There is a long tradition of interrogating the impossibilities of feminist ethnographic practice. See, for example, Abu-Lughod 1990; Stacey 1988; Sandstrom and Opsal 2013.

63. Zussman 2012.

64. Nader 1972.

65. Sprague 2005, 186.

66. Up until January 25, 2016, the National Institutes of Health considered any person under the age of 21 to be a "child" for the purposes of research protocols.

67. One of the problems associated with my choice to make Millerston anonymous is that it prevents me from citing data and sources that would reveal its identity. For this reason, there are places in this text that should include a citation but do not, most notably public health data and archival documents. I have also changed some identifying details about people and places.

CHAPTER 1. RACE, PREGNANCY, AND POWER IN MILLERSTON

1. Collective impact is a collaborative strategy to manage stakeholders from a variety of sectors. The concept has its roots in large-scale philanthropy organizations. See Kania and Karmer 2011.

2. As I explain in more detail in chapter 4, although stakeholders strongly believed that teen pregnancy was a key factor contributing to high rates of school dropout, most teen mothers in Millerston had left or were disconnected from school prior to becoming pregnant.

3. Although my research took place prior to Hurricane Maria, the destruction caused by the 2017 storm, and the US government's woefully inadequate response, prompted another wave of migration to the mainland. Although definitive numbers are difficult to come by, in December 2017 news reports estimated the number of displaced Puerto Ricans settling in the state to be over 3,000. A 2018 internet news video interviewed Puerto Ricans displaced by Maria who were living in Millerston, many of whom had this to say: "¡Hace frío!" (It's cold!).

4. The material in this section is derived from a book produced by a curator at a local museum in conjunction with an exhibit about the history of immigration and migration to Millerston.

5. Whalen and Vázquez Hernández 2005.

6. For a nuanced, astute analysis of the particular forms that the racialization of Puerto Ricans has taken in the contemporary mainland United States, see Vidal-Ortiz 2004.

7. Duany 2000.

8. Gina Pérez (2004) explains that the history of Puerto Rican migration and displacement is a story about gender that is embedded in "development ideologies, labor history, place-making, and ethnic identity construction in a transnational context" (7). And, as Laura Briggs (2002) argues, sexuality and reproduction are central to the colonial project of US involvement in Puerto Rico. Briggs contends that "forms of sexuality are crucial to colonialism, from imperialism to development, from US involvement overseas to the migration of refugees of these processes to the mainland" (4).

9. In the twentieth century, emergent social scientific knowledge about Puerto Rican "difference" justified interventions in the sexuality and reproduction of Puerto Rican women through two overarching modernist narratives: women's rights and scientific progress. See Briggs 2002, 197.

10. The historical discussion in this section is based on my archival research in local historical collections and the database of the *Algonquin Valley News*.

11. As I was first writing this chapter in late 2015 and early 2016, Puerto Rico defaulted on portions of its then $72 million in debt. In June 2016, Congress enacted the Economic Stability Act (or PROMESA, Spanish for "promise"), which created a financial control board charged with attempting to restructure Puerto Rico's massive debt, including implementing austerity measures such as privatization of municipal services, closing more than one hundred schools on the island, and implementing massive cuts to health and human services. The lack of government response to the devastation following Hurricane Maria in the fall of 2017 has significantly exacerbated inequalities and human suffering on the island. See Kishore et al. 2018.

12. Briggs 2002.

13. Briggs 2002, 85. See also Whalen 2005.

14. Pérez 2004, 46.

15. López 2008, 13.

16. Briggs 2002.

17. Vazquez Calzada and Morales del Valle 1982.

18. Nonetheless, as López (2008) suggests, we can best understand sterilization as located on a continuum from freely chosen to fully coerced. Puerto Rican women, then and now, make sterilization decisions under a situation best described as "constrained choice."

19. Menzel 2014.

20. Meckel 1990.

21. Molina 2006, 96.

22. Matthews, MacDorman, and Thomas 2015; Gadson, Akpovi, and Mehta 2017.

23. Singh and van Dyck 2010.

24. Geronimus 1987, 245.

25. The historical discussion in this section is based on the personal archives of a longtime civic leader in Millerston's Puerto Rican community.

26. The task force made a total of 41 recommendations and 22 additional subrecommendations organized into five categories: readiness to learn, excellence in education (including health education), school-to-community linkages, community-to-school linkages, and readiness to earn. A July 1999 implementation report indicated that the task force had completed 24 recommendations while 21 were in process, 12 had not been addressed, and 7 were of an unknown status.

27. Claire 2017; Cole 2012; Spade 2015; Stanley and Smith 2015; Sudbury 2005; Washington 2006.

28. Spade 2015, 3.

29. Clare 2017, 70.

30. Gilson 2011 (overuse); Wacquant 2010 (conceptual clarity).

31. See the 2016 report by Cadena, Rivera, Esparza, and Cadena of Young Women United, "Dismantling Teen Pregnancy Prevention."

32. Spivak 1988.

33. Gilmore 2017; Rodríquez 2017.

34. Stanley 2011, 6.

35. Rodríquez 2017, 21, 31.

36. Mananzala and Spade 2008.

37. For examples, see Chavez 2008; Roberts 2011; Washington 2008; Zuberi and Bonilla-Silva 2008.

38. Because of its proximity to a research university, students and faculty have written a large number of dissertations, theses, journal articles, white papers, and so on about teen pregnancy in Millerston. *Distributing Condoms and Hope* is among the minority that take a critical approach.

39. Lincoln, Jaffe, and Ambrose 1976.

40. Geronimus 2003.

41. See Hoffman 2015; Furstenburg 2003.

42. Solomon-Fears 2016.

43. Barcelos 2014.

44. For a discussion of the biopolitical implications of data construction from the National Campaign, see Barcelos 2014. For feminist analyses of *Teen Mom* and *16 & Pregnant*, see Guglielmo 2013. Pillow (2004) reprints and analyzes the 2001 "Sex Has Consequences" print campaign, featuring a series of mostly young women of color with words like *cheap, dirty,* and *reject* printed over

their bodies in large text. Vinson (2018) also analyzes these ads and reviews counternarratives.

45. Although the project held an annual youth leadership training, as best as I can tell, youth were not involved in a significant or meaningful role in project activities. Adults mainly solicited them for feedback on existing strategies and programs. Occasionally youth would attend coalition meetings or conferences in an observatory role. Adult facilitators seemed to handpick "good" kids to participate in these activities and events. Pregnant and parenting teens participated in Teens Count events only to serve as warning signs.

CHAPTER 2. THE MESSY NARRATIVES OF
DISIDENTIFYING WITH TEEN MOTHERHOOD

1. Reflecting overall teen fertility patterns in the United States, most students at the Towne House had their first pregnancy at age 18 or 19 (as I did), putting them in the liminal category of "teen parents" who were actually legal adults.

2. Pillow 2015.

3. See Clarke, Friese, and Washburn 2018.

4. McClelland and Fine 2008b, 255.

5. By "nonnormative sexual subjects," I am referencing those whose sexual identities, subjectivities, or behaviors do not conform to disciplinary ideals of how one should be, understand themselves, or behave. See Spade and Willse 2016.

6. Camara Phyllis Jones's 2000 article "Levels of Racism: A Theoretic Framework and a Gardener's Tale" is useful for theorizing how structural conditions, rather than individual attributes such as hope, affect health issues. Jones uses the metaphor of a garden to illustrate institutional, interpersonal, and internalized forms of racism; the metaphor works for any form of social oppression. Institutionalized racism, or the condition of the soil in a garden, creates the circumstances in which vulnerable people (or flowers) can thrive or not. Jones emphasizes that the gardener—the person with the power to decide—has substantial influence in determining which flowers get planted in which soil, just as people with social resources wield immense power to govern the life chances of marginalized individuals.

7. Schultz 2001; SmithBattle 2018; Silver 2000. For analysis of the notion that reality TV shows such as MTV's *16 and Pregnant* glamorize or romanticize teen pregnancy and motherhood, see Guglielmo 2013.

8. These programs are generally geared toward a particular (white, middle-class) understanding of proper parenting practices. See Coren, Barlow, and Stewart-Brown 2003; Pillow 2004. Despite calls for greater inclusion of young men in preventing teen pregnancy and participating in childrearing (as noted in the

introduction), the programs for teen fathers in Millerston (as is generally the case) focused on job preparation, but not specifically in terms of their roles or identities as teen fathers. In other words, the programs for teen fathers focused solely on labor market participation and reflected the common social belief about women as caretakers and men as providers.

9. Vinson 2014; Zachry 2005.

10. Temporary Assistance to Needy Families (TANF), more commonly referred to as "welfare," is the means-tested federal program that provides cash assistance to low-income families. TANF replaced the entitlement program Aid to Families with Dependent Children (AFDC) as part of the 1996 Personal Responsibility and Work Opportunity Reconciliation Act of 1996, also known as welfare reform. TANF requires an unmarried, custodial minor parent to participate in school or an approved training program once her baby is 12 weeks old. Evaluation research indicates that this policy succeeded only moderately in increasing school attendance and long-term earnings through employment. See Kaiser Family Foundation 2003.

11. Naples 2004. For a useful discussion on messiness of vulnerability as an ethnographic practice, see Meadow 2018. I originally envisioned the research that became *Distributing Condoms and Hope* as an ethnography of the Towne House. I later shifted the focus of the research to the teen pregnancy prevention industrial complex, using the city of Millerston as the unit of analysis. As I outline in the introduction, this shift was intended in part to avoid reifying "confessional narratives" of teen pregnancy and to instead focus on the discursive workings and material impacts of social power. I found myself, as Wanda Pillow describes this shift in the introduction to *Unfit Subjects: Educational Policy and the Teen Mother*, "dissatisfied with the continued attention [on teen mothers] of a unit of analysis" and instead became interested in the production and circulation of knowledge. As part of a practice of uncomfortable reflexivity, I was increasingly reluctant to insert myself into a small nonprofit organization that was constantly fielding requests from researchers while struggling to meet the day-to-day needs of its students and staff. Although I shared with the students at the Towne House multiple and overlapping marginalized identities and relationships to power, I was nevertheless a community outsider. At the same time that I did not want to become an interloper, I viewed young mothers in Millerston as key figures in making sense of the production of youth sexuality and reproduction in the city. Despite shifting my work to focus on the city of Millerston more generally, I was fortunate and grateful to engage with the Towne House in a variety of ways over several years as a supporter, a researcher, and a friend. I engaged in shorter-term research projects that enabled me to spend more time at the organization and get to know the staff and students. I also attended fund-raising events, graduation ceremonies, and student poetry readings. My engagement with the Towne House was guided by a belief in the importance of its work—even

if it wasn't always perfect—and the organization's commitment to supporting pregnant and parenting teens.

12. See Barcelos and Gubrium 2014; Kelly 1996; Silver 2008; Vinson 2018.

13. In particular, queer of color critique traces its roots to writers, scholars, and activists such as Audre Lorde, Gloria Anzaldúa, Cherríe Moraga, Barbara Smith, and the Combahee River Collective. As Grace Kyungwon Hong and Roderick Ferguson (2012) assert, "Much of what we now call 'women of color feminism' can be seen as queer of color critique, insofar as these texts consistently situate sexuality as constitutive of race and gender. . . . We thus narrate queer of color critique as emerging from women of color feminism rather than deriving from a white Euro-American gay, lesbian, and queer theory tradition. . . . Women of color feminism and queer of color critique reveal the ways in which racialized communities are not homogeneous but instead have always policed and preserved the difference between those who are able to conform to categories of normativity, respectability, and value, and those who are forcibly excluded from such categories" (2).

14. See, for example, Eng 2010; Hong and Ferguson 2012; Ferguson 2003; Gopinath 2005; Johnson 2001; Manalansan 2018; Muñoz 1999; Muñoz 2009.

15. Manalansan 2018, 1288.

16. Manalansan 2018, 1288.

17. With several recent studies finding higher rates of unintended pregnancy among queer youth compared to their heterosexual counterparts, health promotion has increasingly interpellated LGBTQ youth into teen pregnancy prevention efforts. Although it is important to make sexual health education more inclusive and it is laudable to acknowledge that identity and behavior are not commeasurable, these efforts risk focusing on individual behaviors to fix structural LGBTQ health inequities. See Charlton et al. 2018; Goldberg, Reese, and Halpern 2016; Lindley and Walsemann 2015.

In addition, queer of color critique is a strategy for resisting the impossibility and invisibility of Black and brown queerness. Throughout my years working in Millerston, I often heard academics and service providers alike comment that there are "no queer people in Millerston" because, in their view, Latino culture is intrinsically and uniformly homophobic. Queer of color critique makes clear that *erasing* Latinx queers by universalizing Latinx homophobia is itself racist and homophobic. Assuming Latinx cultures are so homophobic as to preclude the existence of Latinx queer people masks homophobia among whites while allowing professional stakeholders to abdicate responsibility for creating queer- and trans-inclusive sexual health promotion.

18. Cohen 2019, 142. In reflecting on her landmark 1997 essay "Punks, Bulldaggers, and Welfare Queens," Cohen articulates the utility of *queer* as provocation that inspires my own use with regard to teen mothers. "In the vision of queer politics that motivated me in 'Punks,'" she writes, "individuals like Michael

Brown and Rekia Boyd are important queer subjects not because of their sexual practice, identity, or performance but because they, as well as other young and poor folks of color, operate in the world as queer subjects: the targets of racial normalizing projects intent on pathologizing them across the dimensions of race, class, gender, and sexuality, simultaneously making them into deviants while normalizing their degradation and marginalization until it becomes what we expect—the norm—until it becomes something that we no longer pay attention to" (142).

19. Ferguson 2003, 2.

20. Muñoz 1999; Muñoz 2009.

21. For example, queer people of color may identify with representations in art, music, or literature that center racial minorities, but disidentify with the homophobic rhetoric they reproduce. Whereas Muñoz's work focused on how minoritarian subjects disidentify with cultural representations and performances, scholars have also used disidentification to demonstrate disidentification with dominant modes of sociological analysis or the whiteness of queer theory. See Ferguson 2003; Johnson 2001.

22. Digital stories are short (2–3 minute) first-person video narratives, created and edited by research participants during a workshop process, that combine recorded voice, still and moving images, and music or other sounds to represent and communicate experience. See StoryCenter, www.storycenter.org; A. Gubrium 2009.

23. Due to the frequent turnover in enrollment at the Towne House—students could take their GED at any time, and new students were always enrolling—the MAMA group had a slightly different configuration each time we met. Sometimes only two or three students were in attendance, other times we had more than ten; a total of about twenty students cycled through the group during the semester. Sometimes we were able to meet in a technology-rich classroom; other times we had to huddle around my laptop to watch a film. During some sessions, students were animated and engaged and other times disinterested and bored. The discontinuity of participants and revolving cast of guest facilitators meant that we frequently had to repeat content. The messiness of the MAMA group mirrors the messiness of its participants' lives. Some days students were tired from lack of sleep at a noisy shelter; other days they were absent due to sick children or suspended because of strict Towne House attendance policies. Despite all these difficulties, the MAMA group was a generative space where young mothers—myself included—found a space of solidarity in which to navigate the messy realities of our lives.

24. Freire 1998.

25. Nonpregnant and parenting young women use similar strategies to shore up their own identities as "unproblematic." For instance, Ranita Ray (2017) analyzes how economically marginalized young women of color construct "identities of distance" by positioning themselves apart from their "risky" pregnant and

parenting peers. This distancing "helps to reproduce dominant race, class, and gender discourses that emphasize the need to police all economically marginalized Black and brown women's bodies" (458).

26. Mann 2018.

27. Ferguson 2003.

28. The Towne House's focus on teen parent resilience likely influenced the students' identification with these narratives. Other research has demonstrated this finding in other groups of teen parents, as well. For a review of these studies, see SmithBattle 2018. The narrative of teen pregnancy as resilience and motivation is one that I myself have (dis)identified with over the years.

29. These contradictory narratives are not germane only to pregnant and parenting young women. For instance, García (2009, 2012) and Mann (2016) find that Latina teens narrate their sexual agency through dominant heteronormative and neoliberal sexual scripts.

30. As I explain in chapter 1, the concept of *teen pregnancy* emerged in public policy as recently as the 1970s.

31. Epidemiologists measure teen birthrates by the number of live births to mothers aged 15–19 per 1,000 women ages 15–19. Sometimes these rates are separated into age groups by 15–17-year-olds and 18–19-year-olds. By using ages 15–19 as the most common measure of teen birth, these data obscure that fact that the rate for women ages 18–19 is four times higher than that of women ages 15–17. For example, in 2015, the rate for 18–19-year-olds was 40.7 births per 1,000, compared to 9.9 births per 1,000 women aged 15–17. In other words, the majority of "teen births" occur to adults.

32. Pillow 2015, 61.

33. The idea of "adolescence" as a particular developmental life stage occurring between childhood and adulthood is a relatively recent social and cultural construction. The concept emerged in the early twentieth century through psychological literature and shifting cultural ideas about child development (e.g., that childhood was a special time in need of nurturance and therefore factory work should be supplanted with compulsory schooling). In contrast to an understanding of adolescence as a biologically or psychologically based, naturally occurring life phase, scholars such as Nancy Lesko (2012) have drawn our attention to the social processes by which race, class, gender, and sexuality construct the meaning of *adolescence*. That is, who is considered an adolescent and what normal adolescent behavior involves are tied to ideas about whiteness, economic status, and masculinity or femininity. Moreover, as Lesko argues, the social construction of adolescence is anchored to ideas about modernity and is therefore a site in which to displace anxieties about shifting racial, economic, and gender formations. Adolescent childbearing becomes a social problem in part because it disrupts chrononormative stages of courtship, marriage, reproduction, and capital accumulation.

34. Amin 2014; Dinshaw et al. 2007; Freeman 2010.

35. Halberstam 2005, 4.

36. For a discussion of how racialized disruptions of normative fertility timing drive white cultural anxieties about teen childbearing, see Geronimus 2003. For an examination of how health care providers draw on and impart to patients discourses of "planned" parenthood marked by achieving having a good job, a steady relationship, and financial stability, see Stevens 2015. Bettie (2012) and Edin and Kefalas (2005) ethnographically demonstrate how parenthood is a way for young women to access adulthood when middle-class markers such as college and financial independence are unavailable.

37. Pillow 2015.

38. Quoted in Dinshaw et al. 2007, 180.

39. This mirrors the view of unmarried white middle-class pregnancy for most of the twentieth century, in which racially and economically privileged women's access to maternity homes shielded them from public condemnation. See Kunzel 1995; Solinger 2000.

40. Pillow (2003a) skillfully illustrates this point: "What would happen if [older, middle-class women were] . . . put under the same scrutiny and regulation as teen mothers? What if our sexual and love lives, our mothering, our relationships, our dietary and health habits, our fiscal responsibility, our familial relationships, our career choices, and moral fortitude were continuously monitored and judged? Who could withstand this type of scrutiny? Would any of us be 'good' mothers?" (154).

41. For a discussion of racism and the child welfare system in the United States, see Roberts 2002.

42. See, for example, Armstrong and Hamilton 2014; Bettie 2012; Bowles and Gintis 1976; Hotz, McElroy, and Sanders 2005; Lareau 2015; Marmot 2005; Phelan, Link, and Tehranifar 2010; Phelan and Link 2015; Rios 2011; Sampson, Morenoff, and Gannon-Rowley 2002; Willis 1981.

43. Pillow 2015.

44. Manalansan 2014, 99.

45. Manalansan 2014, 99. See also Manalansan 2018. In Manalansan's work, the "impossible subjects" are undocumented queers.

46. What's more, numerous kinds of literal and metaphorical mess characterize the lives of young mothers—from the mess of soiled diapers, to the messy systems they must navigate, to the ways their lives mess up easy narratives about teen pregnancy as a social pathology or a source of motivation and resilience.

47. WIC stands for Special Supplemental Nutrition Program for Women, Infants, and Children.

48. As Bettie (2012) demonstrates, the symbolic economy of style among young women is a terrain in which class and racial-ethnic relationships play out. Style can a be a strategy with which to perform or reject normative expectations

around gender, sexuality, age, race, class, and so on. Yet, as Bettie reminds us, style performances are "overdetermined by broader cultural meanings that code women in heavy makeup and tight clothes as low class and oversexed . . . in other words, class differences are often understood as sexual differences" (63).

49. Vargas 2014.

50. Manalansan 2014, 99.

51. Love 2016 (messy method). Vinson (2018) provides a trenchant feminist rhetorical analysis of narratives in each of the three domains.

52. Manalansan 2018.

53. Cohen 1997, 462.

54. Conrad 2014; Duggan 2002.

CHAPTER 3. "IT'S THEIR CULTURE"

1. This is not to say that a greater emphasis on STI prevention would have made youth sexual health promotion in Millerston emancipatory or anti-racist. To the contrary, there is a long history in health promotion of positioning Black and brown bodies as "diseased" or "dirty" (see, for example, Bridges 2011). I point this out, instead, to emphasize the point that teen pregnancy prevention overshadowed stakeholders' stated objectives—even when rates of STI transmission in Millerston far exceeded those of the state as a whole.

2. Fields 2008.

3. Omi and Winant 2015, 13.

4. Omi and Winant 2015, 126.

5. Omi and Winant 2015, 125.

6. See Roberts 2011.

7. The concept of a gendered racial project shares a political investment with intersectionality and responds to Leslie McCall's (2005) call for methodologies and analytics that lend themselves to actually doing intersectional research. Like intersectionality, a gendered racial project is invested in naming and dismantling interlocking systems of oppression. A gendered racial project is a specific strategy for analyzing how race and gender play out in social *processes,* and how those processes correspond to structures of racial domination as well as the everyday experiences of racialized people. For a trenchant analysis of the academic travels and affective dimensions of intersectionality, and related concepts such as "assemblage," see Nash 2019.

8. Kang 2010; Vidal-Ortiz 2009.

9. Mann 2013. For an ethnographic examination of how race and class play out in the context of publicly funded prenatal care, see Bridges 2011.

10. The treatment of unmarried mothers of all ages presaged the racialization of teen pregnancy. For instance, Rickie Solinger details the divergent race-based

approaches to single pregnant women in the post–World War II era preceding the *Roe v. Wade* decision, which legalized abortion. Service providers understood white single pregnant women as having become pregnant through a curable form of neurosis and as possessing a marketable product: a white infant to place in the adoption market. Conversely, they understood Black single pregnancy to be the consequence of an uncontrollable, racially motivated hypersexuality that did not result in a marketable product. This view laid the groundwork for future disciplinary public policy where welfare "reform" positioned Black women as getting something (public assistance) for nothing (another Black baby). See Solinger 2000 and 2005. See also Mink 1998; Roberts 1997.

11. Lincoln, Jaffe, and Ambrose 1976; Pillow 2004.

12. Pillow 2004.

13. Chavez 2008, 72.

14. Erdmans and Black 2015; Fuentes, Bayetti Flores, and Gonzalez-Rojas 2010; García 2012; Mann 2013.

15. García 2009 and 2012.

16. Mann 2013. See also Stevens 2015.

17. López 2014, 3. López's argument focuses on politicians, specifically Republican Party legislators and candidates, but his insights are germane for understanding how actors in Millerston do (not) talk about race.

18. Omi and Winant 2015, 218.

19. Roberts 2011.

20. In referencing this narrative, I specifically use the word *Latino*, rather than *Latinx*, as the narrative is not focused on gender inclusivity or opposition to oppression, as the latter term implies, but is deterministic and homogenous, as the former implies.

21. *Gyp* and *gypping* are slurs that reference Romani people and are used to connote thievery or cheating.

22. Geronimus 2003; López 2008.

23. For an analysis of how white obstetricians use the discourse of "It's their culture" to explain the health behaviors and outcomes of their pregnant patients of color, see Bridges 2011.

24. Fields 2008.

25. Moreover, the imperative to talk freely and openly about sex is situated within white western heteronormativity. On the imperative to speak of sex (and speak of it more and more), see, for example, Foucault (1978) 1990. For analysis of how Latina mothers navigate discourses around race and sexuality in talking with their adolescent daughters about sex, see García 2012.

26. González-López and Vidal-Ortiz 2007, 313.

27. As Elliot (2012) demonstrates, parents across race, class, and gender lines have difficulty talking to their teenagers about sex. In her ethnographic work with a heterogenous group of families, Elliot finds that most parents

viewed their teens as sexually irresponsible and uninterested in talking with them about sex. Parents' views were shaped by an intractable adolescent-adult binary in which adults are autonomous, rational, and responsible, whereas teens are dependent, impulsive, and irresponsible. Moreover, parents relied on raced, classed, and gendered stereotypes to construct their teens' peers as hypersexualized threats to their own child's sexual innocence. Similarly, in her comparative study of white middle-class parents in the United States and the Netherlands, Schalet (2011) distinguishes the particular American culture that dramatizes, rather than normalizes, adolescent sexuality. As part of this dramatization, parents communicate to their teens that sex is dangerous and risky and view communication with their children about sexuality as an adversarial "tug of war."

28. Elizabeth did not indicate whether she believed the large Irish Catholic community in Millerston shared this sentiment.

29. Other scholars have found similar complexities in young Latinas' negotiations of unintended pregnancy. See, for example, Mann, Cardona, and Gómez 2015.

30. Further, as I discuss in the following chapter, there was a great deal of silence around abortion in Millerston on the part of youth sexual health promoters themselves.

31. In 2015, at the culmination of my fieldwork in Millerston, the teen birthrate in the city was 40.5 per 1,000 women ages 15–19. In Puerto Rico, the rate in 2015 was 33.9 per 1,000.

32. I feel the need here to point out the obvious: having babies is part of every human culture. If it weren't, the species would cease to exist.

33. For a review of this literature, see Romo, Nadeem, and Kouyoumdjian 2009.

34. Suseth Valladares and Franco 2010. Similarly, in her ethnographic study of how Latina girls experience their sexual subjectivities and negotiate safer sex, Lorena García (2012) interviewed a series of mother-daughter pairs who problematized an easy characterization of Latinx families as unwilling to talk about sex. García challenges the notion that Latinas are "culturally silent" about sexuality with their daughters, arguing instead that broader discourses about appropriate adolescent sexuality and presumptions of hyperfertility among women of color structure their interactions. Again, the issue is not so much that Latinx families are consistently unable or unwilling to discuss sexuality within their families as that they are embedded in discursive contexts that shape and limit their ability to do so. For an examination of Puerto Rican youth sexual subjectivities and practices at the height of the AIDS crisis, see Asencio 2002.

35. J. Jones, Mosher, and Daniels 2012.

36. Latina Institute for Reproductive Health 2017.

37. Suseth Valladares and Franco 2010.

38. Jerman, Jones, and Onda 2010. As to "Hispanic," abortion data collected by the CDC use US Census Bureau race and ethnicity categories.

39. Pazol, Creanga, and Jamieson 2015. In 2012 the abortion rate for Hispanics was 15.3 per 1,000 women, whereas for white, non-Hispanic women it was 7.6 per 1,000.

40. Kost and Henshaw 2014. The rate of abortion among Black women is higher than both Hispanic and non-Hispanic white women, with a 2012 rate of 28.6 per 1,000.

41. Erickson and Kaplan 1998.

42. Lake Research Associates 2011. As Mann, Cardona, and Gómez (2015) illustrate, young Latinas' decision making around unintended pregnancy, like all people's, is more complicated than binary ways of thinking about it suggest. Although some of their respondents expressed unambiguous opinions about abortion, others wrestled with the options of abortion, adoption, and parenting while constrained by stigma, pressure from male partners, and access to services. Similarly, in a mixed-gender sample of racially diverse young people who did not currently desire a pregnancy, Gómez and colleagues (2018) found that most respondents would nevertheless view an unexpected pregnancy as acceptable. This view was influenced by a more nuanced set of factors than health promoters typically recognize, including perceived readiness based on meeting milestones for adulthood, relationship quality, desire for children, knowledge of parenting realities, and fatalism.

43. Bonilla-Silva and Dietrich 2011; Bonilla-Silva 2014. My research for *Distributing Condoms and Hope* was conducted in 2012–15 and early drafts of chapters were written in 2015–16, prior to the 2016 election of Donald Trump. Since then, the concomitant rising visibility of white nationalism, state-sanctioned Islamophobia, and chants to "build the wall" on the US-Mexico border has called into question whether the Obama-era ideology of colorblindness has indeed passed, as overt forms of racism have become increasingly visible and acceptable. Bonilla-Silva argues that, indeed, colorblind racism remains the hegemonic mode of racism in the United States today. He concedes that multiple modes occur simultaneously and points out that to observe processes of colorblind racism is not to argue that older, more overt forms have ceased to exist. See Bonilla-Silva 2019.

44. Conversely, scholars also point to the expansion of a necropolitical regime that sees certain bodies as expendable (Snorton and Haritaworn 2013). Black Lives Matter, #NoDAPL, and other racial justice movements in the United States have helped to recenter media, scholarly, and activist attention to the ways Black and brown bodies are systematically marked for death. Naming so-called "new" forms of racism does not mean that brutal forms of dispossession and violence have been eliminated.

45. Bonilla-Silva 2014, 26.

46. Omi and Winant 2015, 257.

47. Alexander 2012.

48. However, there is evidence that the California state prison system unlawfully sterilized inmates as recently as 2013 (California State Auditor 2014).

49. There is also evidence suggesting that women of color and low-income women are more likely to experience provider hesitancy or refusal to remove a LARC method. See, for example, Higgins, Kramer, and Ryder 2016.

50. Secura et al. 2014; Weise 2015.

51. Ott et al. 2014.

52. Romero et al. 2015.

53. McClain 2015; Secura et al. 2014; Trussell et al. 2013.

54. Although medical providers and health promoters have come to view LARC as a first-line contraceptive for all potential users, LARC promotion does not play out the same across race, social class, and age. Mann and Grzanka (2018) use commercial, educational, and public-private partnership LARC promotion materials to illustrate this point. Promotion materials aimed at urban middle-class, mostly white consumers use playful messages to communicate LARC as a responsible choice symbolizing freedom. In contrast, materials aimed at economically marginalized, young, and/or women of color are more aggressive in their tone and communicate LARC as the *only* acceptable choice. Across all groups, materials convey what Mann and Grzanka call "agency-without-choice," operating within a neoliberal frame in which "the absence of choice is framed as empowering at the same time that the illusion of choice is preserved" (350).

55. Gold 2014; Gubrium et al. 2016; Higgins 2014; Gómez, Fuentes, and Allina 2014.

56. Gómez, Fuentes, and Allina 2014, 173.

57. Gómez, Fuentes, and Allina 2014, 171. In 2016, SisterSong and the National Women's Health Network released a statement of principles concerning LARC: "We strongly support the inclusion of long-acting reversible contraceptive methods (LARCs) as part of a well-balanced mix of options, including barrier methods, oral contraceptives, and other alternatives. We reject efforts to direct women toward any particular method and caution providers and public health officials against making assumptions based on race, ethnicity, age, ability, economic status, sexual orientation, or gender identity and expression. People should be given complete information and be supported in making the best decision for their health and other unique circumstances." See "Long-Acting Reversible Contraception: Statement of Principles," National Women's Health Network, February 8, 2017, https://www.nwhn.org/wp-content/uploads/2017/02/LARCStatementofPrinciples.pdf.

58. Gold 2014; Roberts 1997; Solinger 2005; Flavin 2008.

59. Briggs 2002; López 2008.

60. See note 49, this chapter.

61. Winters and McLaughlin 2019.

62. Dehlendorf et al. 2010; Downing, LaVeist, and Bullock 2007.

63. Gómez 2014; Gómez and Wapman 2016; Higgins, Kramer, and Ryder 2016; Yee and Simon 2011.

64. See "Contraceptive and Reproductive Health Services for Teens: Evidence-Based Clinical Best Practices," National Center for Chronic Disease Prevention and Health Promotion, accessed June 7, 2020, https://www.cdc.gov/teenpregnancy/pdf/about/fact-sheet-contraceptive-reproductive-health-services-teens_tagged-508.pdf.

65. Gómez, Mann, and Torres 2017; Gubrium et al. 2016.

66. Higgins and Smith 2016; Littlejohn 2012; Littlejohn 2013; Westhoff et al. 2007.

67. Higgins 2014.

68. For a discussion of similar issues among Mexican-origin women, see Gutiérrez 2008.

69. López 2008, xv.

70. According to Briggs (2002), "The women in the film who have been sterilized tell a story of decisions they made based on health, family economies, or beliefs about modernity, while the voice-over inscribes a narrative of the state and social control" (145).

71. Omi and Winant 2014, 256.

72. See, especially, Hoffman 2008. This common view obscures the fact that social welfare programs constitute a much smaller proportion of an individual's tax bill than spending for military, federal prisons, and corporate subsidies. See National Priorities Project, www.nationalpriorities.org.

73. Kearney and Levine 2012.

74. Briggs 2002, 14.

75. Omi and Winant 2014, 256.

CHAPTER 4. SEX, SCIENCE, AND WHAT TEENS DO WHEN IT'S DARK OUTSIDE

1. This is same meeting I describe in the opening vignettes of the introduction.

2. These figures literally make pregnant teenagers' bodies into statistics.

3. The experiences of students at the Towne House are consistent with these findings. See also Fershee 2009; Manlove 1998; MATP 2010; Pillow 2004; and Zachry 2005.

4. Refer to this book's introduction for a review of this literature.

5. Epstein 1994, 145.

6. Fahs and McClelland 2016.

7. Acosta 2013; Carpenter and Epstein 2012; Carrillo 2002; Fields 2008; Fine 1988; Fine and McClelland 2006; Gamson and Moon 2004; Irvine 2004; Pascoe 2012; Schalet 2011.

8. Foucault (1978) 1990, 18.

9. Foucault (1978) 1990, 18.

10. As Steven Epstein (2003) notes, "Power does not so much negate sex as organize it through the proliferation of discourses about it," and "sexual meanings are orchestrated through an injunction that we speak about sex" (490).

11. Confessing that you are or were a teen parent, or the child of one, was a precarious endeavor in Millerston. It was likely to elicit any number of potentially uncomfortable responses. It was rare that anyone would disclose their teen parent status in prevention-focused spaces. For example, Mayor Brown never acknowledged that he was the son of a teen parent except at some Towne House events. I admitted to having been a pregnant teenager only a handful of times during my fieldwork. As part of the redemption narrative, revealing this fact about myself usually communicated that I was interested in this work in order to prevent other young people from doing what I had done. Conversely, due to my "success" story as an academic, others would often implicate me in a progress narrative and use me as an example of what teen parents can do if they "work hard enough."

12. Kristina Myers shared with me that she thought these prompts were "dissing" the students, as many of them were raised by teen parents themselves.

13. For instance, the "stud"-"slut" dichotomy prescribes that boys and young men who are open and active about their sexual behaviors, desires, and pleasures are deemed "studs," whereas girls and young women who do so are "sluts." The "virgin"-"whore" continuum also structures young women's sexual subjectivity by delineating a graduation of socially acceptable sexual behaviors ranging from "good" to "bad." Laina Bay-Cheng (2015) argues that in recent years the virgin-whore continuum has intersected with what she calls the "agency line." Framed through the cultural logics of neoliberalism, the agency line adds another dimension to young women's sexual subjectivity by evaluating their behavior "according to the degree of control they proclaim, or are perceived, to exert over their sexual behavior" (282). Girls stay above the agency line by remaining abstinent, limiting their number of sexual partners, or strictly adhering to contraception. See also Fields 2008; García 2012; Pascoe 2012; Tolman 2002.

14. For a trenchant examination of masculinity in American high schools, see Pascoe 2012.

15. Fields 2008; Fine and McClelland 2006; Tolman 2002. According to psychologist Deborah Tolman (2002), adolescent girls face a "dilemma of desire" that structures their sexual subjectivities. Understood as a choice between safety and enjoying their sexual feelings, the dilemma is framed "as *if* it were an individual rather than a social problem—if a girl has desire, she is vulnerable to per-

sonal physical, social, material, or relational consequences—it is in a way not especially surprising that girls would experience their desire and these resulting difficulties as their own personal problem" (44).

16. Allen 2004; Fine 1988; Fine and McClelland 2006; Gubrium and Shafer 2014.

17. However, stakeholders did not necessarily frame desire or pleasure as something that was the domain of young men. In fact, young men were largely missing from the teen pregnancy prevention industrial complex. It was common to hear stakeholders argue for more programming to engage young men, and some of this programming began after the culmination of my fieldwork. Nevertheless, the duty to prevent teen pregnancy rested mainly on young women.

18. There is, however, considerable debate over Beyoncé's sexual subjectivity in the album, including whether or not her reputation as a feminist is misplaced (see McKenzie 2014).

19. As I discuss in chapter 2, this absence is partially attributable to a notion, held by many white people in Millerston and elsewhere, that few, if any, Latinx people are LGBTQ due to the intractable homophobia in the community.

20. Lindley and Walsemann 2015; Tornello, Riskind, and Patterson 2014.

21. Coker, Austin, and Schuster 2010.

22. For a conceptualization of the emergence, perpetuation, and normalization of abortion stigma, see Kumar, Hessini, and Mitchell 2009. For a discussion of the limitations of the "safe, legal, and rare" argument for abortion access, see Thorne-Thomsen 2010.

23. Sinikka Elliot (2014) uses fieldwork in school-based sex education classrooms to analyze the explicit, neoliberal messages of curricula and the implicit, evaded ones. She identifies abortion and same-sex sexual activity as two of the evaded lessons that "contradict the notion of the free, autonomous agent and emphasize the extent to which we are dependent on others." The responsible sexual agent whom teachers present to students functioned as a "mirage," obscuring both interdependence and social inequalities. Elliot 2014, 222.

24. According to Banu Subramaniam (2009), feminist science studies is "a heterogeneous and amorphous body of work that has emerged and grown organically rather than having been established as a field that has any consensus or cohesion" (952). See also Cipolla et al. 2017; Hammonds and Subramaniam 2003; Haraway 1988; Harding 1986.

25. Mamo and Fishman 2013.

26. See Murphy 2012; Willey 2016; Shim 2005; Mamo 2007. Field-defining edited volumes on feminist and queer science studies include Wyer et al., *Women, Science, and Technology: A Reader in Feminist Science Studies;* Mayberry, Subramaniam, and Weasel, *Feminist Science Studies: A New Generation*; and Cipolla et al., *Queer Feminist Science Studies: A Reader.*

27. Green and Labonte 2007.

28. Glanz, Rimer, and Viswanath 2008; Labonte and Robertson 1996.

29. Popay and Williams 1996, 760.

30. Buchanan 2000; Bowleg 2017; Bowleg et al. 2017; Labonte and Robertson 1996; Labonte et al. 2005.

31. Goldenberg 2006, 2621.

32. Kohatsu, Robinson, and Torner 2004.

33. Murphy 2012, 12.

34. Although "official" scientific racism in medicine, public health, and education in the United States waned in the latter half of the twentieth century, its effects persist in research and practice. For instance, in the nineteenth century the belief that people of African descent had a primitive nervous system that caused them not to feel physical pain was used to justify enslavement and physical abuse. These beliefs persist today; for instance, physicians routinely underprescribe pain medicine for Black patients. For further discussion of the relationship between scientific racism, gender, and sexuality, see Bridges 2011; Roberts 2011; Somerville 2000; and Washington 2008.

35. Academic research also uses and contributes to causal fantasies. For example, the scientific construction of "teen" pregnancy as caused by poverty, lack of access to contraception, and so forth (discussed in detail in the introduction and chapter 1) helped to establish teen pregnancy as a social problem.

36. Crosby and Holtgrave 2006; Kearney and Levine 2012; Penman-Aguilar et al. 2013.

37. For rich descriptions of the social processes by which race, class, and gender inequalities are powerfully reproduced despite how much hope an individual may hold, see Alexander 2012; Bettie 2012; Ray 2018; and Rios 2011.

38. Fershee 2009; Manlove 1998; MATP 2010; Pillow 2004; Zachry 2005.

39. Kearney and Levine 2012; Penman-Aguilar et al. 2013.

40. Wilson and Huntington 2006, 65. For empirical examples, see Barcelos and Gubrium 2014; Graham and McDermott 2006; and Kelly 2000.

41. Ventura, Hamilton, and Mathews 2014.

42. Martin et al. 2017.

43. Boonstra 2014.

44. Mann, Cardona, and Gómez 2015.

45. SEICUS 2015a.

46. SEICUS 2015b.

47. Kirby 2007 and 2008; SEICUS 2015b. The various initiatives created by the changes in federal funding for sex education made under the Obama administration predicated receipt of funds on the use of these externally evaluated, replicable curricula. As of this writing, the Trump administration is in the process of redirecting funding toward AOUM.

48. Kirby 2007.

49. As Norman Denzin (2008) suggests, the politics of research evidence involve the questions of "who has the power to control the definition of evidence, who defines the kinds of materials that count as evidence, who determines what methods best produce the best forms of evidence, and whose criteria and standards are used to evaluate quality evidence" (62). These examples of "embedded science" do not evaluate objective knowledge but rather produce and legitimate what must be known in order to effectively manage the population. For a discussion of AOUM as embedded science, see McClelland and Fine 2008a.

50. Fields 2008. Fields argues that the fight between "abstinence only" and "comprehensive" approaches to sex education works to both elide and reproduce social inequalities. The parents, educators, and school committee members Fields interviewed who advocated for comprehensive approaches employed rhetoric similar to that used by stakeholders in Millerston. They framed the sexuality of young women of color as risky and dangerous to themselves, their potential children, and the community at large. Positioning young people this way enables the promotion of CSE through a savior mentality—they need science to liberate them from the dangers of sexual activity. Fields notes that advocates for comprehensive approaches used raced, classed, and gendered rhetoric that replaced conventional social policy stories about the welfare queen with stories about girls whose parents failed to do their job of educating them about sex, therefore requiring the school to step in. The racialized rhetoric of "children having children"—also deployed in Millerston—even convinced some abstinence-only advocates to switch their minds in favor of a comprehensive approach in order to "save" these kids.

51. For a description of the curriculum, see Advocates for Youth 2008.

52. Advocates for Youth 2008.

53. See, for example, Farmer 1996; Holtgrave and Crosby 2003; Jeffries et al. 2013; Reisner et al. 2016.

54. However, since most of them did not speak Spanish, they frequently had trouble pronouncing it.

55. Villarruel and Eakin 2008, 3.

56. Villarruel and Eakin 2008, 5.

57. Villarruel and Eakin 2008, 7.

58. Fine and McClelland 2006, 325.

59. Fine and McClelland 2006, 325.

60. McClelland and Fine 2008a, 67.

CHAPTER 5. EDUCATED HOPE

1. See http://heymichelfoucault-blog.tumblr.com/image/17750454992.

2. Chaddha and Wilson 2011, 165.

3. Critical health scholars have debated the analytic usefulness of neoliberalism in health promotion, noting its overuse and lack of specificity (Bell and Greene 2016). In the case of Millerston, the economic and cultural logics of neoliberalism are useful lenses through which to make sense of the promotion of hope and condoms in the face of a deindustrialized city with a shredded safety net that was hyperfocused on personal responsibility and individual choice. See also Schrecker 2016; Grzanka, Mann, and Elliot 2016.

4. See Duggan 2003.

5. On femininities, see Gill and Scharf 2011. On sexuality, see Conrad 2014; Duggan 2003; and Edelman and Zimman 2014. On health promotion, see Ayo 2012 and LeBesco 2011. On schooling, see Davies and Bansel 2007.

6. Buchanan 2008.

7. Omi and Winant 2015, 256.

8. This is to say that the majority of salaried, middle- and senior-level public health workers in Millerston were white. As I note in chapter 2, Puerto Ricans were largely concentrated in entry-level, low-wage positions such as medical assistants.

9. McKenzie 2014, 112.

10. INCITE! Women of Color Against Violence 2017.

11. Although my research did not include a needs assessment component, both my interviews with young mothers and the small-scale needs assessments conducted by Teens Count illustrate that young people in Millerston did not see teen pregnancy as a problem in the way that professional stakeholders did. They also did not identify access to contraception and comprehensive sex education as the most pressing issues in their communities. Instead, youth identified interpersonal and community violence, including police harassment, as among the most pressing issues in their communities.

12. Fine and McClelland 2006.

13. Fields 2008.

14. The "Sex Ed the City" project is an exemplar of this approach. An initiative of Forward Together, the project integrated anti-stigma work into its campaign to "make sure that when young people get it on" they have "the power and resources needed to make healthy decisions about their gender, body, and sexuality." The project's report, titled "Let's Get It On: Oakland Youth's Vision for Sex Ed," describes the youth-led participatory action research project that called on the community and school district to implement "sex education justice." In collaboration with adult allies, the group conducted a needs assessment of middle school and high school students' perspectives on the state of sex education in the district and what students wanted their sex education to look like. Throughout the process, youth were the primary writers, thinkers, and facilitators who devised the research methods, conducted surveys and focus groups, analyzed data, wrote up the results, and created a workshop to explain sex education

justice to other students. Their vision of sex education justice includes: forms of contraception relevant to all genders and sexualities; inclusion of all pregnancy options (including parenting, abortion, and adoption); education about healthy and unhealthy relationships; inclusion of all gender identities and sexual orientations; relevant information for youth of color, economically marginalized youth, LGBTQ youth, and youth with disabilities; emphasis on positive body image and self-esteem; and workshops on consent and healthy communication. Their needs assessment revealed that students in the district wanted more time spent on sex education in school and wanted the content to be inclusive of LGBTQ students, non–English speaking students, and students with disabilities. The report's recommendations highlighted the importance of getting youth input in the sex education curriculum planning process, prioritizing sex education teachers who were people of color, and making content and materials inclusive of a range of identities, bodies, and sexualities. See "Let's Get It On: Oakland Youth's New Vision for Sex Ed," Forward Together, accessed June 11, 2020, https://forwardtogether.org/wp-content/uploads/2017/12/2012-Lets-Get-It-On.pdf.

15. On the ethical, moral, and political implications of using disgust as a tool to promote health, see, for example, Lupton 2015.

16. The scholarly journal *Critical Public Health,* established in 1979 as *Radical Community Medicine,* is the journal of record for public health theory and practice that interrogates power relations. On the tradition of community-based participatory research, see Israel et al. 2013 and Wallerstein et al. 2018.

17. See White People Changing Racism, www.wpcr-boston.org. There are important critiques of white-led racial justice organizing, though this work could be a good starting place for white people in Millerston. See DiDi Delgado, "Whites Only: SURJ and the Caucasian Invasion of Racial Justice Spaces," *Huffington Post,* April 3, 2017, https://www.huffpost.com/entry/whites-only-surj-and-the-caucasian-invasion-of-racial_b_58dd5cf7e4b04ba4a5e25209.

18. See https://www.sistersong.net/rj-training-and-leadership-development-programs/.

19. See http://latinainstitute.org/en/what-we-do/leadership-development/trainings.

20. See http://www.caip.us/

21. Muñoz 2009, 18.

22. Here I am indebted to the work of Young Women United and their 2016 report "Dismantling Teen Pregnancy Prevention." See https://youngwomenunited.org/wp-content/uploads/2016/06/ywu-dismantlingtpp-DEC2016-digital-interactive.pdf.

23. Duggan and Muñoz 2009 (emphasis in original). See also Muñoz 2009.

24. Duggan and Muñoz 2009, 279.

25. See Bassichis, Lee, and Spade 2015.

26. Duggan and Muñoz 2009, 279.

27. For example, during the time I was writing this book, the federal government redirected millions of dollars back into abstinence-only sex education, reinstated the gag rule that limits health care providers from talking to their patients about abortion, weakened protections against health care discrimination based on gender and sexuality, refused to provide adequate relief in Puerto Rico following Hurricane Maria, emboldened the behavior of white supremacists in the United States, instituted a policy of forced separation of migrant children and families at the border, and virtually ignored an infectious-disease pandemic that disproportionately killed Black and Latinx people.

APPENDIX B. METHODOLOGICAL NOTES

1. Sprague 2016.
2. Sprague 2016, 6.
3. Emerson, Fretz, and Shaw 2011.
4. Emerson, Fretz, and Shaw 2011, 19.
5. Clarke 2005.
6. Morse 2015, 587.
7. Charmaz 2014.
8. Charmaz 2014, 17.
9. Bernard, Wutich, and Ryan, 2017.
10. Clarke 2005, xxii.
11. Clarke 2005, xxii.
12. Clarke 2005, 155.
13. Perez and Cannella, 2011.
14. Clarke 2005, 175.
15. Clarke 2005, xxvii, xxix.
16. Clarke 2005, 30.
17. Clarke 2005, 87.
18. See Compton, Meadow, and Schilt 2018.

References

Abu-Lughod, Lila. 1990. "Can There Be a Feminist Ethnography?" *Women and Performance: A Journal of Feminist Theory* 5 (1): 7–27.

Acosta, Katie L. 2013. *Amigas y Amantes: Sexually Nonconforming Latinas Negotiate Family*. New Brunswick, NJ: Rutgers University Press.

Advocates for Youth. 2008. *Science and Success: Sex Education and Other Programs That Work to Prevent Teen Pregnancy, HIV, and Sexually Transmitted Infections*. 2nd ed. Washington, DC.

Alexander, Michelle. 2012. *The New Jim Crow: Mass Incarceration in the Age of Colorblindness*. New York: New Press.

Alford, Sue, and Debra Hauser. 2011. *Adolescent Sexual Health in Europe and the U.S.—Why the Difference?* 3rd ed. Washington, DC: Advocates for Youth. https://www.advocatesforyouth.org/wp-content/uploads/storage//advfy /documents/fsest.pdf.

Allen, Louisa. 2004. "Beyond the Birds and the Bees: Constituting a Discourse of Erotics in Sexuality Education." *Gender and Education* 16 (2): 151–67.

Amin, Kadji. 2014. "Temporality." *TSQ: Transgender Studies Quarterly* 1 (1–2): 219–22.

Armstrong, Elizabeth A., and Laura T. Hamilton. *Paying for the Party: How College Maintains Inequality*. Cambridge, MA: Harvard University Press, 2013.

Asencio, Marysol. 2002. *Sex and Sexuality among New York's Puerto Rican Youth*. Boulder, CO: Lynne Rienner.

Asian Communities for Reproductive Justice (ACRJ). 2005. "A New Vision for Advancing Our Movement for Reproductive Health, Reproductive Rights, and Reproductive Justice." Strong Families Movement. Accessed February 14, 2016. http://strongfamiliesmovement.org/assets/docs/ACRJ-A-New-Vision.pdf.

Ayo, Nike. 2012. "Understanding Health Promotion in a Neoliberal Climate and the Making of Health Conscious Citizens." *Critical Public Health* 22 (1): 99–105.

Barcelos, Chris A. 2014. "Producing (Potentially) Pregnant Teen Bodies: Biopower and Adolescent Pregnancy in the USA." *Critical Public Health* 24 (4): 476–88.

Barcelos, Chris A., and Aline C. Gubrium. 2014. "Reproducing Stories: Strategic Narratives of Teen Pregnancy and Motherhood." *Social Problems* 61 (3): 466–81.

Barcelos, Chris A., and Aline C. Gubrium. 2018. "Bodies That Tell: Embodying Teen Pregnancy through Digital Storytelling." *Signs: Journal of Women in Culture and Society* 43 (4): 905–27.

Bassichis, Morgan, Alexander Lee, and Dean Spade. 2015. "Building an Abolitionist Trans and Queer Movement with Everything We've Got." In *Captive Genders: Trans Embodiment and the Prison Industrial Complex*, 2nd edition, edited by Eric Stanley and Nat Smith, 21–46. Chico, CA: AK Press.

Bay-Cheng, Laina Y. 2003. "The Trouble of Teen Sex: The Construction of Adolescent Sexuality through School-Based Sexuality Education." *Sex Education: Sexuality, Society, and Learning* 3 (1): 61–74.

Bay-Cheng, Laina Y. 2015. "The Agency Line: A Neoliberal Metric for Appraising Young Women's Sexuality." *Sex Roles* 73 (7–8): 279–91.

Bayetti Flores, Verónica. 2011. "Teen Pregnancy Prevention and Reproductive Justice: What's the Real Problem?" *Rewire News*, June 1, 2011. https://rewire.news/article/2011/06/01/teen-pregnancy-prevention-reproductive-justice-what-real-problem/.

Bell, Kirsten, and Judith Green. 2016. "On the Perils of Invoking Neoliberalism in Public Health Critique." *Critical Public Health* 25 (3): 239–43.

Bernard, H. Russell, Amber Wutich, and Gery W. Ryan. 2017. *Analyzing Qualitative Data: Systematic Approaches*. Thousand Oaks, CA: Sage.

Bettie, Julie. 2012. *Women without Class: Girls, Race, and Identity*. Oakland: University of California Press.

Bhatia, Sunil. 2013. "Nicholas Kristof and the Politics of Writing About Women's Oppression in Darker Nations." *Feminist Wire*, February 13, 2013. http://www.thefeministwire.com/2013/03/op-ed-nicholas-kristof-and-the-politics-of-writing-about-womens-oppression-in-darker-nations/

Bonell, Chris. 2004. "Why Is Teenage Pregnancy Conceptualized as a Social Problem? A Review of Quantitative Research from the USA and UK." *Culture, Health, and Sexuality* 6 (3): 255–72.

Bonilla-Silva, Eduardo. 2003. "'New Racism,' Color-Blind Racism, and the Future of Whiteness in America." In *White Out: The Continuing Significance of Racism*, edited by Ashely W. Doane and Eduardo Bonilla-Silva, 271–84. New York: Routledge.

Bonilla-Silva, Eduardo. 2014. *Racism without Racists: Color-Blind Racism and the Persistence of Racial Inequality in the United States*. 4th edition. Lanham, MD: Rowman and Littlefield.

Bonilla-Silva, Eduardo. 2019. "'Racists,' 'Class Anxieties,' Hegemonic Racism, and Democracy in Trump's America." *Social Currents* 6 (1): 14–31.

Bonilla-Silva, Eduardo, and David Dietrich. 2011. "The Sweet Enchantment of Color-Blind Racism in Obamerica." *Annals of the American Academy of Political and Social Science* 634(1): 190-206.

Boonstra, Heather D. 2014. "What Is Behind the Declines in Teen Pregnancy Rates?" *Guttmacher Policy Review* 17 (3): 15–21.

Bowleg, Lisa. 2017. "Towards a Critical Health Equity Research Stance: Why Epistemology and Methodology Matter More than Qualitative Methods." *Health Education and Behavior* 44 (5): 677–84.

Bowleg, Lisa, Ana Maria del Rio–Gonzalez, Sidney L. Holt, Carolin Pérez, Jenne S. Massie, Jessica E. Mandell, and Cheriko A. Boone. 2017. "Intersectional Epistemologies of Ignorance: How Behavioral and Social Science Research Shapes What We Know, Think We Know, and Don't Know about US Black Men's Sexualities." *Journal of Sex Research* 54 (4–5): 577–603.

Bowles, Samuel, and Herbert Gintis. 2011. *Schooling in Capitalist America: Educational Reform and the Contradictions of Economic Life*. Boston: Haymarket Books.

Bridges, Khiara. 2011. *Reproducing Race: An Ethnography of Pregnancy as a Site of Racialization*. Berkeley: University of California Press.

Briggs, Laura. 2002. *Reproducing Empire: Race, Sex, Science, and U.S. Imperialism in Puerto Rico*. Berkeley: University of California Press.

Buchanan, David R. 2000. *An Ethic for Health Promotion*. New York: Oxford University Press.

Buchanan, David R. 2008. "Autonomy, Paternalism, and Justice: Ethical Priorities in Public Health." *American Journal of Public Health* 98 (1): 15-21.

Cadena, Micaela, Raquel Z. Rivera, Tannia Esparza, and Denicia Cadena. 2016. *Dismantling Teen Pregnancy Prevention*. Albuquerque: Young Women United. https://youngwomenunited.org/wp-content/uploads/2016/06/ywu-dismantlingtpp-DEC2016-digital-interactive.pdf.

California State Auditor. 2014. "Sterilization of Female Inmates." June. 2016. https://www.auditor.ca.gov/pdfs/reports/2013-120.pdf.

Candie's Foundation. 2015. "Mission." Accessed February 24, 2016. http://www.candiesfoundation.org/aboutUs_Mission.

Carpenter, Laura, and Steven Epstein. 2012. "Sexual Health and Science." Paper presented at American Sociological Association conference Sociology of Sexualities: Assessing the State of the Field, Denver.

Carrillo, Hector. 2002. *The Night Is Young: Sexuality in Mexico in the Time of AIDS*. Chicago: University of Chicago Press.

Chaddha, Anmol, and William Julius Wilson. 2011. "'Way Down in the Hole': Systemic Urban Inequality and *The Wire.*" *Critical Inquiry* 38, (1): 164–88.

Charlton, Brittany M., Andrea L. Roberts, Margaret Rosario, Sabra L. Katz-Wise, Jerel P. Calzo, Donna Spiegelman, and S. Bryn Austin. 2018. "Teen Pregnancy Risk Factors among Young Women of Diverse Sexual Orientations." *Pediatrics* 141 (4): 1–10.

Charmaz, Kathy. 2014. *Constructing Grounded Theory*. 2nd edition. Thousand Oaks, CA: Sage.

Chavez, Leo. 2008. *The Latino Threat: Constructing Immigrants, Citizens, and the Nation*. Stanford, CA: Stanford University Press.

Cipolla, Cyd, Kristina Gupta, David A. Rubin, and Angela Willey, eds. 2017. *Queer Feminist Science Studies: A Reader*. Seattle: University of Washington Press.

Claire, Eli. 2017. *Brilliant Imperfection: Grappling with Cure*. Durham, NC: Duke University Press.

Clarke, Adele E. 2005. *Situational Analysis: Grounded Theory after the Postmodern Turn*. Thousand Oaks, CA: Sage.

Clarke, Adele E., Carrie Friese, and Rachel Washburn, eds. 2015. *Situational Analysis in Practice: Mapping Research with Grounded Theory*. Walnut Creek, CA: Left Coast Press.

Cohen, Cathy J. 1997. "Punks, Bulldaggers, and Welfare Queens: The Radical Potential of Queer Politics?" *GLQ: A Journal of Lesbian and Gay Studies* 3 (4): 437–65.

Cohen, Cathy J. 2019. "The Radical Potential of Queer?: Twenty Years Later." *GLQ: A Journal of Lesbian and Gay Studies* 25 (10): 140–44.

Coker, Tumaini R., S. Bryn Austin, and Mark A. Schuster. 2010. "The Health and Health Care of Lesbian, Gay, and Bisexual Adolescents." *Annual Review of Public Health* 31: 457–77.

Cole, Teju. 2012. "The White-Savior Industrial Complex." *Atlantic*. March 21. https://www.theatlantic.com/international/archive/2012/03/the-white-savior-industrial-complex/254843/.

Collins, Patricia Hill. 2000. *Black Feminist Thought: Knowledge, Consciousness, and the Politics of Empowerment*. New York: Routledge.

CSDH (Committee on the Social Determinants of Health). 2008. *Closing the Gap in a Generation: Health Equity through Action on the Social Determinants of Health; Final Report of the Commission on the Social Determinants of Health.* Geneva: World Health Organization.

Compton, D'Lane, Tey Meadow, and Kristin Schilt. 2018. *Other, Please Specify: Queer Methods in Sociology.* Oakland: University of California Press.

Connell, Catherine, and Sinnika Elliot. 2009. "Beyond the Birds and the Bees: Learning Inequality through Sexuality Education." *American Journal of Sexuality Education* 4 (2): 83–102.

Conrad, Ryan, ed. 2014. *Against Equality: Queer Revolution, Not Mere Inclusion.* Chico, CA: AK Press.

Coren, Ester, Jane Barlow, and Sarah Stewart-Brown. 2003. "The Effectiveness of Individual and Group-Based Parenting Programmes in Improving Outcomes for Teenage Mothers and Their Children: A Systematic Review." *Journal of Adolescence* 26 (1): 79–103.

Crosby, Richard A., and David R. Holtgrave. 2006. "The Protective Value of Social Capital against Teen Pregnancy: A State-Level Analysis." *Journal of Adolescent Health* 38 (5): 556–59.

Cunnington, Aubrey J. 2001. "What's So Bad about Teenage Pregnancy?" *Journal of Family Planning and Reproductive Health Care* 27(1): 36–41.

Daniel, Clare. 2017. *Mediating Morality: The Politics of Teen Pregnancy in the Post-welfare Era.* Amherst: University of Massachusetts Press.

Danziger, Sandra K. 2010. "The Decline of Cash Welfare and Implications for Social Policy and Poverty." *Annual Review of Sociology* 36: 523–45.

Davies, Bronwyn, and Peter Bansel. 2007. "Neoliberalism and Education." *International Journal of Qualitative Studies in Education* 20 (3): 247–59.

Dehlendorf, Christine, Rachel Ruskin, Kevin Grumbach, Eric Vittinghoff, Kirsten Bibbins-Domingo, Dean Schillinger, and Jody Steinauer. 2010. "Recommendations for Intrauterine Contraception: A Randomized Trial of the Effects of Patients' Race/Ethnicity and Socioeconomic Status." *American Journal of Obstetrics and Gynecology* 203 (4): 319-e1–319-e8.

Denzin, Norman K. 2008. *Qualitative Inquiry under Fire.* Walnut Creek, CA: Left Coast Press.

Dinshaw, Carolyn, Lee Edelman, Roderick A. Ferguson, Carla Freccero, Elizabeth Freeman, Judith Halberstam, Annamarie Jagose, Christopher S. Nealon, and Tan Hoang Nguyen. 2007. "Theorizing Queer Temporalities: A Roundtable Discussion." *GLQ: A Journal of Lesbian and Gay Studies* 13 (2): 177–95.

Downing, Roberta, Thomas A. LaVeist, and Heather E. Bullock. 2007. "Intersections of Ethnicity and Social Class in Provider Advice Regarding Reproductive Health." *American Journal of Public Health* 97 (10): 1803–7.

Duany, Jorge. 2000. "Nation on the Move: The Construction of Cultural Identities in Puerto Rico and the Diaspora." *American Ethnologist* 27 (1): 5–30.

Duggan, Lisa. 2003. *The Twilight of Equality? Neoliberalism, Cultural Politics, and the Attack on Democracy.* Boston: Beacon Press.

Duggan, Lisa, and José Esteban Muñoz. 2009. "Hope and Hopelessness: A Dialogue." *Women and Performance: A Journal of Feminist Theory* 19 (2): 275–83.

Edelman, Elijah Adiv, and Lal Zimman. 2014. "Boycunts and Bonus Holes: Trans Men's Bodies, Neoliberalism, and the Sexual Productivity of Genitals." *Journal of Homosexuality* 61 (5): 673–90.

Edin, Kathryn, and Maria Kefalas. 2005. *Promises I Can Keep: Why Poor Women Put Motherhood before Marriage.* Berkeley: University of California Press.

Edin, Kathryn, and H. Luke Shaefer. 2016. "20 Years since Welfare 'Reform.'" *Atlantic,* August 22, 2016. https://www.theatlantic.com/business/archive/2016/08/20-years-welfare-reform/496730/.

Elia, John P., and Jessica Tokunaga. 2015. "Sexuality Education: Implications for Health, Equity, and Social Justice in the United States. *Health Education* 115 (1): 105–20.

Elliott, Sinikka. 2012. *Not My Kid: What Parents Believe about the Sex Lives of their Teenagers.* New York: New York University Press.

Elliott, Sinikka. 2014. "'Who's to Blame?' Constructing the Responsible Sexual Agent in Neoliberal Sex Education." *Sexuality Research and Social Policy* 11 (3): 211–24.

Emerson, Robert M., Rachel I. Fretz, and Linda L. Shaw. 2011. *Writing Ethnographic Fieldnotes.* 2nd edition. Chicago: University of Chicago Press.

Eng, David L. 2010. *The Feeling of Kinship: Queer Liberalism and the Racialization of Intimacy.* Durham, NC: Duke University Press.

Epstein, Steven. 1994. "A Queer Encounter: Sociology and the Study of Sexuality." *Sociological Theory* 12: 188–202.

Epstein, Steven. 2003. "An Incitement to Discourse: Sociology and the History of Sexuality." *Sociological Forum* 18 (3): 485–502.

Epstein, Steven. 2018. "Governing Sexual Health: Bridging Bio-citizenship and Sexual Citizenship." In *Bio-citizenship: The Politics of Bodies, Governance, and Power,* edited by Kelly E. Happe, Jenell Johnson, and Marina Levina, 21–50. New York: New York University Press.

Epstein, Steven, and Laura Mamo. 2017. "The Proliferation of Sexual Health: Diverse Social Problems and the Legitimation of Sexuality." *Social Science and Medicine* 188: 176–90.

Erdmans, Mary Patrice, and Timothy Black. 2015. *On Becoming a Teen Mom: Life before Pregnancy.* Oakland: University of California Press.

Erickson, Pamela I., and Celia P. Kaplan. 1998. "Latinas and Abortion." In *The New Civil War: The Psychology, Culture, and Politics of Abortion,* edited by Linda J. Beckman and S. Marie Harvey, 133–55. Washington, DC: American Psychological Association.

Fahs, Breanne, and Sara I. McClelland. 2016. "When Sex and Power Collide: An Argument for Critical Sexuality Studies." *Journal of Sex Research* 53 (4–5): 392–416.

Farmer, Paul. 1996. "On Suffering and Structural Violence: A View from Below." *Daedalus* 125 (1): 261–83.

Ferguson, Roderick A. 2003. *Aberrations in Black: Toward a Queer of Color Critique.* Minneapolis: University of Minnesota Press.

Fershee, Kendra. 2009. "Hollow Promises for Pregnant Students: How the Regulations Governing Title IX Fail to Prevent Pregnancy Discrimination in School." *Indiana Law Review* 43: 79–237.

Fessler, Kathryn Bondy. 2003. "Social Outcomes of Early Childbearing: Important Considerations for the Provision of Clinical Care." *Journal of Midwifery and Women's Health* 48 (3): 178–85.

Fields, Jessica. 2008. *Risky Lessons: Sex Education and Social Inequality.* New Brunswick, NJ: Rutgers University Press.

Fine, Michelle. 1988. "Sexuality, Schooling, and Adolescent Females: The Missing Discourse of Desire." *Harvard Educational Review* 58 (1): 29–54.

Fine, Michelle, and Sara McClelland. 2006. "Sexuality Education and Desire: Still Missing after All These Years." *Harvard Educational Review* 76 (3): 297–338.

Flavin, Jeanne. 2008. *Our Bodies, Our Crimes: The Policing of Women's Reproduction in America.* New York: New York University Press.

Foucault, Michel. (1978) 1990. *The History of Sexuality,* Volume 1: *An Introduction.* Translated by Robert Hurley. New York: Vintage Books.

Foucault, Michel. 1980. "Truth and Power." In *Power/Knowledge: Selected Interviews and Other Writings, 1972–1977,* edited by Colin Gordon, 109–33. New York: Random House.

Fraser, Nancy, and Linda Gordon. 1994. "A Genealogy of Dependency: Tracing a Keyword of the US Welfare State." *Signs: Journal of Women in Culture and Society* 19 (2): 309–36.

Freeman, Elizabeth. 2010. *Time Binds: Queer Temporalities, Queer Histories.* Durham, NC: Duke University Press.

Freire, Paolo. 1998. *The Paulo Freire Reader,* edited by Ana Maria Araújo Freire and Donaldo Macedo. New York: Continuum.

Fuentes, Liza, Verónica Bayetti Flores, and Jessica Gonzalez-Rojas. 2010. *Removing Stigma: Toward a Complete Understanding of Young Latinas' Sexual Health.* New York: National Latina Institute for Reproductive Health.

Furstenberg, Frank E. 2003. "Teenage Childbearing as a Public Issue and Private Concern." *Annual Review of Sociology* 29: 23–39.

Furstenberg, Frank E. 2016. "Reconsidering Teenage Pregnancy and Parenthood." *Societies* 6 (4): 1–33.

Gadson, Alexis, Eloho Akpovi, and Pooja K. Mehta. 2017. "Exploring the Social Determinants of Racial/Ethnic Disparities in Prenatal Care Utilization and Maternal Outcome." *Seminars in Perinatology* 41 (5): 308–17.

Gamson, Joshua, and Dawne Moon. 2004. "The Sociology of Sexualities: Queer and Beyond." *Annual Review of Sociology* 30: 47–64.

García, Lorena. 2009. "Now Why Do You Want to Know about That? Heteronormativity, Racism, and Sexism in the Sexual (Mis)education of Latina Youth." *Gender & Society* 23 (4): 520–41.

García, Lorena. 2012. *Respect Yourself, Protect Yourself: Latina Girls and Sexual Identity.* New York: New York University Press.

Geronimus, Arline T. 1987. "On Teenage Childbearing and Neonatal Mortality in the United States." *Population and Development Review* 13 (2): 245–79.

Geronimus, Arline. T. 1996. "Black/White Differences in the Relationship of Maternal Age to Birthweight: A Population-Based Test of the Weathering Hypothesis." *Social Science and Medicine* 42 (4): 589–97.

Geronimus, Arline. T. 1997. "Teenage Childbearing and Personal Responsibility: An Alternative View." *Political Science Quarterly* 112 (3): 405–30.

Geronimus, Arline T. 2001. "Understanding and Eliminating Racial Inequalities in Women's Health in the United States: The Role of the Weathering Conceptual Framework." *Journal of the American Medical Women's Association* 56 (4): 133–36.

Geronimus, Arline. T. 2003. "Damned If You Do: Culture, Identity, Privilege, and Teenage Childbearing in the United States." *Social Science and Medicine* 57 (5): 881–93.

Geronimus, Arline. T. 2004. "Teenage Childbearing as Cultural Prism." *British Medical Bulletin* 69 (1): 155–66.

Geronimus, Arline T., and Sanders Korenman. 1993. "Maternal Youth or Family Background? On the Health Disadvantages of Infants with Teenage Mothers. *American Journal of Epidemiology* 137 (2): 213–25.

Gill, Rosalind, and Christina Scharff, eds. 2013. *New Femininities: Postfeminism, Neoliberalism, and Subjectivity.* New York: Springer.

Gilson, Dave. 2011. "Our Industrial-Complex Complex." *Mother Jones.* January 17.http://www.motherjones.com/mojo/2011/01/eisenhower-military-industrial-complex.

Gilmore, Ruth Wilson. 2017. "In the Shadow of the Shadow State." In *The Revolution Will Not Be Funded: Beyond the Non-profit Industrial Complex,* edited by INCITE! Women of Color Against Violence, 41–52. Durham, NC: Duke University Press.

Glanz, Karen, Barbara Rimer, and K. Viswanath, eds. 2008. *Health Behavior and Health Education: Theory, Research, and Practice.* 4th edition. San Francisco: Jossey-Bass.

Gold, Rachel B. 2014. "Guarding against Coercion While Ensuring Access: A Delicate Balance." *Guttmacher Policy Review* 17 (3): 8–14.

Goldberg, Shoshana K., Bianka M. Reese, and Carolyn T. Halpern. 2016. "Teen Pregnancy among Sexual Minority Women: Results from the National Longitudinal Study of Adolescent to Adult Health." *Journal of Adolescent Health* 59 (4 (): 429–37.

Goldenberg, Maya. J. 2006. "On Evidence and Evidence-Based Medicine: Lessons from the Philosophy of Science." *Social Science and Medicine* 62 (11): 2621–32.

Gómez, Anu Manchikanti. 2014. "To Control or Be Controlled: Young Black and Latina Women's Perspectives on Intrauterine Devices." *Contraception* 90 (3): 348.

Gómez, Anu Manchikanti, and Mikaela Wapman. 2017. "Under (Implicit) Pressure: Young Black and Latina Women's Perceptions of Contraceptive Care." *Contraception* 96 (4): 221–26.

Gómez, Anu Manchikanti, Emily S. Mann, and Vanessa Torres. 2018. "'It would have control over me instead of me having control': Intrauterine Devices and the Meaning of Reproductive Freedom." *Critical Public Health* 28 (2): 190–200.

Gómez, Anu Manchikanti, Liza Fuentes, and Amy Allina. 2014. "Women or LARC First? Reproductive Autonomy and the Promotion of Long-Acting Reversible Contraceptive Methods." *Perspectives on Sexual and Reproductive Health* 46 (3): 171–75.

Gómez, Anu Manchikanti, Stephanie Arteaga, Natalie Ingraham, Jennet Arcara, and Elodia Villaseñor. 2018. "It's Not Planned, but Is It Okay? The Acceptability of Unplanned Pregnancy among Young People." *Women's Health Issues* 28 (5): 408–14.

González-López, Gloria, and Salvador Vidal-Ortiz. 2008. "Latinas and Latinos, Sexuality, and Society: A Critical Sociological Perspective." In *Latinas/os in the United States: Changing the Face of America,* edited by H. Rodríguez, R. Sáenz, and C. Menjívar, 308–24. New York: Springer.

Gopinath, Gayatri. 2005. *Impossible Desires: Queer Diasporas and South Asian Public Cultures.* Durham, NC: Duke University Press.

Graham, Hilary, and Elizabeth McDermott. 2006. "Qualitative Research and the Evidence Base of Policy: Insights from Studies of Teenage Mothers in the UK." *Journal of Social Policy* 35 (1): 21–37.

Green, Judith, and Ronald Labonte. 2007. "Introduction: From Critique to Engagement; Why Critical Public Health Matters." In *Critical Perspectives in Public Health,* edited by Judith Green and Ronald Labonte, 1–12. New York: Routledge.

Grzanka, Patrick R., Emily S. Mann, and Sinikka Elliott. 2016. "The Neoliberalism Wars, or Notes on the Persistence of Neoliberalism." *Sexuality Research and Social Policy* 13 (4): 297–307.

Gubrium, Aline C. 2009. "Digital Storytelling: An Emergent Method for Health Promotion Research and Practice." *Health Promotion Practice* 10 (2): 186–91.

Gubrium, Aline C., Amy L. Hill, and Sarah Flicker. 2014. "A Situated Practice of Ethics for Participatory Visual and Digital Methods in Public Health Research and Practice: A Focus on Digital Storytelling." *American Journal of Public Health* 104(9): 1606–14.

Gubrium, Aline C., and Mim Shafer. 2014. "Sensual Sexuality Education with Young Parenting Women." *Health Education Research* 29 (4): 649–61.

Gubrium, Aline C., Emily S. Mann, Sonya Borrero, Christine Dehlendorf, Jessica Fields, Arline T. Geronimus, Anu M. Gómez, et al. 2016. "Realizing Reproductive Health Equity Needs More than Long-Acting Reversible Contraception (LARC)." *American Journal of Public Health* 106 (1): 18–19.

Gubrium, Jaber F., and James A. Holstein. 2009. *Analyzing Narrative Reality.* Thousand Oaks, CA: Sage.

Guglielmo, Letizia. 2013. *MTV and Teen Pregnancy: Critical Essays on 16 and Pregnant and Teen Mom.* Lanham, MD: Scarecrow Press.

Gutiérrez, Elena R. 2008. *Fertile Matters: The Politics of Mexican-Origin Women's Reproduction.* Austin: University of Texas Press.

Halberstam, Jack. 2005. *In a Queer Time and Place: Transgender Bodies, Subcultural Lives.* New York: New York University Press.

Hammonds, Evelynn, and Banu Subramaniam. 2003. "A Conversation on Feminist Science Studies." *Signs: Journal of Women in Culture and Society* 28 (3): 923–44.

Hao, Lingxin, and Andrew J. Cherlin. 2004. "Welfare Reform and Teenage Pregnancy, Childbirth, and School Dropout." *Journal of Marriage and Family* 66 (1): 179–94.

Haraway, Donna. 1988. "Situated Knowledges: The Science Question in Feminism and the Privilege of Partial Perspective." *Feminist studies* 14 (3): 575–99.

Harding, Sandra G. 1986. *The Science Question in Feminism.* Ithaca, NY: Cornell University Press.

Hesse-Biber, Sharlene Nagy. 2007. "The Practice of In-Depth Feminist Interviewing." In *Feminist Perspectives on Social Research,* edited by Sharlene Nagy Hesse-Biber and Michelle L. Yaiser, 111–48. New York: Oxford University Press.

Higgins, Jenny A. 2014. "Celebration Meets Caution: Long Acting Reversible Contraception (LARC)'s Boons, Potential Busts, and the Benefits of a Reproductive Justice Approach." *Contraception* 89 (4): 237–41.

Higgins, Jenny A., and Nicole K. Smith. 2016. "The Sexual Acceptability of Contraception: Reviewing the Literature and Building a New Concept." *Journal of Sex Research* 53 (4–5): 417–56.

Higgins, Jenny A., Renee D. Kramer, and Kristin M. Ryder. 2016. "Provider Bias in Long-Acting Reversible Contraception (LARC) Promotion and Removal: Perceptions of Young Adult Women." *American Journal of Public Health* 106 (11): 1932–37.

Hoffman, Saul. 2008. *By the Numbers: The Public Costs of Teen Childbearing.* Washington, DC: National Campaign to Prevent Teen Pregnancy.

Hoffman, Saul. 2015. "Teen Childbearing and Economics: A Short History of a 25-year Research Love Affair." *Societies* 5(3): 646–63.

Hoffman, Saul, and Rebecca Maynard, eds. 2008. *Kids Having Kids: Economic Costs and Social Consequences of Teen Pregnancy.* Washington, DC: Urban Institute.

Hofrichter, Richard. 2003. "The Politics of Health Inequities: Contested Terrain." In *Health and Social Justice: Politics, Ideology, and Inequity in the Distribution of Disease,* edited by Richard Hofrichter, 1–56. San Francisco: Jossey-Bass.

Holtgrave, David R., and Richard A. Crosby. 2003. "Social Capital, Poverty, and Income Inequality as Predictors of Gonorrhea, Syphilis, Chlamydia, and AIDS Case Rates in the United States." *Sexually Transmitted Infections* 79 (1): 62–64.

Hong, Grace Kyungwon, and Roderick A. Ferguson, eds. 2011. *Strange Affinities: The Gender and Sexual Politics of Comparative Racialization.* Durham, NC: Duke University Press.

Hotz, V. Joseph, Susan McElroy, and Seth Sanders. 2005. "Teenage Childbearing and Its Life Cycle Consequences." *Journal of Human Resources* 40 (3): 683–715.

INCITE! Women of Color Against Violence. 2017. *The Revolution Will Not Be Funded: Beyond the Non-profit Industrial Complex.* Durham, NC: Duke University Press.

Irvine, Janice M. 2004. *Talk about Sex: The Battles over Sex Education in the United States.* Berkeley: University of California Press.

Israel, Barbara, Eugenia Eng, Amy J. Schultz, and Edith A. Parker. 2018. *Methods for Community-Based Participatory Research for Health.* 2nd edition. San Francisco: Jossey Bass.

Jeffries, William L., Gary Marks, Jennifer Lauby, Christopher S. Murrill, and Gregorio A. Millett. 2013. "Homophobia Is Associated with Sexual Behavior That Increases Risk of Acquiring and Transmitting HIV Infection among Black Men Who Have Sex with Men." *AIDS and Behavior* 17 (4): 1442–53.

Jerman, Jenna, Rachel K. Jones, and Tsuyoshi Onda. 2010. *Characteristics of U.S. Abortion Patients in 2014 and Changes since 2008.* New York: Guttmacher Institute.

Johnson, E. Patrick. 2001. "'Quare' Studies, or (Almost) Everything I Know about Queer Studies I Learned from My Grandmother." *Text and Performance Quarterly* 21 (1): 1–25.

Jones, Camara Phyllis. 2000. "Levels of Racism: A Theoretic Framework and a Gardener's Tale." *American Journal of Public Health* 90 (8): 1212–15.

Jones, Jo, William Mosher, and Kimberly Daniels. 2012. "Current Contraceptive Use in the United States, 2006–2010, and Changes in Patterns of Use since 1995." *National Health Statistics Reports* 18 (60): 1–25.

Kaiser Family Foundation. 2003. "Teen and TANF: How Adolescents Fare under the Nation's Welfare Program." December 2003. https://kaiserfamily foundation.files.wordpress.com/2013/01/teens-and-tanf-how-adolescents-fare-under-the-nation-s-welfare-program.pdf.

Kalil, Ariel, and Sandra K. Danziger. 2000. "How Teen Mothers Are Faring under Welfare Reform." *Journal of Social Issues* 56 (4): 775–98.

Kang, Miliann. 2010. *The Managed Hand: Race, Gender, and the Body in Beauty Service Work.* Berkeley: University of California Press.

Kania, John, and Mark Kramer. 2011. "Essentials of Social Innovation: Collective Impact." *Stanford Social Innovation Review* (winter).

Kaye, Kelleen, Katherine Suellentrop, and Corinna Sloup. 2009. *The Fog Zone: How Misperceptions, Magical Thinking, and Ambivalence Put Young Adults at Risk for Unintended Pregnancy.* Washington, DC: National Campaign to Prevent Teen and Unplanned Pregnancy.

Kearney, Melissa S., and Phillip B. Levine. 2012. "Why Is the Teen Birth Rate in the United States So High and Why Does It Matter?" *Journal of Economic Perspectives* 26 (2): 141–63.

Kearney, Melissa S., and Phillip B. Levine. 2015. "Media Influences on Social Outcomes: The Impact of MTV's *16 and Pregnant* on Teen Childbearing." *American Economic Review* 105 (12): 3597–3632.

Kelly, Deirdre M. 1996. "Stigma Stories: Four Discourses about Teen Mothers, Welfare, and Poverty." *Youth and Society* 27 (4): 421–49.

Kelly, Deirdre. M. 2000. *Pregnant with Meaning: Teen Mothers and the Politics of Inclusive Schooling.* New York: Peter Lang.

King, Jamilah. 2013. "New York City Tries to Shame Its Teens into Not Having Babies." *Colorlines,* March 6. https://www.colorlines.com/articles/new-york-city-tries-shame-its-teens-not-having-babies.

Kirby, Douglas B. 2007. *Emerging Answers 2007: Research Findings on Programs to Reduce Teen Pregnancy and Sexually Transmitted Diseases.* Washington, DC: National Campaign to Prevent Teen and Unplanned Pregnancy.

Kirby, Douglas B. 2008. "The Impact of Abstinence and Comprehensive Sex and STD/HIV Education Programs on Adolescent Sexual Behavior." *Sexuality Research and Social Policy* 5 (3): 18–27.

Kishore, Nishant, Domingo Marqués, Ayesha Mahmud, Mathew V. Kiang, Irmary Rodriguez, Arlan Fuller, Peggy Ebner, et al. 2018. "Mortality in Puerto Rico after Hurricane Maria." *New England Journal of Medicine* 379 (2): 162–70.

Klein, Johnathan D. 2005. "Adolescent Pregnancy: Current Trends and Issues." *Pediatrics* 116 (1): 281–86.

Kohatsu, Neal D., Jennifer G. Robinson, and James C. Torner. 2004. "Evidence-Based Public Health: An Evolving Concept." *American Journal of Preventive Medicine* 27 (5): 417–21.

Kost, Kathryn, and Stanley Henshaw. 2014. *US Teenage Pregnancies, Births, and Abortions, 2010: National and State Trends by Age, Race and Ethnicity.* New York: Guttmacher Institute.

Kramer, Karen L., and Jane B. Lancaster. 2010. "Teen Motherhood in Cross-Cultural Perspective." *Annals of Human Biology* 37 (5): 613–28.

Kristof, Nicholas. 2014. "Politicians, Teens, and Birth Control." *New York Times,* November 12, 2014. http://www.nytimes.com/2014/11/13/opinion/nicholas-kristof-politicians-teens-and-birth-control.html?_r=0.

Kristof, Nicholas, and Sheryl WuDunn. 2010. *Half the Sky: Turning Oppression into Opportunity for Women Worldwide.* New York: Vintage.

Kumar, Anuradha, Leila Hessini, and Ellen M. Mitchell. 2009. "Conceptualising Abortion Stigma." *Culture, Health, and Sexuality* 11 (6): 625–39.

Kunzel, Regina. 1993. *Fallen Women, Problem Girls: Unmarried Mothers and the Professionalization of Social Work, 1890–1945.* New Haven, CT: Yale University Press.

Labonte, Ronald, and Ann Robertson. 1996. "Delivering the Goods, Showing Our Stuff: The Case for a Constructivist Paradigm for Health Promotion Research and Practice." *Health Education Quarterly* 23 (4): 431–47.

Labonte, Ronald, Michael Polanyi, Nazeem Muhajarine, Tom McIntosh, and Allison Williams. 2005. "Beyond the Divides: Towards Critical Population Health Research." *Critical Public Health* 15 (1): 5–17.

Lake Research Associates. 2011. "Poll: Latino Voters Hold Compassionate Views on Abortion." National Latina Institute for Reproductive Justice. November 30. http://latinainstitute.org/sites/default/files/Latino AbortionAttitudesPolling.pdf.

Lareau, Annette. 2015. "Cultural Knowledge and Social Inequality." *American Sociological Review* 80 (1): 1–27.

Lawlor, Debbie, and Mary Shaw. 2002. "Too Much Too Young? Teenage Pregnancy Is Not a Public Health Problem." *International Journal of Epidemiology* 31 (3): 552.

LeBesco, Kathleen. 2011. "Neoliberalism, Public Health, and the Moral Perils of Fatness." *Critical Public Health* 21 (2): 153–64.

Lesko, Nancy. 2012. *Act Your Age! A Cultural Construction of Adolescence.* 2nd edition. New York: Routledge.

Lincoln, Richard, Frederick S. Jaffe, and Linda Ambrose. 1976. *11 Million Teenagers: What Can Be Done about the Epidemic of Adolescent Pregnancies in the United States*. New York: Alan Guttmacher Institute.

Lindley, Lisa, and Katrina Walsemann. 2015. "Sexual Orientation and Risk of Pregnancy among New York City High-School Students." *American Journal of Public Health* 105 (7): 1379–86.

Littlejohn, Krystale E. 2012. "Hormonal Contraceptive Use and Discontinuation Because of Dissatisfaction: Differences by Race and Education." *Demography* 49 (4): 1433–52.

Littlejohn, Krystale E. 2013. "'It's those pills that are ruining me': Gender and the Social Meanings of Hormonal Contraceptive Side Effects." *Gender and Society* 27 (6): 843–63.

López, Ian Haney. 2014. *Dog Whistle Politics*. New York: Oxford University Press.

López, Iris Ofelia. 2008. *Matters of Choice: Puerto Rican Women's Struggle for Reproductive Freedom*. New Brunswick, NJ: Rutgers University Press.

Love, Heather. 2016. "Queer Messes." *WSQ: Women's Studies Quarterly* 44 (3): 345–49.

Luker, Kristin. 1997. *Dubious Conceptions: The Politics of Teenage Pregnancy*. Cambridge, MA: Harvard University Press.

Luna, Zakiya, and Kristin Luker. 2013. "Reproductive Justice." *Annual Review of Law and Social Science* 9: 327–52.

Lupton, Deborah. 2015. "The Pedagogy of Disgust: The Ethical, Moral, and Political Implications of Using Disgust in Public Health Campaigns." *Critical Public Health* 25 (1): 4–14.

Luttrell, Wendy. 2003. *Pregnant Bodies, Fertile Minds: Gender, Race, and the Schooling of Pregnant Teens*. New York: Routledge.

Malone, Gloria. 2013. "I Was a Teen Mom and the NYC Teen Pregnancy Ads Miss the Point." *Rewire News*, March 13, 2013. https://rewire.news /article/2013/03/13/i-was-a-teen-mom-and-the-nyc-teen-pregnancy-ads-miss-the-point/.

Mamo, Laura. 2007. *Queering Reproduction: Achieving Pregnancy in the Age of Technoscience*. Durham, NC: Duke University Press.

Mamo, Laura, and Jennifer R. Fishman. 2013. "Why Justice? Introduction to the Special Issue on Entanglements of Science, Ethics, and Justice." *Science, Technology, and Human Values* 38 (2): 159–75.

Manalansan, Martin. 2014. "The 'Stuff' of Archives: Mess, Migration, and Queer Lives." *Radical History Review* 120: 94–107.

Manalansan, Martin. 2018. "Messing Up Sex: The Promises and Possibilities of Queer of Color Critique." *Sexualities* 21 (8): 1287–90.

Mananzala, Rickie, and Dean Spade. 2008. "The Nonprofit Industrial Complex and Trans Resistance." *Sexuality Research and Social Policy* 5 (1): 53–71.

Manlove, Jennifer. 1998. "The Influence of High School Dropout and School Disengagement on the Risk of School-Age Pregnancy." *Journal of Research on Adolescence* 8 (2): 187–220.

Mann, Emily S. 2013. "Regulating Latina Youth Sexualities through Community Health Centers: Discourses and Practices of Sexual Citizenship." *Gender and Society* 27 (5): 681–703.

Mann, Emily S. 2016. "Latina Girls, Sexual Agency, and the Contradictions of Neoliberalism." *Sexuality Research and Social Policy* 13 (4): 330–40.

Mann, Emily S. 2018. "Sexual Citizenship and Everyday Feelings." In *Youth Sexualities: Public Feelings and Contemporary Cultural Politics*, Volume 1, edited by Susan Talburt, 183–206. Santa Barbara, CA: Praeger.

Mann, Emily S., and Patrick R. Grzanka. 2018. "Agency-Without-Choice: The Visual Rhetorics of Long-Acting Reversible Contraception Promotion." *Symbolic Interaction* 41 (3): 334–56.

Mann, Emily S., Vanessa Cardona, and Cynthia A. Gómez. 2015. "Beyond the Discourse of Reproductive Choice: Narratives of Pregnancy Resolution among Latina/o Teenage Parents. *Culture, Health and Sexuality* 17 (9): 1090–104.

Marmot, Michael. 2005. "Social Determinants of Health Inequalities." *Lancet* 365 (9464): 1099–1104.

Marmot, Michael. 2007. "Achieving Health Equity: From Root Causes to Fair Outcomes." *Lancet* 370 (9593): 1153–63.

Martin, Joyce A., Brady E. Hamilton, Michelle J. K. Osterman, Anne K. Driscoll, and T. J. Matthews. 2017. "Births: Final data for 2015." *National Vital Statistics Reports* 66 (1): 1–70.

MATP (Massachusetts Alliance on Teen Pregnancy). 2010. *Expecting Success: How Policymakers and Educators Can Help Teen Parents Stay in School.* Boston: MATP.

Matthews, T. J., Marian F. MacDorman, and Marie E. Thomas. 2015. "Infant Mortality Statistics from the 2013 Period Linked Birth/Infant Death Data." *National Vital Statistics Reports* 64 (9): 1–30.

Mayberry, Maralee, Banu Subramaniam, and Lisa H. Weasel, eds. 2003. *Feminist Science Studies: A New Generation.* New York: Routledge.

McCall, Leslie. 2005. "The Complexity of Intersectionality." *Signs: Journal of Women in Culture and Society* 30 (3): 1771–1800.

McClain, Dani. 2015. "Birth-Control Experts Are Wary of Coercive Tactics in the Push for IUD Use." *Nation*, December 15. http://www.thenation.com /article/birth-control-experts-wary-of-coercive-tactics-in-push-for-iud-use/.

McClelland, Sara I., and Michelle M. Fine. 2008a. "Embedded Science: Critical Analysis of Abstinence-Only Evaluation Research." *Cultural Studies Critical Methodologies* 8 (1): 50–81.

McClelland, Sara I., and Michelle M. Fine. 2008b. "Writing on Cellophane: Studying Teen Women's Sexual Desires, Inventing Methodological Release Points." In *The Methodological Dilemma: Creative, Critical, and Collaborative Approaches to Qualitative Research*, edited by Sara I. McClelland and Michelle M. Fine, 232–60. New York: Routledge.

McKenzie, Mia. 2014. *Black Girl Dangerous: On Race, Queerness, Class, and Gender*. Oakland, CA: BGD Press.

Meadow, Tey. 2018. "The Mess: Vulnerability as Ethnographic Practice." In *Other, Please Specify: Queer Methods in Sociology*, edited by D'Lane Compton, Tey Meadow, and Kristen Schilt, 154–66. Oakland: University of California Press.

Meckel, Richard. 1990. *Save the Babies: American Public Health Reform and the Prevention of Infant Mortality, 1850–1929*. Baltimore: Johns Hopkins University Press.

Menzel, Annie. 2014. "The Political Life of Black Infant Mortality." PhD dissertation, University of Washington.

Metzel, Jonathan, and Anna Kirkland, eds. 2010. *Against Health: How Health Became the New Morality*. New York: New York University Press.

Mink, Gwendolyn. 1998. *Welfare's End*. Ithaca, NY: Cornell University Press.

Molina, Natalia. 2006. *Fit to Be Citizens? Public Health and Race in Los Angeles, 1879–1939*. Berkeley: University of California Press.

Morse, Janice M. 2015. "Data Were Saturated." *Qualitative Health Research* 25 (5): 587–88.

Muñoz, José Esteban. 1999. *Disidentifications: Queers of Color and the Performance of Politics*. Minneapolis: University of Minnesota Press.

Muñoz, José Esteban. 2009. *Cruising Utopia: The Then and There of Queer Futurity*. New York: New York University Press.

Murphy, Michelle. 2012. *Seizing the Means of Reproduction: Entanglements of Feminism, Health, and Technoscience*. Durham, NC: Duke University Press.

Nader, Laura. 1972. "Up the Anthropologist: Perspectives Gained from Studying Up." In *Reinventing Anthropology*, edited by Dell Hymes, 284–311. New York: Vintage Books.

Naples, Nancy A. 2004. "The Outsider Phenomenon." In *Feminist Perspectives on Social Research*, edited by Sharlene Nagy Hesse-Biber and Michelle L. Yaiser, 373–81. New York: Oxford University Press.

Nash, Jennifer C. 2019. *Black Feminism Reimagined: After Intersectionality*. Durham, NC: Duke University Press.

National Campaign to Prevent Teen and Unplanned Pregnancy. 2016. "Why It Matters." *Power to Decide*. Accessed March 14, 2016. https:// thenationalcampaign.org/why-it-matters.

National Latina Institute for Reproductive Health. 2017. "Contraception: Issue Brief." July. Accessed February 19, 2019. http://latinainstitute.org/sites/default/files/NLIRH-Contraception-IssueBrief-R2.pdf.

Nettleton, Sarah, and Robin Bunton. 1995. "Sociological Critiques of Health Promotion." In *The Sociology of Health Promotion: Critical Analyses of Consumption, Lifestyle, and Risk*, edited by Robin Bunton and Roger Burrows, 41–57. London: Routledge.

North, Anna. 2012. "The Anti–Nicolas Kristof Backlash." *Buzzfeed*, October 3, 2012. http://www.buzzfeed.com/annanorth/the-anti-nicholas-kristof-backlash#.fha9lJaQD.

Omi, Michael, and Howard Winant. 2015. *Racial Formation in the United States*. 3rd edition. New York: Routledge.

Ott, Mary A., Gina S. Sucato, Paula K. Braverman, William P. Adelman, Elizabeth M. Alderman, Cora C. Breuner, et al. 2014. "Contraception for Adolescents." *Pediatrics* 134 (4), e1257–e1281.

Pascoe, C. J. 2012. *Dude, You're a Fag: Masculinity and Sexuality in High School*. With a new preface. Berkeley: University of California Press.

Pazol, Karen, Andreea Creanga, and Denise Jamieson. 2015. "Abortion Surveillance—United States, 2012." *Morbidity and Mortality Weekly Report Surveillance Summary* 64 (November 27): 1–40.

Penman-Aguilar, Ana, Marion Carter, Christine Snead, and Athena Kourtis. 2013. "Socioeconomic Disadvantage as a Social Determinant of Teen Childbearing in the US." *Public Health Reports* 128 (1): 5–22.

Pérez, Gina. 2004. *The Near Northwest Side Story: Migration, Displacement, and Puerto Rican Families*. Berkeley: University of California Press.

Perez, Michelle Salazar, and Gaile S. Cannella. 2011. "Using Situational Analysis for Critical Qualitative Research Purposes." In *Qualitative Inquiry and Global Crises*, edited by Norman K Denzin and Michael D. Giardina, 97–117. Walnut Creek, CA: Left Coast Press.

Petersen, Alan. R., and Deborah Lupton. 1996. *The New Public Health: Health and Self in the Age of Risk*. London: Sage.

Phelan, Jo C., and Bruce G. Link. 2015. "Is Racism a Fundamental Cause of Inequalities in Health?" *Annual Review of Sociology* 41: 311–30.

Phelan, Jo C., Bruce G. Link, and Parisa Tehranifar. 2010. "Social Conditions as Fundamental Causes of Health Inequalities: Theory, Evidence, and Policy Implications." *Journal of Health and Social Behavior* 51 (1): S28–S40.

Pillow, Wanda S. 2003a. "'Bodies Are Dangerous': Using Feminist Genealogy as Policy Studies Methodology." *Journal of Education Policy* 18 (2): 145–59.

Pillow, Wanda S. 2003b. "Confession, Catharsis, or Cure? Rethinking the Uses of Reflexivity as Methodological Power in Qualitative Research." *International Journal of Qualitative Studies in Education* 16 (2): 175–96.

Pillow, Wanda S. 2004. *Unfit Subjects: Educational Policy and the Teen Mother.* New York: Routledge.

Pillow, Wanda S. 2006a. "Exposed Methodology: The Body as a Deconstructive Practice." In *Emergent Methods in Social Research,* edited by Sharlene Nagy Hesse-Biber and Patricia Leavy, 213–29. San Francisco: Sage.

Pillow, Wanda S. 2006b. "Teen Pregnancy and Education." *Educational Policy* 20 (1): 59–84.

Pillow, Wanda S. 2015. "Policy Temporality and Marked Bodies: Feminist Praxis amongst the Ruins." *Critical Studies in Education* 56 (1): 55–70.

Pillow, Wanda S., and Cris Mayo. 2007. "Toward Understandings of Feminist Ethnography." In *Handbook of Feminist Research: Theory and Praxis,* edited by Sharlene Nagy Hesse-Biber, 155–71. Thousand Oaks, CA: Sage.

Popay, Jennie, and Gareth Williams. 1996. "Public Health Research and Lay Knowledge." *Social Science and Medicine* 42 (5): 759–68.

Rankin, Lauren. 2014. "New York's Teen Pregnancy Campaign Quietly Gets Made Over, Still Misses the Mark." *Rewire News,* March 21, 2014. https://rewire.news/article/2014/03/21/new-yorks-teen-pregnancy-campaign-quietly-gets-made-still-misses-mark/.

Ray, Ranita. 2017. "Identity of Distance: How Economically Marginalized Black and Latina Women Navigate Risk Discourse and Employ Feminist Ideals." *Social Problems* 65 (4): 456–72.

Ray, Ranita. 2018. *The Making of a Teenage Service Class: Poverty and Mobility in an American City.* Oakland: University of California Press.

Reisner, Sari L., Tonia Poteat, JoAnne Keatley, Mauro Cabral, Tampose Mothopeng, Emilia Dunham, Claire E. Holland, Ryan Max, and Stefan D. Baral. 2016. "Global Health Burden and Needs of Transgender Populations: A Review." *Lancet* 388 (10042): 412–36.

Rich-Edwards, Janet W. 2002. "Teen Pregnancy Is Not a Public Health Crisis in the United States. It Is Time We Made It One." *International Journal of Epidemiology* 31 (3): 555–56.

Rich-Edwards, Janet W., Stephen L. Buka, Robert T. Brennan, and Felton Earls. 2003. "Diverging Associations of Maternal Age with Low Birthweight for Black and White Mothers." *International Journal of Epidemiology* 32 (1): 83–90.

Rios, Victor. 2011. *Punished: Policing the Lives of Black and Latino Boys.* New York: New York University Press.

Roberts, Dorothy. 1997. *Killing the Black Body: Race, Reproduction, and the Meaning of Liberty.* New York: Pantheon.

Roberts, Dorothy. 2002. *Shattered Bonds: The Color of Child Welfare.* New York: Basic Books.

Roberts, Dorothy. 2011. *Fatal Invention: How Science, Politics, and Big Business Re-create Race in the Twenty-First Century.* New York: The New Press.

Rodríquez, Dylan. 2017. "The Political Logic of the Non-profit Industrial Complex." In *The Revolution Will Not Be Funded: Beyond the Non-profit Industrial Complex,* edited by INCITE! Women of Color Against Violence, 21–40. Durham, NC: Duke University Press.

Romero, Lisa, Karen Pazol, Lee Warner, Lorrie Gavin, Susan Moskosky, Ghenet Besera, et al. 2015. "Vital Signs: Trends in Use of Long-Acting Reversible Contraception among Teens Aged 15–19 Years Seeking Contraceptive Services—United States, 2005–2013." *Morbidity and Mortality Weekly Report* 64 (13): 363–69.

Romo, Laura F., Erum Nadeem, and Claudia Kouyoumdjian. 2009. "Latina/o Parent-Adolescent Communication about Sexuality." In *Latina/o Sexualities: Probing Powers, Passions, Practices, and Policies,* edited by Marysol Asencio, 62–73. New Brunswick, NJ: Rutgers University Press.

Ross, Loretta. 2006. "Understanding Reproductive Justice: Transforming the Pro-choice Movement." *Off Our Backs* 36 (4): 14–19.

Ross, Loretta, and Rickie Solinger. 2017. *Reproductive Justice: An Introduction.* Oakland: University of California Press.

Rothman, Kenneth, Sander Greenland, and Timothy L. Lash. 2008. *Modern Epidemiology.* Philadelphia: Lippincott, Williams and Wilkins.

Ryan, Susan M. 2004. *The Grammar of Good Intentions: Race and the Antebellum Culture of Benevolence.* Ithaca, NY: Cornell University Press.

Sampson, Robert J., Jeffrey D. Morenoff, and Thomas Gannon-Rowley. 2002. "Assessing 'Neighborhood Effects': Social Processes and New directions in Research." *Annual Review of Sociology* 28 (1): 443–78.

Sandstrom, Kent, and Tara Opsal. 2013. "Introduction to the Special Issue: Grappling with 'The Feminist Ethnographer's Dilemma.'" *Journal of Contemporary Ethnography* 42 (4): 383–93.

Santelli, John, Mary A. Ott, Maureen Lyon, Jennifer Rogers, Daniel Summers, and Rebecca Schleifer. 2006. "Abstinence and Abstinence-Only Education: A Review of US Policies and Programs." *Journal of Adolescent Health* 38 (1): 72–81.

Scally, Gabriel. 2002. "Too Much Too Young? Teenage Pregnancy Is a Public Health, Not a Clinical, Problem." *International Journal of Epidemiology* 31 (3): 554–55.

Schalet, Amy. 2011. *Not under My Roof: Parents, Teens, and the Culture of Sex.* Chicago: University of Chicago Press.

Scharrón-Del Río, María R., and Alan A. Aja. 2015. "The Case FOR 'Latinx: Why Intersectionality Is Not a Choice." *Latino Rebels,* December 5, 2015. http://www.latinorebels.com/2015/12/05/the-case-for-latinx-why-intersectionality-is-not-a-choice/.

Schrecker, Ted. 2016. "'Neoliberal Epidemics' and Public Health: Sometimes the World Is Less Complicated Than It Appears." *Critical Public Health* 26 (5): 477–80.

Schroder, Elizabeth. 2013. "Chicago's 'Pregnant Men' Ads: Flipping the Dialogue on Men and Teen Pregnancy Prevention." *Rewire News,* May 22, 2013. https://rewire.news/article/2013/05/22/chicagos-pregnant-men-ads-flipping-the-dialogue-on-men-and-teen-pregnancy-prevention/.

Schultz, Katherine. 2001. "Constructing Failure, Narrating Success: Rethinking the 'Problem' of Teen Pregnancy." *Teachers College Record* 103 (4): 582–607.

Secura, Gina M., Tessa Madden, Colleen McNicholas, Jennifer Mullersman, Christina M. Buckel, Qiuhong Zhao, and Jeffrey F. Peipert. 2014. "Provision of No-Cost, Long-Acting Contraception and Teenage Pregnancy." *New England Journal of Medicine* 371 (14): 1316–23.

SEICUS 2015a. "Abstinence Only until Marriage Q & A." Sexuality Information and Educator Council of the United States. Accessed January 4, 2016. http://www.siecus.org/index.cfm?fuseaction=page.viewpage&pageid=522&grandparentID=477&parentID=523.

SEICUS. 2015b. "Sexuality Education Q & A." Sexuality Information and Educator Council of the United States. Accessed January 4, 2016. http://www.siecus.org/index.cfm?fuseaction=page.viewpage&pageid=521&grandparentID=477&parentID=514.

Shim, Janet K. 2014. *Heart-Sick: The Politics of Risk, Inequality, and Heart Disease.* New York: New York University Press.

Silliman, Jael, Marlene Gerber Fried, Loretta Ross, and Elena Gutiérrez. 2016. *Undivided Rights: Women of Color Organize for Reproductive Justice,* 2nd edition. Chicago: Haymarket Books.

Silver, Lauren. 2008. "The Politics of Regulation: Adolescent Mothers and the Social Context of Resiliency." *Voices* 8 (1): 1–11.

Singh, Gopal K., and Peter C. van Dyck. 2010. *Infant Mortality in the United States, 1935–2007: Over Seven Decades of Progress and Disparities.* Rockville, MD: Health Resources and Services Administration, Maternal and Child Health Bureau, US Department of Health and Human Services.

Sisson, Gretchen. 2012. "Finding a Way to Offer Something More: Reframing Teen Pregnancy Prevention." *Sexuality Research and Social Policy* 9 (1): 57–69.

SmithBattle, Lee. "Teen Mothering in the United States: Fertile Ground for Shifting the Paradigm." In *Re/Assembling the Pregnant and Parenting Teenager: Narratives from the Field(s),* edited by Annelies Kamp and Majella McSharry, 75–104. Oxford: Peter Lang, 2018.

Snorton, C. Riley, and Jin Haritaworn. 2013. "Trans Necropolitics: A Transnational Reflection on Violence, Death, and the Trans of Color Afterlife." In *The*

Transgender Studies Reader, Volume 2, edited by Susan Stryker and Aren Aizura, 66–76. New York: Routledge.

Solinger, Rickie. 2000. *Wake Up, Little Susie: Single Pregnancy and Race before Roe v. Wade.* 2nd edition. New York: Routledge.

Solinger, Rickie. 2005. *Pregnancy and Power: A Short History of Reproductive Politics in America.* New York: New York University Press.

Solomon-Fears, Carmen. 2016. *Teenage Pregnancy Prevention: Statistics and Programs.* Washington, DC: Congressional Research Service. https://fas.org /sgp/crs/misc/RS20301.pdf.

Somerville, Siobhan B. 2000. *Queering the Color Line: Race and the Invention of Homosexuality in American Culture.* Durham, NC: Duke University Press.

Spade, Dean. 2015. *Normal Life: Administrative Violence, Critical Trans Politics, and the Limits of Law.* Durham, NC: Duke University Press.

Spade, Dean, and Craig Willse. 2016. "Norms and Normalization." In the *Oxford Handbook of Feminist Theory,* edited by Lisa Disch and Mary Hawkesworth, 551–71. New York: Oxford University Press.

Spivak, Gayatri Chakravorty. 1988. "Can the Subaltern Speak?" In *Can the Subaltern Speak? Reflections on the History of an Idea,* edited by Rosalind Morris, 21–78. New York: Columbia University Press.

Sprague, Joey. 2016. *Feminist Methodologies for Critical Researchers: Bridging Differences.* 2nd edition Lanham, MD: Rowman & Littlefield.

Stacey, Judith. 1988. "Can There Be a Feminist Ethnography?" *Women's Studies International Forum* 11 (1): 21–27.

Stanley, Eric, and Nat Smith. 2015. *Captive Genders: Trans Embodiment and the Prison Industrial Complex.* 2nd edition. Chico, CA: AK Press.

Stevens, Lindsay M. 2015. "Planning Parenthood: Health Care Providers' Perspectives on Pregnancy Intention, Readiness, and Family Planning." *Social Science and Medicine* 139: 44–52.

Subramaniam, Banu. 2009. "Moored Metamorphoses: A Retrospective Essay on Feminist Science Studies." *Signs: Journal of Women in Culture and Society* 34 (4): 951–80.

Sudbury, Julia. 2005. *Global Lockdown: Race, Gender, and the Prison-Industrial Complex.* New York: Routledge.

Suseth Valladares, Ena, and Marisol Franco. 2010. *Unearthing Latina/o Voices on Family, Pregnancy, and Reproductive Justice.* Los Angeles: California Latinas for Reproductive Justice. http://www.californialatinas.org/wp-content /uploads/2013/01/CLRJ-Unearthing-Latina-o-Voices.pdf.

Thompson, Lee, and Anjeela Kumar. 2011. "Responses to Health Promotion Campaigns: Resistance, Denial, and Othering." *Critical Public Health* 21 (1): 105–17.

Thorne-Thomsen, Aimée. 2010. "Keep Abortion Safe and Legal? Yes. Make it Rare? Not the Point." Rewire.com. April 26. https://rewire.news/article/2010/04/26/safe-legal-rare-another-perspective/.

Tolman, Deborah L. 2002. *Dilemmas of Desire: Teenage Girls and Sexuality.* Cambridge, MA: Harvard University Press.

Tornello, S. L., R. G. Riskind, and C. J. Patterson. 2014. "Sexual Orientation and Sexual and Reproductive Health among Adolescent Young Women in the United States." *Journal of Adolescent Health* 54 (2): 160–68.

Trussell, James, Nathaniel Henry, Fareen Hassan, Alexander Prezioso, Amy Law, and Anna A. Filonenko. 2013. "Burden of Unintended Pregnancy in the United States: Potential Savings with Increased Use of Long-Acting Reversible Contraception." *Contraception* 87 (2): 154–61.

Vargas, Deborah R. 2014. "Ruminations on *Lo Sucio* as a Latino Queer Analytic." *American Quarterly* 66 (3): 715–26.

Vazquez Calzada, J. L., and Z. Morales del Valle. 1982. "Female Sterilization in Puerto Rico and its Demographic Effectiveness." *Puerto Rico Health Sciences Journal* 1 (2): 68–79.

Ventura, Stephanie J., Brady E. Hamilton, and T. J. Mathews. 2014. "National and State Patterns of Teen Births in the United States, 1940–2013." *National Vital Statistics Reports* 63 (4): 1–34.

Vidal-Ortiz, Salvador. 2004. "On Being a White Person of Color: Using Autoethnography to Understand Puerto Ricans' Racialization." *Qualitative Sociology* 27 (2): 179–203.

Vidal-Ortiz, Salvador. 2009. "The Figure of the Transwoman of Color through the Lens of 'Doing Gender.'" *Gender and Society* 23 (1): 99–103.

Villarruel, Antonia M., and Brenda L. Eakin. 2008. "*Cuídate:* A Culturally-Based Program to Reduce HIV Sexual Risk Behavior among Latino Youth (Starter Kit)." New York: Select Media.

Vinson, Jenna. 2018. *Embodying the Problem: The Persuasive Power of the Teen Mother.* New Brunswick, NJ: Rutgers University Press.

Wacquant, Loïc. 2010. "Prisoner Reentry as Myth and Ceremony." *Dialectical Anthropology* 34 (4): 605–20.

Wallerstein, Nina, Bonnie Duran, John Oetzel, and Meredith Minkler. 2013. *Community-Based Participatory Research for Health: Advancing Social and Health Equity.* San Francisco: Jossey Bass.

Ward, Martha C. 1995. "Early Childbearing: What Is the Problem and Who Owns It?" In *Conceiving the New World Order: The Global Politics of Reproduction,* edited by Faye D. Ginsburg and Rayna Rapp, 140–158. Berkeley: University of California Press.

Washington, Harriet. 2006. *Medical Apartheid: The Dark History of Medical Experimentation on Black Americans from Colonial Times to the Present.* New York: Harlem Moon.

Weise, Karen. 2015. "Warren Buffett's Family Secretly Funded a Birth Control Revolution." *Bloomberg News.* July 30. http://www.bloomberg.com/news /articles/2015-07-30/warren-buffett-s-family-secretly-funded-a-birth-control-revolution.

Westhoff, Carolyn L., Stephen Heartwell, Sharon Edwards, Mimi Zieman, Gretchen Stuart, Carrie Cwiak, Anne Davis, Tina Robilotto, Linda Cushman, and Debra Kalmuss. 2007. "Oral Contraceptive Discontinuation: Do Side Effects Matter?" *American Journal of Obstetrics and Gynecology* 196 (4): 412-e1.

Whalen, Carmen. 2005. "Colonialism, Citizenship, and the Making of the Puerto Rican Diaspora: An Introduction." In *The Puerto Rican Diaspora: Historical Perspectives,* edited by Carmen Whalen and Victor Vázquez-Hernández, 1–42. Philadelphia: Temple University Press.

Whalen, Carmen, and Víctor Vázquez-Hernández, eds. 2008. *The Puerto Rican Diaspora: Historical Perspectives.* Philadelphia: Temple University Press.

WHO. 2019. "Defining Sexual Health." World Health Organization. Accessed August 14, 2019. https://www.who.int/reproductivehealth/topics/sexual_health/sh_definitions/en/.

Wilkinson, Richard, and Michael Marmot, eds. 2003. *Social Determinants of Health: The Solid Facts.* 2nd Edition. Copenhagen: World Health Organization, Regional Office for Europe.

Willey, Angela. 2016. *Undoing Monogamy: The Politics of Science and the Possibilities of Biology.* Durham, NC: Duke University Press.

Willis, Paul. 1981. *Learning to Labor: How Working Class Kids Get Working Class Jobs.* New York: Columbia University Press.

Wilson, Helen, and Annette Huntington. 2006. "Deviant (M)others: The Construction of Teenage Motherhood in Contemporary Discourse." *Journal of Social Policy* 35 (1): 59–76.

Winters, Della J., and Adria Ryan McLaughlin. 2019. "Soft Sterilization: Long-Acting Reversible Contraceptives in the Carceral State." *Affilia,* December 11. https://doi.org/10.1177/0886109919882320.

World Bank. 2015. "Adolescent Fertility Rates." World Bank Group. Accessed March 5, 2016. http://data.worldbank.org/indicator/SP.ADO.TFRT /countries.

Wyer, Mary, Mary Barbercheck, Donna Cookmeyer, Hatice Ozturk, and Marta Wayne. 2013. *Women, Science, and Technology: A Reader in Feminist Science Studies.* New York: Routledge.

Yee, Lynn M., and Melissa A. Simon. 2011. "Perceptions of Coercion, Discrimination and Other Negative Experiences in Postpartum Contraceptive Counseling for Low-Income Minority Women." *Journal of Health Care for the Poor and Underserved* 22 (4): 1387–1400.

Zachry, Elizabeth M. 2005. "Getting My Education: Teen Mothers' Experiences in School before and after Motherhood." *Teachers College Record* 107 (12): 2566–98.

Zoila-Pérez, Miriam. 2011. "Teen Moms Look for Support, but Find Only Shame." *Colorlines,* May 6. https://www.colorlines.com/articles/teen-moms-look-support-find-only-shame.

Zuberi, Tukufu, and Eduardo Bonilla-Silva, eds. 2008. *White Logic, White Methods: Racism and Methodology.* Lanham, MD: Rowman & Littlefield.

Zussman, Robert. 2012. "Narrative Freedom." *Sociological Forum* 27 (4): 807–24.

Index

Note: *Millerston* is a pseudonym, as are all names of interviewees

Founded in 1893,
UNIVERSITY OF CALIFORNIA PRESS
publishes bold, progressive books and journals
on topics in the arts, humanities, social sciences,
and natural sciences—with a focus on social
justice issues—that inspire thought and action
among readers worldwide.

The UC PRESS FOUNDATION
raises funds to uphold the press's vital role
as an independent, nonprofit publisher, and
receives philanthropic support from a wide
range of individuals and institutions—and from
committed readers like you. To learn more, visit
ucpress.edu/supportus.